To: Donnie

D0095208

11/23/02

I Remember
PAUL "BEAR" BRYANT

I Remember
PAUL "BEAR" BRYANT

*Personal Memories of College Football's
Most Legendary Coach,
as Told by the People Who Knew Him Best*

AL BROWNING

**Cumberland House
Nashville, Tennessee**

Published by Cumberland House Publishing, Inc., 431 Harding Industrial Drive, Nashville, TN 37211 • www.cumberlandhouse.com

Cover design by Gore Studio, Inc.

Library of Congress Cataloging-in-Publication Data

Browning, Al.
   I remember Paul "Bear" Bryant : personal memories of college football's most legendary coach, as told by the people who knew him best / Al Browning.
      p. cm.
   Includes index.
   ISBN 1-58182-159-X (pbk. : alk. paper)
      1. Bryant, Paul W. 2. Bryant, Paul W.--Friends and associates. 3. Football coaches--United States--Biography. 4. Football--Coaching.

   GV939.B79 B76 2001
   796.332'092--dc21
   [B]   2001032315

Printed in the United States of America
1 2 3 4 5 6 7—06 05 04 03 02 01

To all the "boys of autumn" from Alabama,
Texas A&M, Kentucky, and Maryland,
who Paul "Bear" Bryant truly loved.

Contents

PREFACE

Paul William "Bear" Bryant was near the end of a speech to the Birmingham Quarterback Club when he said, "I want to share something with you that has been most beneficial to me. It's a little poem entitled 'What Have I Traded.' I read it every morning to help me through the day. I'll share it with you if you'll give me a minute."

This is the beginning of a new day.
God has given me this day to use as I will.
I can waste it or I can use it for good.

What I do today is very important because
I'm exchanging a day of my life for it.
When tomorrow comes this day will be gone, forever,
leaving something in its place I have traded for it.

I want it to be gain, not loss, good, not evil,
success, not failure, in order that I shall not
forget the price I paid for it.

Those words were on Bryant's desk at Memorial Coliseum at the University of Alabama. He read them daily, he professed, for the last three years he coached football. He said the poem inspired him to make the most of each day.

Likewise, his life was an inspiration to countless people who knew him directly and indirectly.

*In memory of Mary Harmon Bryant,
who was not afraid to make a coaching
suggestion or two to her husband.*

Acknowledgments

I'd like to express gratitude to every individual who has taken time to help with the preparation of this book. Some of the reflections offered were the result of interviews conducted during the 1970s, 1980s and 1990s, including conversations that came when I was employed as a sports columnist at the *Tuscaloosa News* and the *Knoxville News-Sentinel*.

I offer special appreciation to the Paul Bryant Museum on the University of Alabama campus. Each employee there was most helpful during the research process. Special thank-yous go to Taylor Watson, Jan Adams, Gary Shores, and Clem Gryska.

I've attempted to credit all other newspapers and magazines in the text of this book. An exception is the Associated Press news service, which distributed some newspaper articles that did not carry a byline from which information was secured.

INTRODUCTION

July 12, 1979

After exchanging pleasantries, Paul "Bear" Bryant and I settled into our seats on the University of Alabama airplane departing Tuscaloosa, Alabama, en route to Little Rock, Arkansas. I was then a 29-year-old sports columnist and saw Bryant almost daily during football season—the first of August to mid-January. On this day the sixty-five-year-old famous football coach was unusually quiet as he pored through documents stashed in his trademark oversized brown briefcase. As was his custom, his plastic-rimmed eyeglasses rested near the point of his nose.

He was going to Little Rock for an afternoon meeting at a hotel to visit with Collins Kilgore, his cousin, Ike Murry, a former Arkansas attorney general, and some other business associates. I was going deep into backwoods Arkansas to explore his childhood home and talk to the people who knew him when he was the poor country boy who showed up barefoot for junior high school—long before he left huge footprints as a sports icon who walked side by side with the rich and famous.

By that point in his career, Bryant had won 284 games as a college coach at Maryland, Kentucky, Texas A&M, and Alabama. He was twenty-one victories away from becoming the most prolific winner in the sport at that level of competition. Also, he was less than two months from the start of a season in which the Crimson Tide would win for him a sixth national championship, a back-to-back accomplishment for the second time during what would become his quarter of a century in Tuscaloosa, from 1958 through 1982.

Bryant looked refreshed as the airplane traversed Mississippi. In fact, he looked better than he had in years. He had lost weight, started walking for the sake of exercise, and softened his consumption of vodka and gin. As he read through a business plan, I flowed through the pages of a book, albeit while glancing up now and then at the massive man seated a few feet in front of me.

After a little more than an hour in the air, all in silence except for the soft purr of airplane engines, I noticed Bryant gazing out of the window beside him. He looked pensive, immersed in thought, and I wondered what was going through his mind. He startled me when he said, "Alfred, there's home."

I glanced out of my window and observed the landscape, patches of pasture and trees with few buildings in sight.

"I guess coming back to Arkansas brings back a lot of memories," I said, searching for something appropriate to say without overstepping boundaries.

Bryant nodded and said, "Yeah, a ton of 'em—mostly about Mama and how I hooked up our old mule and we rode that damn wagon from Smith Chapel to Fordyce on Saturday mornings to sell vegetables to the city slickers."

I had heard Bryant talk many times about Ida Bryant, his mother, and how she had been strong after his father, Monroe, developed high blood pressure and was unable to work much.

"There were eleven of us in a little ol' house in the woods, nine kids," Bryant said, his thoughts running free. "When Papa got sick, it was up to Mama to make us work and to teach us the difference between right and wrong.

"Damn, we didn't have anything back then. But the hell of it is none of us knew it, at least not until we got out of grade school in Kingsland and started junior high school in Fordyce. That's when I realized how poor we were."

My reporter instincts told me to ask the coach if I could turn on a tape recorder. But decency prevailed and I left a tough man with an earned reputation for pushing football players toward championships alone with his sentimental thoughts. I swallowed hard and turned the pages of my book more quickly when I saw tears forming in his eyes. Earlier, he told me he held his mother's small hands in his enormous ones as she was near death in a New Orleans hospital. I figured he was thinking about that at that moment, plus a lot more, and nothing more was said until the airplane came to a halt on a runway at the Little Rock airport.

We were met by Kilgore at a private hangar. He drove us to the hotel where the business meeting would be held, told me I would have dinner that evening with him and his wife, Edith, and Murry and his wife, Catherine, and he would drive me seventy miles to Fordyce the next morning so I could interview anybody I wanted.

"Alfred, you're on your own," Bryant said with a grin as I shook his hand and told him goodbye. "You can believe everything you see and about half of what you hear—and don't spread a bunch of lies about me among my homefolks. Just tell 'em hello for me and tell 'em I'll be coming for a visit soon."

Bryant made good on that vow—with an ironic twist. He became the most prolific winner in college football history on November 28, 1981, when Alabama defeated Auburn 28–17 for victory number 315. He won his final game on December

29, 1982, when the Crimson Tide defeated Illinois 21–15 in the Liberty Bowl for victory number 323. It was just after that game that he and his driver and confidant, Billy Varner, made a trip to Arkansas by automobile. On January 26, 1983, at just past noon, he died at age sixty-nine from a massive heart attack at Druid City Hospital in Tuscaloosa. His funeral was held on January 28, almost exactly one month after he coached his final game.

Ronald Reagan, president when Bryant died, said in a most appropriate manner, "Americans have lost a hero who always seemed larger than life, a coach who made legends out of ordinary people. He was a hard, but loved, taskmaster. He was patriotic to the core, devoted to his players, and he was inspired by a winning spirit that would not quit. 'Bear' Bryant gave his country the gift of life unsurpassed. In making the impossible seem easy, he lived what we strive to be."

When I studied that statement, it took me back to Smith Chapel, where Bryant was reared deep in the woods, with only three tiny unpainted wooden houses and a white, one-room church within the eight miles between Fordyce, five miles away, and Kingsland, three miles away. For him to advance from what was commonly known as Moro Bottom, named for the creek that ran through the area, to become the most successful college coach in history does seem impossible, as the president said, and he did make it appear easy.

Where Bryant's concerned, a lot of people have tried to explain how a pauper became a king—the American Dream personified if you will—and to my thinking nobody has come closer than Edith Kilgore. An imperturbable lady, she said little during the three hours I visited with her and her husband, Collins, and Ike Murry and his wife, Catherine, in Little Rock on July 12, 1979. But near the end of our evening together, she said something I believe holds more truth than most of the other theories that have been offered.

"It goes back so far, even to his first day peddling groceries with his mother off that wagon," Edith said. "She was an iron woman who gave him direction in life. She probably made him realize that through hard work, there was a better way to live.

"The answer can be found there. I don't think Bear wanted to plow the rest of his life."

More evidence of that can be found later in this book, as individuals who knew Bryant well share their personal memories of him. They include childhood friends, family members, players at Maryland, Kentucky, Texas A&M, and Alabama, assistant coaches and athletics department associates, and more common folks like me. They all have stimulating moments to reveal, reflections that provide previously unseen glimpses of a true sports superstar.

From my point of view, the trip to Arkansas in 1979 pieced together the early pieces of a puzzle relating to Bryant's triumphant life. The picture was made complete in a more sobering setting, his funeral in 1983, during which time I was working for him as an administrative assistant and was honored to speak on behalf of his widow, Mary Harmon Bryant, his son, Paul Bryant Jr., his daughter, Mae Martin Tyson, and other members of his family.

My first contact with Bryant dates back to 1959, when I was in the third grade at East Three Notch Elementary School in Andalusia, Alabama. He was in his second season as coach at Alabama and even a youngster like me got caught up in his mission to restore the dignity of a proud football program that had fallen on dismal times.

As part of a plan to reach out to the children of Alabama, Bryant used a football uniform giveaway tied to his Sunday afternoon television program that reviewed the game played the previous day. He accepted questions from kids and chose one to answer on air.

I watched the weekly television program because I liked

hearing Denny Chimes on the Alabama campus toll four times at its beginning. Of course, I was into football, too, because my father, Al, and mother, Hilda, were faithful followers, and almost all of my other relatives, from grandparents to aunts and uncles on both sides of the family, favored the Crimson Tide.

During one of the television shows, I asked my father, "Who calls defensive signals for Alabama?" He suggested I send a letter to Coach Bryant and ask him.

I should have known something unusual was going on a couple of weeks later when about a dozen members of our family showed up at our house on College Street on Sunday afternoon to watch the *Bear Bryant Show*. I was sure of that when my father and mother literally hauled me inside by the seat of my pants from an afternoon of play in the back yard.

Well, lo and behold, Bryant announced that the question he had selected had been sent by Butch Browning of Andalusia, Alabama. He said the middle linebacker called defensive signals. Later that week, I received a Hutch football uniform that consisted of shoulder pads, a red helmet with a white stripe, gold pants, and a red jersey.

At the urging of my father, I wrote Bryant a thank you letter. He responded with an autographed picture. I wrote another letter. He responded with an Alabama football brochure. I wrote another letter after the Crimson Tide defeated Auburn that season, 10–0, to end a five-game losing streak to the intrastate rival. He responded with a hastily torn page from a note pad on which he wrote, "Hi, Butch . . . Come to see us . . . Paul Bryant."

I still have that torn page. Also, I still have the helmet from the football uniform. But I never told Bryant about our correspondence until 1982, when he was a couple of weeks away from the start of his last season.

"Yeah, I remember giving away those uniforms," Bryant said with a chuckle before drawing hard on an unfiltered

Chesterfield cigarette in his office. "In fact, now that I think back, when I met you I remember thinking how the name Browning sounded familiar."

I never did buy into that line. But I accepted his compliment with a grin and said, "Hell, Coach, that name should've sounded familiar. I wrote you a thousand times between the third and sixth grades."

My first personal contact with Bryant came in 1972, four years after my dream of playing for him ended because of a lack of ability at T.R. Miller High School in Brewton, Alabama. I was a student at Alabama, entering my senior year, when I was asked to start a sports section for a liberal campus publication known as the *Boll Weevil*, an alternative to the more established *Crimson-White*. I had only written poetry and a few short stories at the time, but I accepted the challenge.

My first interview was with Bryant. It was arranged by Kirk McNair, then the assistant sports information director at Alabama under Charley Thornton and the man who more than anybody helped me get started in sports journalism.

About a week before the start of football practice that year, McNair took me to the second floor at Memorial Coliseum and introduced me to Bryant. People have suggested I must have been frightened out of my mind that morning, but that was not the case. I was excited and either too naive or full of myself to be nervous. Also, I was prepared, with the questions I wanted to ask written on blue index cards.

In reflection, I asked every question that should have been asked—even the socially unacceptable ones.

Did Bryant think any of his players were using marijuana?

Did Bryant cheat while recruiting prospects?

Did Bryant teach brutal tactics in football, as alleged after a game against Georgia Tech during the 1960s by the

Atlanta Journal *and* Saturday Evening Post?

Did Bryant fix the outcome of a game against Georgia during the 1960s, as alleged by the Saturday Evening Post?

Bryant patiently listened to every question and answered every question. The *Boll Weevil*, in its first sports section, got a story the *New York Times* would have welcomed.

I got a career in journalism because the *Tuscaloosa News* offered me a job as a sports reporter on February 13, 1973, and, except for a brief respite, I was employed by that newspaper until August 1, 1982.

Being in Tuscaloosa during that time allowed me to see the legend of Paul "Bear" Bryant grow, even to witness its rejuvenation after Alabama produced 6–5 and 6–5–1 records in 1969 and 1970, respectively. He attempted to resign at that time, but his resignation was not accepted by the school president, Dr. David Matthews. The Crimson Tide won 103 games during the 1970s, at the time a national record, and three national championships. Also, the coach was closing in on Amos Alonzo Stagg (314 victories), and Glenn "Pop" Warner (313 victories), in his quest to become the most prolific winner in history.

There were numerous memorable moments, some to be offered later, plus a few times when Bryant just plain got mad at me.

In 1975 the Alabama State Legislature advanced a proposal to change the name of Denny Stadium on campus to Bryant-Denny Stadium. Mike McKenzie, then the sports editor at the *Tuscaloosa News*, as well as my chief mentor, wrote a column applauding the impending action. I wrote one stating the name of the stadium should remain intact, that it was wrong to tamper with distinguished Alabama football tradition.

Bryant never said anything to me about my opinion on the issue, but Charley Thornton was quick to relay how he really felt. As Thornton said, "Coach Bryant asked me what that stringy-haired, young punk sports writer at the

Tuscaloosa News was trying to prove. Maybe you better stay clear of him for a while."

That says a lot about Bryant. He was always gracious in victory, as well as fiercely determined in defeat. But it is foolish for anybody to believe he did not delight in the accolades that came his way. In that regard, he had superb timing—stepping into the spotlight at precisely the proper moment and playing the role of unassuming champion when that approach worked best.

In 1980, Bryant had a team that seemed to lack discipline, at least in my estimation, and I wrote a column to that effect. It appeared in print on Sunday morning. Somebody within the athletics department warned me that he was on the rampage and was ready to chew me out.

I went to football practice Monday afternoon and interviewed Bryant one-on-one afterwards. He did not bring up the column. The same thing happened Tuesday afternoon and Wednesday afternoon. By the time we had our one-on-one session Thursday afternoon, I thought I was in the clear. Then as I was leaving, he said, "Alfred, do you believe those things you said in that column?" I told him I did. He said, "Okay, as long as that's your honest opinion." I nodded, smiled, waved, and started walking away. He said, "But, Alfred, that doesn't mean I don't think what you wrote is a crock of shit."

I left that confrontation with one thought in mind: Wow, I managed to escape with a sense of dignity, at least I think I did.

Bryant knew how to work the news media better than anybody I have seen. There were a few exceptions, but he normally got what he wanted from writers and broadcasters while maintaining the warm relationships he desired.

My relationship with Bryant grew more secure as the years passed and finally reached a degree of closeness that even now I find unfathomable. I think that as Bryant grew older and more reflective, he appreciated my forthrightness when talking with him because a lot of people started treating him more like a glorified god than a somewhat normal person when he approached and eclipsed the record for wins.

One evening in his office in 1981, he said, "You know, as I look back on my life, the biggest regret I have is I haven't gotten to know my neighbors good enough. My life has been consumed by football, trying to win. It has always been football this and football that, work this and work that. I should've taken the time to get to know a lot of good people a whole lot better."

I suggested that part of the problem rested in the fact people did not reach out to him enough, that too many considered him something more than merely human.

"Maybe so, at least in some cases," Bryant said. "But I'm the one who should've reached out. Remember, Alfred, you've got to treat other people the way you want to be treated."

That adequate yet mistated pass at the Golden Rule considered, a lot of people find it surprising Bryant displayed a more spiritual side during his latter years. They recall a cussing and fussing coach on the field and a man who liked to have a good time fishing, hunting, and drinking off the field. Most people do not want to consider a more gentle person.

In his house, Bryant had these framed words: "Ask God to bless your work. Do not ask Him to do it for you."

In his office, Bryant had these framed words: "What have you traded for what God has given you today?" As previously mentioned, he read the entire poem at the start of each work day and used it as a prayer that his life be more productive in every way.

I got to see that side of Bryant with much more depth during his last season as a coach because he gave me a break on August 2, 1982, for which I will forever be thankful.

The previous night I had resigned as sports editor and

sports columnist at the *Tuscaloosa News* because I had become disenchanted with part of the newspaper management team. Rather than let Bryant learn about my departure from somebody else, I stopped by his office on Sunday afternoon. I found him watching a baseball game on one television and a golf tournament on another. I told him about the professional decision I had made.

"What are you going to do?" he said.

"I don't know. It'll work out."

Bryant sat for a couple of moments in silence and puffed on an unfiltered Chesterfield.

"Did you shave this morning?" he said.

"Yes sir."

"When you looked in the mirror, did you like what you saw?"

"If you're asking me if I'll regret leaving the newspaper, the answer is no."

He nodded, took another puff and thought for a couple of minutes.

He told me Gary White, an assistant athletics director at Alabama was attempting to become the athletics director at Gadsden State Junior College, that I could have his job if he made that move. I asked what the job entailed. He told me it dealt with working to ensure the academic good standing of athletes and handling some athletics department accounting chores. I told him I could handle the first part, but I was not qualified to handle the second part, that maybe I should look elsewhere.

After a few more minutes of silent contemplation, Bryant told me he needed an administrative assistant to help him with athletics department communications and many of his personal endeavors. I asked for a more detailed job description and got one. I accepted the offer.

"Don't you want to know what I'm thinking about paying you?" Bryant said.

"No sir. It's more than I'm making now."

"I'm giving you $500 a week and you can do other things to add to it," Bryant said. "It won't take you ten hours to do what I've got in mind."

"Then why not pay me $100 a week for starters?" I said.

"You let me handle the finances," Bryant said.

"Yes sir."

I reported to work the next morning at 5:30. I was sitting on the steps of Memorial Coliseum when Bryant arrived. He laughed heartily and said, "Alfred, I've got to get you a damn key if you're going to beat me to work every day."

When we got upstairs, Bryant gave me some instructions.

"I want you to work under the guidance of Young Boozer (one of his former teammates at Alabama and a successful Tuscaloosa businessman) to launch a drive aimed at bringing about the construction of a museum on campus named in my honor," Bryant said. "I don't want a damn shrine built for me. But some people want to build something, so I've agreed as long as its a shrine built in honor of all of my former players, assistant coaches, and a lot of other people at Alabama, Texas A&M, Kentucky, and Maryland. It's going to be like that or we aren't going to do it."

Bryant asked if I understood. I told him I did.

"I want you to help me with my responses to some of the letters I'm getting from all over the world," Bryant said. "That record business from last season opened the floodgates. We'll talk about 'em and you'll write 'em. Then I'll review 'em. What I need is for you to make me sound smarter than an old plowhand from Arkansas."

I worked about sixty hours that week. When I saw Bryant the following Monday morning, he instructed his secretary, Linda Knowles, to write me a check out of his personal account. It was for $100, as I had foolishly suggested.

But Lynne and Kirk McNair quickly came to my rescue, hiring me at *Bama: Inside The Crimson Tide* magazine, even giving me a nice office, and Paul Bryant Jr. offered me the opportunity to do some public relations work for Greenetrack, the dog racing establishment in which he owned stock.

It was a whirlwind six months, without question, and my relationship with the coach got even warmer—even as his health began deteriorating badly.

Linda Knowles has said Bryant "literally willed himself through that last season." I concur with that thought. Billy Varner said the man he served was "losing step quickly." I agree with that statement. The three of us watched almost daily as Dr. William Hill, a Tuscaloosa cardiologist, Dr. Bill deShazo, an Alabama team physician, and Jim Goostree, the Crimson Tide team trainer, came and went in an effort to make him feel better.

As for the season, it started grand and faded. Alabama won its first five games, achieving a Number 1 national ranking, then lost four of its next six. After LSU won, 20–10, on November 6, 1982, dropping the record to a more than respectable 7–2, Bryant announced during his postgame press conference that "maybe it was time to turn over the leadership of the program to someone else." Sports writers and sports broadcasters laughed, but I could tell he was serious by the look on his face.

I walked with Bryant, Varner, and two Alabama State Troopers to a car just after the press conference. I said, "Coach Bryant, you're serious about this, aren't you?" He nodded and said, "Yes, Alfred, I'm afraid the time has come."

About an hour later I had a drink with Jack Perry, the Alabama sports information director, at the Tide & Tiger bar across the street from Legion Field in Birmingham. I told him he better prepare himself, that the coach was serious. I cautioned him to stay quiet about it and I would let him know more when I could.

Frankly, I was mad at Bryant because I thought he was

bailing out on his players as the season started unwinding. I was more angry after a Saturday night of sleep and went to Memorial Coliseum at just after dawn the next morning to let him know how I felt. When I arrived, assistant head coach Ken Donahue told me he thought the coach had stayed in Birmingham the night previous and was returning to Tuscaloosa after taping his weekly television program. I went to a nearby Shoney's restaurant, where he sometimes stopped for breakfast, but did not find him.

I was waiting for Bryant when he arrived at Memorial Coliseum early Monday morning. We walked upstairs and put on some coffee. He went into his office, and I stood just outside chatting with Varner. Finally, I knocked on the closed door, heard him say come in and opened it.

"Coach, have you got a minute for me?"

"Sure, Alfred. Come on in."

I entered the room and said nothing.

"What have you got on your mind?" Bryant said.

I fired it at him. Let him have it. I told him he had taught players not to quit when times get bad and he was setting a terrible example for them. I talked without pause for about three minutes, stopped and said, "I guess I'm over my time limit."

Bryant smiled and asked me take a seat. He unbuttoned his left shirt sleeve and pulled it up, exposing a badly swollen and bluish-gray arm. Then he said, "Alfred, Dr. Hill said I'm going to croak if I don't quit. I really don't have a choice."

I looked hard at the arm. I felt about six inches tall. My eyes were tearing when I looked at his face. Thank God, he was smiling. Then he said, "Alfred, I appreciate everything you just told me. But maybe you ought to get all the facts straight before you start running off at the mouth."

At that moment, Bryant broke into a loud chuckle. It was music to my ears.

"This is between us," Bryant said, his voice firm.

"Yes sir."

"I won't be coaching after the bowl game, provided we make one."

"Yes sir."

"I need to talk to Paul [his son] about a few things first, but I want you to stop by for another visit after practice later this week," Bryant said. "We've got to make some decisions about where Billy, Linda, you, and me are going be head-quartered after my days around here are over."

It was about two weeks, actually, before Bryant told me he would probably serve Alabama as athletics director for about six months after his replacement as coach was named. He said he planned to deposit $100,000 in my checking account so I could get an office built, that I could deed it to him after the construction was completed and a move into it was under way.

"Coach Bryant, if you put $100,000 in my checking account, you won't ever see me again," I said.

"Shit."

Ray Perkins was named the next coach at Alabama.

A game against Illinois in the Liberty Bowl was arranged.

Bryant conducted his last practice on Thomas Field just before Christmas Day in 1982. Surprisingly, only three people were there to watch, *Huntsville Times* sports editor and sports columnist John Pruett, Pruett's son, and me.

Bryant called it "the last roundup" as he walked away from the practice field.

On December 29, 1982, Alabama defeated Illinois 21-15 on a bitter cold evening in Memphis, Tennessee. After conducting his last official press conference as Crimson Tide coach, Bryant walked from an interview tent and started to get into an automobile. About two dozen Alabama fans were standing nearby, with many of them saying the same thing, "We'll miss you, Bear. Thanks for the memories."

Bryant got out the automobile, turned toward the fans

and said, "Ya'll keep cheering for Alabama, ya'll hear?"

It was not an eloquent remark, no doubt, but I cannot think of a more appropriate last statement for Bryant to make before departing the scene of his final game.

I will always think it unusual, to say the least, that Bryant spoke in terms of days, weeks, months, and years when talking about what he would do during his retirement, even during his final press conference in Memphis, Tennessee. "That'll depend on how long the Good Lord gives me," he said.

On January 24, 1983, Bryant complained of chest pains while visiting in the home of his good friend and business associate Jimmy Hinton in Tuscaloosa. He was taken to Druid City Hospital and placed in the intensive care unit. His pulse rate was extremely low and Hill, the cardiologist, and other physicians were concerned.

During the next day and a half, Bryant met frequently with family members, especially his son, Paul Jr., and his daughter, Mae Martin Tyson, and began making decisions like those a man who knew his time was about up would make. He was getting things in order, so to speak.

On January 26, 1983, at about 12:10 P.M., I telephoned Linda Knowles, his secretary, to check on his condition. I was in my office at *Bama: Inside The Crimson Tide* magazine.

"Al, he's gone," she said.

"Where has he gone?" I said.

"Al, he's gone," she said, her voice choked by sobs.

She had just heard the news. He had died a few minutes earlier. Her world was standing still. So was mine.

"I'll be there in a few minutes," I said.

Strangely, I telephoned my mother in Huntsville, Alabama, and told her about the passing.

Then I walked into the office next to mine and broke the news to a dear friend: "Kirk, Coach Bryant is dead."

I will never forget the look on Kirk McNair's face. Also,

bless him, I will always remember the first words out of his mouth: "Are you okay?" Here was a man who knew Bryant well and had served him skillfully and much longer than I. Yet, at that moment, he was a friend first.

I arrived at Memorial Coliseum at about 12:25 P.M. and found Linda Knowles and Sam Bailey, the associate athletics director and longtime Bryant friend, conversing in hushed tones. After a couple of minutes, he said, "Al, we've got players working out downstairs in the weight room. You've got to go tell them what has happened."

I completed that chore, then went back upstairs and announced I was going to the Bryants' house. I did not think I would be able to see Mrs. Bryant, but I wanted to let her know I was there to offer condolence. When Mae Martin Tyson greeted me, she told me her mother wanted me to represent the family that afternoon at a press conference at Druid City Hospital. I conferred for several minutes with Paul Jr. and departed.

The following morning I was summoned to a meeting at the Rose Administration Building on the University of Alabama campus. I was there with Dr. Roger Sayers, a vice president, Sam Bailey, Jim Goostree, and Mike Ellis, director of university public relations. We had been charged with the duty of planning a funeral that we knew would be large, though we could not imagine how massive, and the task was arduous.

My responsibilities were to make sure Mrs. Bryant's wishes were followed to the letter; to coordinate with Dr. Joe Elmore, the minister at First United Methodist Church, who eventually conducted an exemplary service; and to handle a multitude of requests from the news media.

It was a blur then and is a blur now.

Alabama State Troopers estimated that more than 100,000 mourners were in the streets of downtown Tuscaloosa when the service was conducted. They said more than 60,000 mourners lined streets and highways when the funeral processional traveled from First United Methodist Church to Elmwood Cemetery in Birmingham. They said more than 20,000 mourners were in the area of the gravesite.

Not until December 1, 2000, did I read all of the newspaper reports from that funeral in the *Tuscaloosa News* and the *Birmingham News*. They made me more convinced Bryant was a man who mastered life in such a manner that his passing literally united an entire state in grief.

So comes to mind a conversation Bryant and I had in his office on July 17, 1981.

He said, "Alfred, they'll forget me as soon as I croak and I'm buried."

I offered a strong objection. I told him his accomplishments as a football coach and his ability to lead people, even a throng who had never met him, would ensure that his life would not be forgotten. I told him years would come and go, even decades, and people would pass along stories about him.

"No, that's not the way it is," Bryant said. "Life moves on and people find interest in other things."

Only a fool would dispute that thought.

But the remembrances included in this text, plus thousands more that remain unprinted, indicate one thing: if only once, I was right and Paul "Bear" Bryant was wrong.

I Remember

PAUL "BEAR" BRYANT

1
THE BOY

Even when he was young, Bear had an ability to attract
attention and lead. But certainly when he came out of Moro
Bottom, you never would have thought he would become
famous. In fact, you would have wondered if he would end up
in the pen.

—IKE MURRY, former
Arkansas attorney general

It is obvious Paul "Bear" Bryant made a lasting impression on
individuals residing in Fordyce, Arkansas, and the surrounding area, most notably Smith Chapel and Kingsland, long
before he earned his nickname by wrestling a bear at the Lyric
Theater.

The young boy who dispensed vegetables with his mother
from the back of a mule-drawn wagon was gifted at show-
manship. Maybe he had a chip on his shoulder, an under-
standable psychological condition given the almost impover-
ished condition of his family at that time. Regardless, he was
not unlike a person in a strange country when he started
junior high school in Fordyce after attending elementary

school in Kingsland, the childhood home of country music recording star Johnny Cash. He arrived from deep in the backwoods, without shoes, and he had to overcome a cultural shock.

Maybe that is why he decided to show off for everybody in town by wrestling a bear.

Here is the story of how, at age twelve, Bryant wrestled a bear, by his own acknowledgement to impress Drucilla Smith, an older girl with red hair. The opening reflection comes from **Chester Darling**, a high school football teammate who later owned a service station in downtown Fordyce:

I was in the theater selling peanuts and popcorn when Bear arrived. The place was packed because word had been put out that somebody was going to wrestle a bear owned by a traveling showman who went from town to town and promised to pay anybody who would tangle with his grizzly. I think everybody in town must have been there—or wanted to be there.

Bear tells it he crawled up on stage because Drucilla Smith smiled at him. That could be true because Drucilla was a beauty with quite a figure. But I think Bear knew all along he was going to wrestle that day. I think everybody knew he was.

The match itself was over in a jiffy, less than a minute. Bear grabbled hold of the bear like he was going to throw it down and the muzzle came off. His sisters must have seen what happened first because they all started screaming: "The bear is gonna kill him . . . the bear is gonna kill him."

They were getting out of that door as they hollered, flying like birds. It was worse than a fire. Everybody was moving as fast as they could go.

Bear was on the move, too. He came off that stage like a man who had seen a ghost.

In his latter years, Bryant acknowledged he was frightened. He laughed when remembering how Ike Murry, a childhood friend who later became attorney general in Arkansas, called the bear "one of the scrawniest he had ever seen."

However, Bryant said, "He looked like he was thirty feet tall to me."

Bryant made a deal to wrestle the bear for $1 per minute. He said he pinned the bear for several minutes and kept getting poked by the bear owner with a stick. He said he would have stayed there "for a week, if he had let me, because we needed the money." But when the muzzle came off, as Darling described, the boy jumped from the stage and landed on the third row of seats, damaging his shins so severely he had scars on them the rest of his life.

"I went to get my money after things settled down inside the Lyric Theater and the bear owner had skipped town," Bryant said. "All I got out of it was a nickname."

Murry added, "Actually, the bear owner asked for a rematch as long as Bear would agree to wear the muzzle."

Collins Kilgore, a cousin to Bryant who lived in Fordyce at the time, remembered the wrestling match well. He smiled and said, "To tell the truth, I'm not sure who had fan support during the match. I think the real bear had more people pulling for him than Paul did."

ॐ

There is little doubt Bryant was physically equipped to wrestle the bear. His childhood was filled with farm chores, commencing at 4 A.M., followed by a mule and wagon ride or a walk through woods to elementary school in Kingsland.

In fact, he battled beasts of another kind a long time before he pinned a bear in the Lyric Theater.

ॐ

Paul had to grow up quickly, just to survive. None of us in the Moro Bottom area had any money. We had to work hard for what we ate, and that wasn't always very much.

—SENORA BRYANT, a sister-in-law

Senora Bryant, who married Paul's much older brother Harley, recalls an extremely young Bryant:

> Harley and Paul were always close, despite their age difference. Paul was four years old when Harley and I got married, but we always did a lot of things together. In fact, we lived in their house our first three months as man and wife.
>
> The first thing I remember about Paul was the day Harley, Paul, and I went hog hunting. Harley called up the hogs with an old horn and put Paul in the pen to fight them off while he marked them. I can still see that little boy in there battling those hogs. He was so small then. He could've have been killed. He was scared to death, too, but he stayed in that pen and tried.

ॐ

He was was so damn country it was unbelievable. He had never been around anybody except mules and chickens.

—IKE MURRY, former
Arkansas attorney general

A little later in his youth, between ages eight and twelve, Bryant did not make such an effort when it came to blending in with people from Fordyce, population about 3,800. He did not feel comfortable around "city slickers" when he saw them on weekends. When his mother went to visit with her brother who owned the only hotel and restaurant in town, he stayed to himself.

Collins Kilgore, a cousin, remembers how standoffish Bryant could be when visiting:

> Aunt Ida [Bryant's mother] usually had lunch with us before she and Paul started back home on the mule-drawn wagon. Paul was always welcomed, but he never ate with us, not once.
>
> Instead, Paul bought a big slab of cheese at the general store, paying a nickel, as I recall, and drove the wagon down by the Cotton Belt Railroad Depot. He'd get under a train car and eat cheese and crackers while we had a feast at the restaurant.
>
> I liked Paul a lot, even back then, but he was a peculiar person. I'd go to the railroad depot and beg him to come eat with us. But he wouldn't do it. One day I asked him why. He shrugged his shoulders and said he liked sitting and dreaming about becoming a train engineer.
>
> Isn't that something? The boy who became the greatest football coach in history didn't want to do anything the rest of life except drive a train.

Kilgore laughed heartily at the absurdity of the thought of his cousin driving a train for a living, then said, "But, you know, a few years later a lot of folks wished Paul had stayed that way. Instead, he became a showman, a guy who seemed to thrive on creating havoc for folks."

ॐ

Bear was so timid when he first arrived in Fordyce that he would barely talk to anybody. He was a nice-looking guy, about six feet tall and extremely handsome, who ended up having a girl in every town. But he was so bashful during those first few months that he walked around school with his head down to keep from meeting anybody.

—CATHERINE MURRY, a former girlfriend

Because of his background—maybe because of feelings of inferiority—Bryant did have an interesting way of dealing with junior high school classmates. After his father died, his mother moved the family to Fordyce, where they resided during the school year in a diminutive boarding house at the corner of Charlotte Street and East First Street. Many of his new friends remembered him as being shy, to an extreme, as well as mischievous.

One of the first people Bryant took an interest in at junior high was Catherine Murry, who eventually would marry one of his friends, Ike Murry. Catherine recalls how bewildered she was to find out she was the object of his affection:

Once Bear got some confidence, thanks to a lot of help from his cousin, Collins Kilgore, he was almost unbearable.

He first showed interest in me by sending a box of chocolate-coated cherries. He put them in my seat at school for me to find. When I thanked him for them, I thought he was going to knock over every desk in that classroom trying to get out of the door. He said, "Catherine, I didn't give you those cherries." Then he sent me a note later that day saying he did give them to me. Then he sent me another note saying he didn't.

It took a full day for the truth to surface, maybe even two, but Bear finally admitted he gave me those cherries. He said the reason he couldn't tell the truth up front was because he stole them and he knew he'd get in a lot of trouble.

After that experience, it didn't take Bear long to become accustomed to city ways. It was a shocking change in direction. Early on, in those first few weeks at our school, he was a guy who would walk across the hall and slip along the wall to keep from having to talk to anybody. But after he got more comfortable, in large part because of his cousin, Collins Kilgore, his devilish ways began to surface.

Bear was always sort of quiet, but it didn't take long for

us to realize we wouldn't be able to predict what he'd do next. He became a showoff who craved attention. He was always into mischief, at times unbearably, like putting bugs on girls, pulling practical jokes, and starting fights.

֍

Paul had a lot of Barnum and Bailey in him before he wrestled the bear at the Lyric Theater. He was a showman. He wanted to prove his worth and he enjoyed the spotlight. He got ridiculed a lot. He fought that with his fists. He got challenged a lot. Normally, he'd answer every one of them. Then there were times when he'd brag about being able to do this or do that. An example is the day he said he could run five miles in about half of an hour along a rocky country road.

—COLLINS KILGORE, cousin

W. R. "Footsie" Benton, a childhood friend of Bryant and one of his football teammates at Fordyce High School, remembers the "five-mile boast," too:

Bear always had a competitive spirit, the same fire that made him a great leader as a football coach. We all noticed that just after he and his family moved to Fordyce from Smith Chapel.

I'll never forget the afternoon he vowed he could run in his bare feet from the railroad depot to some place near Kingsland, beyond Moro Creek, in half an hour. I don't remember how far it was, not exactly, but it was at least five miles and maybe six.

Word spread like a wildfire and everybody was snickering. Then a fairly large crowd gathered to see if he could do it. In fact, we pooled a few dollars and bet him he couldn't do it.

Well, off he went, running along a gravel road, and, lo and behold, he came sprinting toward the finish line right on time. It must have been 100 degrees that day, but Bear made it with a minute or two to spare. That big rascal collapsed as soon as he reached the finish line. Had it not been for one of the guys knowing first aid, Bear might have died.

As fate would have it, Bear didn't have many doubters from that day forward.

☙

One of the funnier things about Paul as a child was his big feet. I can remember him soaking them in Epsom salt because he thought that would make them shrink. He was self-conscious about being such a big boy at a young age.

—LOUISE GOOLSBY, sister

Louise Goolsby of Nashville, Tennessee, is Bryant's only living sibling. She tells a couple of interesting stories about her brother and her family:

Our oldest sister, Ouida, ruled the family when we were children. I remember when we were out picking potatoes one day. This was when Paul was seven or eight. He wasn't doing much. He didn't want to pick. So Ouida got a switch and whipped him. He was howling, "No, Ouida, don't hit me any more until the blisters go down."

Another memorable time was the day our brother Jack offered Paul fifty cents to go slap a tombstone in a graveyard about a hundred yards behind our house. We got this man, Mr. Duke, to go lie down under a sheet.

Paul slapped the tombstone and Mr. Duke jumped up. It really scared Paul. He fell down running and couldn't get back on his feet because he was so frightened. He literally crawled back to the house.

That really upset Mama because she was afraid Paul was about to go into convulsions. He did look that bad at the time.

૭

Paul was a showboat, no doubt about that. From the time he started playing football at Fordyce High School, every newspaper clipping said Bryant this and Bryant that. He loved every minute of it. I think he loved the attention he got as a coach, too, every accolade that came his way.

—COLLINS KILGORE, cousin

The introduction Bryant received to football remains a mystery of sorts. There is no doubt he had to beg his mother for years before she would allow him to try out for the Fordyce High School Red Bugs team. Whether he played in the first game he saw, as has been stated, cannot be substantiated.

However, it is true that once Ida Bryant gave Paul Bryant the go ahead, he went to a local cobbler without her permission and had cleats put on the bottom of his only pair of shoes. He wore them to school. He wore them to church. He wore them on the football field.

Chester Darling, the starting quarterback on a state championship team, recalls Bryant being a super end and tackle for the Red Bugs, as well as a player who craved attention:

We were playing a game up in Little Rock against a big rival. Bear had a bruised knee and he wanted everybody to know about it. He really made a show of it. He wrapped it heavy with tape and limped around the field during pregame warmups. You would've thought that damn knee was broken in half.

I remember that game like it was yesterday, one play more

than all of the others. We punted the football and Bear took off stiff-legged down the field. He got there about the time this skinny punt returner caught the ball, and he really bowled that guy over. The crowd went crazy and Bear got up and limped to the sideline like he was in terrible pain.

But that's the way Bear played football. He was damn good, as tough as nails, but he had a lot of movie star in him, too. The dustier the playing field, the better for him because that meant he could make a run at a defender, hurl himself through the air, roll on the ground, with dust flying everywhere, and bowl over the guy like a tank.

Then he'd come back to the huddle with a big grin on his face and talk about how the crowd must have loved that block.

🌀

Bear kept saying it was time for him to score a touchdown, that all he needed was the football. I told him if he scored it'd be over my dead body. I had already had enough of him messing around with Catherine, at the time my girlfriend, later the woman I married, and I wasn't going to let him get in the end zone.

—**IKE MURRY,** a high school teammate

Ike Murry grins broadly as he tells how his teammate yearned for his first touchdown, noting that he and Bryant had discussed the story numerous times through the years:

We were playing the team from Warren, Arkansas, and pretty much had them whipped. As I recall, the score was 58–0. Knowing we had the game won, our coach took out most of the regulars to hold down the score.

But Bear would have no part of that. Instead, he sent his

substitute back to the bench and put himself in at quarterback. We had the ball on the Warren 2-yard line, so it was obvious to me what he planned to do.

When we got in the huddle, Bear was grinning. He said, "Boys, I'm a tackle and an end, but I'm about to score me a touchdown. This is my big chance."

Well, I was the center and, since I was already mad at him about him carrying on about Catherine, I said, "Let me tell you something, you son of a bitch. If you score a touchdown, you'll be the first person to do it without the football."

I centered the ball fifteen feet over his head and laughed my butt off when he ran back to the 40-yard line to retrieve it. He made it back to the 10-yard line, but he sure as hell didn't score. I would've tackled him myself to keep that from happening.

§

Bryant was good enough as a Fordyce Red Bugs player to be recruited by colleges, particularly Arkansas and Alabama. The Crimson Tide became his choice for two reasons.

1. Don Hutson, soon to be a great pass receiver as a collegian and a professional, was a Pine Bluff, Arkansas, native who had enrolled at Alabama a year earlier.

2. Bryant had been mesmerized while listening to radio broadcasts of the Crimson Tide playing in the Rose Bowl in 1926, 1927, and 1931.

Interestingly, Hutson and Bryant were stars for Alabama in the 1935 Rose Bowl, a victory over Stanford, with the latter dubbed "the other end" because of the abilities of the former.

2

THE COLLEGE PLAYER

Coach Hank [Crisp] started this long spiel in the dressing room, and I didn't have any idea where he was going with it. I don't think anybody did, with the possible exception of Coach [Frank] Thomas. Ultimately, he worked himself into a frenzy, reached a high pitch, and the most shocked player in the stadium at that moment was Paul Bryant.

—PAUL BURNUM, Alabama assistant coach

A broken bone is a broken bone, we must assume, and that is serious enough. But there is a definitive difference in a cracked fibula and a cracked hip, although football fans across the nation were led to believe otherwise after the University of Alabama defeated Tennessee 25–0 on October 19, 1935.

That game, played in Knoxville, Tennessee, made Paul "Bear" Bryant, a senior Alabama end, a hero from coast to coast.

The week started quietly, as well as romantically, with Bryant holding hands with Mary Harmon Black, a campus beauty queen. They were seated in a swing on the front porch of an Alabama sorority house. A set of crutches lay on the floor nearby.

Forty-five years later, Mary Harmon Bryant reminisced about their dating days:

> I was so excited because Paul told me he would be able to escort me to a dance that weekend. I was thrilled because I didn't get to see him much during football season because it took up all of his time.
>
> We were a couple of lovebirds, something Coach Thomas didn't like much, so it was nice hearing that I would be first in his life on a football weekend.
>
> Then I learned otherwise.

Bryant had cracked the fibula the previous weekend during a loss to Mississippi State, one of two defeats the Crimson Tide had during his senior season. He was ruled unavailable for the game against Tennessee. During a meeting on Thursday afternoon, the day before the team was to travel to Knoxville, Coach Frank Thomas told him he would make the trip to provide moral support for his teammates.

"You'll dress for the game and help us keep your teammates motivated," Thomas said. "This is Tennessee. We'll need all the help we can muster."

Bryant offers his recollections of how he went from "sick bay" to stardom:

> I was on crutches and had no idea I'd play against Tennessee. The night before the game, at the hotel in Knoxville, our team physician took off the cast. He said I'd be able to dress for the game, if nothing else, as Coach Thomas wanted.
>
> I was a yellow belly. I asked him if there was any chance of the bone sticking out without the cast on it. He assured me that wouldn't happen.
>
> A few minutes before the game, when Coach Thomas was making his pep talk to the squad, he asked Coach Hank if

he had anything to say. Coach Hank said he did, then got up to talk to us. He had a cigarette dangling from his mouth when he said, "I'll tell you one thing. I don't know about the rest of you, you or you or you, but I know ol' Number 34 will be after them today."

In those days they changed players' numbers almost every week, basically so Coach Hank could sell a lot of game programs. So he's up there talking ol' number 34. I looked down to see what my jersey number was, just to see, and there it was as plain as day, ol' 34.

I had cold chills running up my spine. I was shocked. When I looked up, Coach Thomas and Coach Hank were looking at me. I guess everybody in the dressing room was. Then Coach Thomas said, "Bryant, can you play?"

What could I have said? I just ran on out there.

I was as lucky as a priest because I played the rest of the year on that broken leg. It wasn't much of a break, but it was broken, and I was fortunate to have a good game against Tennessee that afternoon.

In that game Bryant caught a pass that helped along the first touchdown drive; caught a pass, pitched the football to a teammate and made a block to get him into the end zone for the second touchdown; and made numerous tackles as Alabama shut out Tennessee.

The next morning, the *Knoxville News-Sentinel* featured a column written by **Bob Wilson** that said:

A magician must serve as physician for the Alabama football squad. Nothing less than a hokus-pokus [sic] man could have done the miracle in healing the lame, hurt, and sick in such a quick time.

Bear Bryant, an end, had a broken leg. That is, as late as Saturday morning.

But the magician medicine man waved his wand shortly

before the game. Those Tidesmen, who a few hours before had been using crutches, walking sticks and rolling chairs, suddenly became strong, husky, vicious athletes.

A few days later, **Ralph McGill**, writing in the *Atlanta Constitution*, said, "As far as this season is concerned, Paul Bryant has first place in the courage league. Bryant displayed true courage and determination. Putting aside all thoughts of

Paul "Bear" Bryant was a strapping young man as a University of Alabama offensive and defensive end during the 1930s.

Courtesy of Paul Bryant Museum

pain, he went on to play what is thought to be one of the best games of his career."

McGill was skeptical before writing. He even asked to view x-rays of the leg with the cracked fibula.

The fame of Bryant spread and he received an ovation from Georgia fans the next weekend in Athens, Georgia. "That's the only one I ever got as a player," he said.

Actually, Bryant was a better than average player. He arrived on campus from Fordyce, Arkansas, and had to take a foreign language course at Tuscaloosa High School before enrolling at Alabama. He played on Crimson Tide teams that produced 7–1–1, 10–0, and 6–2–1 records, 23–3–2 overall. His favorite victory came in the 1935 Rose Bowl, when Alabama defeated Stanford 29–13 with Millard "Dixie" Howell and Don Hutson starring.

Bryant talked about the Rose Bowl trip and how excited he was to be a part of it:

People ask me if I remember anything about the 1935 Rose Bowl, and I tell them I remember everything about it.

I remember how cold chills ran up my back, and still do, when I think about a telegram our team received from Stanford before our final regular season game with Vanderbilt. The telegram said, "If you win decisively, where can we reach you after the game?"

I remember the train trip. How long it was—and all of that free food they fed us.

I remember falling in love with California.

I remember there were movie stars all over the place.

I remember every minute of the game—their great tailback Bobby Grayson running for a touchdown in the first quarter to give them a 7–0 lead.

I remember "Dixie" Howell hitting off me [his block] and spinning out and running for the touchdown that should have tied the game. But Riley Smith missed the point-after kick.

Most of all, I remember we had the game won by the fourth quarter.

Bryant had a couple of other recollections of that Rose Bowl that were humorous. Each player was allowed to invite a female guest to Pasadena, California, as his sponsor. **Bryant** offered an invitation to Barbara Del Simmons, a girlfriend from Pine Bluff, Arkansas, then went one over the limit when he offered an invitation to Mary Harmon Black, whom he had started dating that year at Alabama:

> I had no idea both Mary Harmon and Barbara Del would show up. In fact, it looked for a while like I wouldn't have a sponsor at all. But that's what happened, two girls at the Rose Bowl, and I had to do a lot of explaining. After she heard me out, I don't guess Barbara Del and I said two words to each other the entire time we were on the West Coast. As for Mary Harmon, well, I was trying to balance the scales a little because she was so pretty she had what seemed like a million boys after her. That whole escapade almost cost me two girlfriends and, of course, a lifelong mate.

Late in the fourth quarter of the game, **Bryant** discovered something unusual on the playing field:

> Stanford was in a huddle and I looked down to the ground. Right next to my knee was a big pile of silver. There were dimes, quarters, and half dollars. I don't know where it came from, but I knew somebody up there not only liked me but was leaning my way. It was a lot of money, probably about three dollars in change.
>
> I scooped it up real fast and was holding it to take to the bench between plays. Then, lo and behold, here comes Bobby Grayson on a run around my end. It was the only decent tackle I made all day—and I lost my money doing it.

On April 17, 1981, **Bryant** told another good story on himself about the 1935 Rose Bowl. It provides insight into how he was as a college player, interestingly, not all that different from his high school years:

We were full of ourselves when we got to Pasadena for the Rose Bowl, and Coach Thomas knew it. So he sort of reeled us in by putting a hard curfew on us. He'd let us go out, but we had to be in extremely early. Mostly, we were just practicing and sitting.

Don Hutson, "Dixie" Howell, Riley Smith, Young Boozer, and I organized some crap games and some card games—you know, something to do to pass the hours. The games got larger, longer, and louder until Coach Thomas had enough. We looked like a bunch of quail scurrying for underbrush when he came through the door and let us have it about gambling like that.

Then that night a few of us stayed out way too late, down on The Strip, where the lights were bright. I don't think we made it back to the hotel until almost daylight.

Well, the next afternoon Coach Hank [Crisp] called a few of us aside and said Coach Thomas was mad as hell and was thinking about sending about a dozen of us home. He went down the list of names and mine was on it. I almost threw up—and I was about to cry. There we were, living a dream, and it was about to be over for us before the game.

Later, Coach Hank told me Coach Thomas didn't know a thing about us missing curfew. In fact, he said he wasn't sure about that himself, but that he knew we weren't thinking about football. It worked like a charm. No more craps, no more cards and no more long nights on the town. It was just football from that point on.

༄

Paul wrote me a letter when he was playing at Alabama and said he was thinking about coming home. He was worried about his mother and his brothers and sisters.

—COLLINS KILGORE, cousin

Collins Kilgore, Bryant's cousin, describes how Bryant worried about his family back home:

When Paul was playing football at Alabama, he constantly fretted over what was happening back home in Fordyce. I told him everybody was proud of him, that's what was happening, and he should be happy about all the talk he was prompting. But he worried that his family needed him at home working.

I asked Paul if he was enjoying himself, and he said, "Yeah, it's the best thing that ever happened to me. I'm learning things about football from Coach Thomas that I never dreamed."

Paul told me Coach Thomas would lecture the team one day and then the next day make players go up to a chalkboard and explain what he had said. Paul said almost everybody was scared to death that Coach Thomas was going to call on them and make them diagram plays and explain how they worked. But he said he loved being in that position because he knew the offenses and defenses from top to bottom.

I suggested to Paul that day that maybe he would become a coach. He said, "Yeah, Collins, that's come to mind a few times." So I asked him how in the world he thought he could become a coach if he quit and came home to work. I told him it seemed to me his best bet to never have to farm again would be to learn all he could about football.

That's the last time I remember hearing him say anything about quitting the team.

❦

Paul hopped a freight train and rode it home for a visit.

—**LOUISE GOOLSBY,** sister

Louise Goolsby, Bryant's sister who resides in Nashville, Tennessee, remembers her brother's early days as a player and how he struggled with a determined sense of independence.

Paul got his introduction to football in Fordyce and became quite a player. When he was in high school, some men from the University of Alabama showed up and asked him if he wanted to go to college and play. He said, "Yeah, I really do."

People have said those men approached Paul while he was running home from high school, which was his way of staying in shape, put him in the car and took off for Tuscaloosa. I don't recall it happening just that way, but I do know Paul completed his high school requirements after getting to Alabama.

Players didn't get much in those days, so Paul swept floors and worked in the campus dining hall to make some money. I've been told he didn't have many clothes, just a few some people gave him, and didn't have sheets for his bed.

I was in Dallas going to business school to learn how to be a secretary when I got a letter from Paul. He said he was disappointed he didn't have enough money to buy our mother a card on Mother's Day. It was obvious he didn't have some things he should have, that he was struggling a little, so I borrowed $100 and bought him all sorts of things. I think it took me two years to pay back that loan, but we were so close there wasn't any way I was going let him go without some things he needed.

At some point during that time, Paul hopped a freight

train and rode it home for a visit. A few of us where there at the time, our mother and a couple of his other sisters. We listened to him talk about playing football and what it was like at Alabama. Finally, our mother asked him if he had any money. He said, "Sure. I've got all I need."

Later, our mother saw his pants hanging over a chair. She went through the pockets and all she found was three pennies. She put twenty dollars in a pocket before he left to go back to Tuscaloosa. It wasn't long before she got a letter from him with the twenty dollars in it. After seeing our mother struggle like she did to make ends meet, there wasn't any way Paul was going to take that money from her.

3

THE SUPERSTAR

So this must be what God looks like.

—**GEORGE BLANDA,** Kentucky
and professional player

George Blanda said he thought that when he first met Paul "Bear" Bryant, who coached football at the University of Kentucky from 1946 through 1953.

Earlier Bryant had coached at Maryland (1945), and later he coached at Texas A&M (1954 through 1957), and at Alabama (1958 through 1982). His overall record as a head coach was 323-85-17, including six wins at Maryland, sixty wins at Kentucky, twenty-five wins at Texas A&M, and 232 wins at Alabama.

Bryant won six national championships, all while leading the Crimson Tide. He won fourteen Southeastern Conference championships, one at Kentucky and thirteen at Alabama. He won one Southwest Conference championship at Texas A&M. He led Kentucky to four bowl games, Texas A&M to one bowl game, and the Crimson Tide to twenty-four bowl games, consecutive appearances between 1959 and 1982.

While Blanda might have been guilty of an overstatement

upon his introduction to Bryant, there is no doubt the coach had a way of impressing people and, of course, of inspiring his players, assistant coaches, and other staff members to strive to be the best they could in their pursuits of football championships.

The impact has lingered. In 1981, the afternoon before victory number 314 in State College, Pennsylvania, 31–16 over Penn State, **Washington Serini**, another of Bryant's Kentucky stars, sat in a Holiday Inn and waited for his former coach to arrive. More than two decades after his playing career had ended, he had driven to the site of the game with the idea of a surprise reunion with Bryant.

"That man taught everybody he coached at Kentucky everything we needed to make it through life," Serini said as he waited anxiously for Bryant to arrive. "He was tough and demanding on the football field, to the point he pushed us as far as we could go, but he was like a second father off the football field. I owe a great debt to Paul Bryant, the greatest coach who ever lived."

When Bryant strolled into the lobby, Serini rose to his feet. Tears rolled down his cheeks as he ran to the coach, embraced him warmly and, as a show of the strength he claimed to have garnered as a player, lifted him off the floor.

"It's great to see you, George Washington Serini," Bryant said. "I'm glad to see an ol' Kentucky gent here today."

Serini introduced Bryant to his wife and daughter, who was a Penn State student. The coach greeted them with Southern warmth then said, "Your father was a tough ol' player, a great one. In fact, Wash is the only player to ever block three punts in the Blue-Gray All-Star Game."

Serini smiled, proudly, obviously delighted the coach remembered, and said something about Bryant being an impenetrable taskmaster. They sat and talked about old times for about half an hour.

"Coach Bryant, I'll never forget how you made us attempt

to knock down power poles during blocking drills because you didn't like the way we were scrimmaging," Serini said. "We knew there wasn't any way we'd move those poles, but we darn sure tried to do that for you."

Bryant chuckled and said, "Wash, I'd rather you not tell those kinds of stories about me. Remember, I'm the coach everybody accused of teaching brutal football."

"It wasn't brutal, but it was hard," Serini said.

There was a pause.

"I'm here to thank you, Coach Bryant."

The following afternoon, after Alabama had won, Penn State fans offered gratitude, too. They formed a tunnel at least six people deep on both sides under the grandstands in "Happy Valley" and applauded Bryant, who that day tied Amos Alonzo Stagg as the most winning coach in collegiate history.

ॐ

Coach Bryant, the man, was bigger than life. He reminded me a lot of a character in an old John Wayne movie—or John Wayne himself. He lived hard. He played hard. He coached hard. He was a giant man, no doubt. After I graduated from Alabama and went to the NFL, I was amazed by how many people asked me what he was like and what it was like playing for him. He had a following across the nation, maybe around the world.

—BOB BAUMHOWER,
Alabama and professional player

ॐ

We were at a charity golf tournament in Los Angeles and

they had all kinds of movie stars there. But Coach Bryant always had the biggest crowd following him—and he hit the ball better when they gathered up around him. He wasn't what you'd term a great golfer, but when he was under the spotlight, had that crowd watching, he'd hit the ball 200 or more yards off the tee, straight as an arrow. Now, he might end up making a 10 on the hole, or some bad score, but he always looked a lot better when people were watching. I always thought he thrived on that type attention, got pumped up and usually rose to the occasion.

—**BILLY VARNER,** confidant,
friend, and driver

Bryant took a liking to Billy Varner after frequent conversations with him in the 19th hole at Indian Hills Country Club in Tuscaloosa, Alabama, where he worked as a bartender. He said he liked his smile and how the normally quiet man talked a lot about his family. So as his fame in football grew, the coach got him a job at the University of Alabama Police Department with the idea he would become his personal driver.

The relationship was long-lasting, more than a decade, until the coach died. Varner was forever amazed by the way people from all walks of life reacted to Bryant, who treated him much more like a confidant and friend than an employee:

Not long before Coach Bryant died, he wanted to go to Fordyce, Arkansas, for a funeral. Neil Morgan, a close friend from Tuscaloosa, agreed to make the trip with us.

When we started to leave, Coach Bryant grabbed some fish he had caught and said, "Billy, maybe we can stop somewhere along the way and get somebody to fry these for us." I got a cooler, iced the fish and away we went.

We got over in Mississippi, in a small town, a place so little I can't remember the name, and came up on a restaurant on the side of the highway. It had a bunch of cars in the parking lot and Coach Bryant said, "Billy, that must be a good place to eat. Let's stop over there and see if they can cook our fish."

Well, he walked in the door and everybody froze. The loud talk stopped and the whispers started. It was like, my goodness, The Bear is here among us. Coach Bryant greeted everybody, something like, "I hope ya'll are doing good," and went to the counter and asked a lady if she could fry the fish. She said, "Oh yeah, my pleasure."

Then Coach Bryant started making the rounds, shaking hands and talking. In a matter of minutes he had a big crowd in the corner. They stopped shooting pinball and gathered around him. To my amazement, he started inviting everybody to eat with us. I was thinking, "Oh no, we've only got a few fish in a bag and he's lining up dinner guests."

When he got up to ten or twelve folks, I decided to make something happen. I walked over to the lady who owned the restaurant, the one he had asked to fry the fish, and asked if she could cook us something else, like several hamburgers and a lot of fried chicken. I suggested she might want to put some trimmings on the side because it looked like we were going have a giant crowd at the table.

Meanwhile, Coach Bryant and Neil Morgan were enjoying themselves talking about football and farming with those people.

Well, she brought out the food and I quickly grabbed a hamburger and got out of the way. I wasn't going to touch that fish because that's what The Man wanted to eat. I didn't want him getting on me for eating all the fish, making fun of me for being fat, so I took my hamburger and sat and listened while I ate.

That setting was unusual, to say the least, but that's how it was with Coach Bryant. He loved being around people who recognized him and made a big deal over him. But he also loved the few times he had with down-to-earth people, folks a lot like him, at least like he said he was growing up.

෪

The minute the guy saw Coach Bryant, he went crazy. He started screaming, "Hey, I know you. Yes I do. Oh, my gosh. It's him. Yes, it is. Oh, my goodness, I can't wait to tell people who I ran into today." He kept pacing and chanting, clapping his hands and shaking his head—never calling Coach Bryant by name, just screaming that he knew who he was.

—Terry Henley, Auburn player

Terry Henley played running back for Auburn University from 1969 through 1972. He was a star for the Tigers as a senior, the Southeastern Conference player of the year for a team that defeated Alabama 17–16 by blocking two punts for touchdowns late in the fourth quarter.

Bryant did not take kindly to losing to Auburn, the intrastate rival, but he respected Henley, was impressed by his ability and liked the quick wit he displayed as a player:

It was in 1976 and I was flying out of Birmingham for a meeting in Atlanta. When I got on the airplane, I immediately saw Coach Bryant sitting in first class and spoke to him as I made my way to the coach section. I was surprised when he called me by my name because I had no idea he'd know me.

Before I could sit down, he hollered for me to join him in first class. I sort of shook my head, but he got louder and demanded I take the vacant seat beside him.

Coach Bryant had a couple of drinks en route to Atlanta and we talked about a little of everything. I believe he was going to a reunion with his Kentucky players, maybe his Maryland players, and I know he was really looking forward to it.

When we got off the airplane in Atlanta and started walking along the concourse, I told him I enjoyed the visit, that it was a real pleasure. He said, "Terry, come on with me. I've got a little layover. Let's go in one of these bars."

The minute we stepped inside, the bartender recognized Coach Bryant and started chanting. He went on and on— "Yes sir, I know you . . . You're the best . . . By golly, I recognized that face as soon as I saw it." He was like a little kid. Then he said, "I'm gonna buy you a drink. Yep, that's what I'm gonna do."

Coach Bryant said, "Fine, thank you. I'll have a double vodka and tonic."

Then the bartender said, "Yes sir, Coach Bryant. It's coming up—and I'm gonna buy half of it."

Coach Bryant got a kick out of that—"I'm gonna buy half of it." He was still laughing when we parted.

☙

We were gathered around the craps table rolling away when somebody said The Coach has disappeared. I looked up and Coach Bryant was gone. I noticed a big stack of chips at his position and figured he had gone to the restroom. We kept playing until Billy Varner walked up and asked if any of us knew where Coach Bryant was. He looked worried. Suddenly, everybody was more than a little concerned about his safety.

—"BROTHER" HARRIS,
Tuscaloosa friend

In stark contrast to the pleasant time he had at a restaurant in a small town in Mississippi, **Billy Varner** recounts how Bryant liked bright lights, too, such as occasional trips to Las Vegas with power broker friends from Tuscaloosa and Birmingham, Alabama:

I remember the night Coach Bryant disappeared because I was convinced somebody had kidnapped him.

Coach Bryant disappeared at some point after I went to the restroom. When I came back, he wasn't in sight. I told his friends to keep their eyes out for him, then took off on a long walk around the casino to see if I could find him. After about an hour of searching, I got scared and went to find a security officer.

The folks in Las Vegas knew Coach Bryant well, and they really liked having him out there. He was like an attraction who didn't have to get on a stage to entertain fans. People just loved being in his presence.

The security people went to work. They had a full force looking long and hard for Coach Bryant. As time passed, I was getting more worried that somebody had kidnapped him. Then a house detective came to tell me The Man was okay.

Coach Bryant had gone to the restroom, like we thought at first, but instead of walking all the way back to the craps table he was playing, he joined another game. He was doing good at that table, too, because he had another big pile of chips in front of him when I first saw him.

⊛

When Coach Bryant opened the door to the hotel suite, I was standing there with some coffee, orange juice, and breakfast. He said, "Billy, where in hell have you been? I've been worried about you." He didn't crack a smile, but I know he realized he had locked me out of the suite at some point during the night.

—**BILLY VARNER,** confidant,
friend, and driver

One of the funnier things that happened when I was traveling with Coach Bryant came in Las Vegas. He was out there for some function, an appearance, and, as usual, he mixed a little pleasure with his business.

After spending a few hours on the gambling floor, he decided to go upstairs to bed. I guess it was about 11 P.M. He said I could stay behind and have some fun, if I wanted, but I told him I'd go up with him and get some sleep.

Coach Bryant went to bed, and I sat in the suite for a while watching television. I got the urge to go downstairs, you know, to look around and take in some of the action. I was probably down there about an hour, maybe two.

When I got back to the suite, I discovered Coach Bryant had put on the security lock. There wasn't any way for me to get inside without waking him, so I decided to go back downstairs. I checked the door about every hour, and it remained locked.

Now, I knew about what time Coach Bryant would get up, so I came up with a plan. Ultimately, at about six A.M. I went to a restaurant adjacent to the casino and got a breakfast tray, with orange juice and coffee included. A waitress told me they would be glad to deliver the food through room service, but I declined her offer and said I'd take it up.

I stood in the hallway for a while, then heard Coach Bryant unhooking the security lock. I waited a few more minutes, knocked on the door and said, "Coach Bryant, how about some breakfast?"

Coach Bryant and I never did discuss how I left the suite and he locked me out. But he had a big grin on his face when we sat down and ate breakfast.

ॐ

Few people knew Paul "Bear" Bryant was a fan of Ann Landers, the syndicated newspaper columnist who provides advice for wayward souls from all walks of life. He read her column every morning, before turning to the stock market report and the sports pages.

Often, Bryant read her column to his football players, at least those he thought would make a positive impact. He and Landers exchanged letters and had at least one telephone conversation.

Whether Bryant and Landers ever met personally is unknown. But the admiration was mutual, as **Ira Berkow** of the *New York Times* discovered on December 10, 1982.

Berkow interviewed Bryant in New York City. Interestingly, that was the same week he confirmed his replacement as Alabama's coach. He was having dinner with New York Giants Coach Ray Perkins, when he leaned toward him and said, "Walter, it's time to come home."

Berkow had no reason to believe Bryant was about to retire, or else his column would have had another slant. But the words he wrote explained much about the admiration the coach had for the wisdom Landers expressed.

Here is a portion of that column:

Several times over the years, Paul "Bear" Bryant, an academician at the University of Alabama, has penned letters to Ann Landers. They are not the conventional ones she gets that seek advice for the lovelorn.

The old football coach with a face lined like a walnut is still tough at age sixty-nine, but he does not seem lorn of love.

When he writes Ann, America's equivalent of the Oracle of Delphi, it is generally to compliment her on a column. He says he had read jillions of 'em to his football players. He says he appreciates her moral stance and her sense of humor.

Ann Landers replies quickly, not only because she is the most dedicated of respondents, but, she says, she was flattered by the Bear's attention.

Even though she has never been able to learn football—"I just can't hack it," she says. "I keep looking for the ball while everyone else is cheering"—she is aware that the Bear has won more games than any other coach in college football history.

Once she dropped him a note of thanks and said if he were ever in Chicago, where she lives, to please call, that she'd love to meet him.

Last August, she received an unexpected telephone call. "It was from the Bear," she said. "He didn't growl, as I thought he might, he purred like a pussycat."

He was calling from Tuscaloosa and requested a column she had done twelve years ago. The column, which he reads every fall to his freshman football players, had been misplaced and, as he said, he didn't know where in the world it was.

The column is entitled "Dead at 17." It's a hypothetical account of a boy who takes the family car, drives carelessly, has a wreck and sees himself declared dead and buried.

"It's a story that really gets to you," Bryant said. "And Ann very graciously said she'd rerun it."

One may not expect Bear Bryant to be reading the letters of La Rochefoucauld or Montesquieu at breakfast. But not epistles beginning "Dear Ann" either.

"I'll take advice from anyone if I think it's good," Bryant said. "And anyone who's been in business as long as she has, has to be good."

As for football coaches, she is impressed with Bear Bryant.

"He must be a very sensitive, warm person to care so

much about the kids who pass through his life," she said. "I have a feeling he cares more about them than he does his record of being the coach with all of those wins."

If he were to write a letter to Ann Landers asking for advice, what would he say?

He replied, "Dear Ann: Help. Bear."

And how would Ann Landers respond? "I'd say, hang in there, Bear. They need you. Don't let a bum season discourage you. You've still got plenty to give."

I really haven't gotten over the inferiority complex I had as a kid. I'm nervous around a lot of people, in awe of what they've accomplished. I've just learned to hide it better.

—PAUL "BEAR" BRYANT, in 1982,
just before his last season
as Alabama's coach

Bryant certainly *seemed* comfortable in all settings, whether with the rich and famous or the poor and uncelebrated. One of his dear friends was Bob Hope, the comedian. He and Bryant played a lot of golf together. Also, he came to Tuscaloosa during the 1970s and filmed a skit entitled "Thunder Foot" for his annual *Look Magazine All-America* television special with the coach and Joe Namath, a former Alabama and New York Jets quarterback.

John Wayne adored Bryant and sometimes joked about how similarities between the two were often mentioned. Numerous entertainers who passed through Tuscaloosa stopped by his office for visits or to pick up autographed pictures. When singer Olivia Newton-John requested an autograph, the coach studied the hyphenated last name and asked his secretary, "Am I suppose to put a dash in this last name?"

Former United States presidents Richard Nixon, Gerald Ford, Jimmy Carter, and Ronald Reagan were corresponding friends. So was syndicated columnist Ann Landers. New York Yankees owner George Steinbrenner often invited Bryant to the "Big Apple" as his special guest.

Bryant had two meaningful meetings with President John Fitzgerald Kennedy. The first came just after Alabama won a national championship in 1961, when the coach, quarterback Pat Trammell, and university president Dr. Frank Rose went to New York City to be honored. The second came after the Crimson Tide defeated Oklahoma in the 1963 Orange Bowl, 17–0; it was the last football game Kennedy attended before he was assassinated in Dallas, Texas.

The list of famous friends is much longer, too lengthy to complete.

Perhaps the crowning evening for the superstar coach, came not long after he became the most prolific winner in college football history with victory number 315. "America's Tribute to Paul 'Bear' Bryant" was staged in Washington, D.C., in a large hotel ballroom that was filled to capacity despite a steep price per admission.

On the day before the black tie affair, Bryant had two meetings that meant a lot to him.

During the afternoon he went to the White House for a meeting with Vice President George Bush, who was subbing for President Ronald Reagan, who was out of the country. The entourage was small. Paul Bryant Jr., his son, Billy Varner, his confidant, and I accompanied him. The meeting was held in the Old Executive Office Building.

During the evening I sat with him and had a few drinks for about an hour in his hotel suite as Mary Harmon Bryant, his wife, relaxed in their bedroom. He was waiting for the arrival of a contingent of players from his years at Texas A&M.

"I'm really looking forward to seeing those guys," Bryant

said. "They paid a hard price to become winners. There won't be a soft one among those from our team in 1954 because I almost killed them during preseason practice."

The coach grew pensive.

Then he said, "The ones who survived, and there damn sure weren't many, gave me this ring after they won the Southwest Conference championship in 1956. It's a prized possession."

There was a knock on the door at the top of the hour. The Aggies had arrived precisely on time.

"Alfred, if you've got the stomach for a lot of bullshit, stay and listen to us reminisce about those days at A&M," Bryant said after making numerous introductions.

I excused myself, stating it would be best for Aggies to enjoy their reunion in private.

All of Bryant's football programs were represented by large numbers at the festive banquet the following evening, with Terrapins, Wildcats, Aggies, and Crimson Tiders in the audience. The Reverend Billy Graham, a friend of Mary Harmon Bryant, presented the invocation. The musical group Alabama provided entertainment. Then when it ended, Bryant led a processional out of the ballroom. At his side was Billy Varner.

It was at that moment that Bill "Brother" Oliver, a former Alabama defensive halfback under Bryant in the early 1960s and an assistant coach numerous years under Bryant, observed and heard something interesting that should tell us a lot about the coach honored that night.

"As they walked out of the ballroom, Coach Bryant was signing autographs on the left side and Billy Varner was signing autographs on the right side," Oliver said. "It was obvious Billy was a little uncomfortable, but he was signing away as fast as he could. This went on from the time they left the head table until they reached the exit. Suddenly, Coach Bryant noticed Billy signing autographs. He stopped, looked at Billy and said, 'Take your time, Billy, I'll get the car.'

"That's the man I remember. Coach Bryant was as loyal to the people who worked for him as the people who served under his leadership were to him. That's truly a mark of greatness."

While that exchange with a confidant, friend and driver speaks volumes about Bryant and his memory of his past, when things did not come so triumphantly, only people close to him got to see that side of the man—or else took time to notice.

But with that stated, it is bewildering how the Bryant legend was built for reasons other than out of the ordinary winning.

Controversy seemed to follow Bryant at every stop he made as a coach: Maryland for one season, Kentucky for eight seasons, Texas A&M for four seasons and Alabama for twenty-five seasons. As a crisis festered, then subsided, he grew in stature. Observers across the nation wanted to know more about a coach who seemed to come and go routinely in the spotlight.

In that regard, the superstar threatened time and again to become a fallen star—only to rise and to glow more brilliantly.

Bryant produced a 6-2-1 record in 1946, his only season at Maryland. He had the Terrapins' players and fans at a feverish pitch after years of losing until the school president, Dr. Curly Byrd, abruptly instructed him to reinstate a player he had kicked off the team for drinking in a bar because the chief executive of the university was a friend of the banished young man's family.

Bryant considered the proposition for roughly one hour, although he said he slept on it a night, and decided to resign. He broke the news to Byrd the next morning, during a heated exchange, and a newspaper man overheard the remark.

Suddenly, Byrd was on the defensive. Students were so outraged by the resignation that they threatened to boycott classes. Also, there was talk of students rioting until Bryant addressed the student body on campus and urged restraint.

"I could've won that battle," Bryant said. "But I was stubborn and I was going to make my point. The whole thing was based on the fact I would've lost my entire team if I had taken back that player who didn't have the discipline I preached about. Then it came down to me backing down, telling Curly Byrd I wanted to keep my job at Maryland. I wasn't going to do that because I knew I wouldn't be able to look at my face in the mirror.

"It wasn't a comfortable time. I'd be lying if I said I didn't shed some tears agonizing over that job. Hell, anybody would've felt that way not knowing what might happen."

Bryant put to rest that storm, returned to his office and discovered a telegram on his desk from the president of the University of Kentucky. Dr. Herman Donovan invited him to lead that program. "As feelings of relief go, the one I had at that moment was about as big as they come," he said.

ᔕ

I've never seen a person work so hard in my life. Coach Bryant demanded the same thing from all of us.

—STEVE MEILINGER, Kentucky player

Steve Meilinger discovered the coach at Kentucky, Bryant, was a man who knew football and did not mind working almost around the clock to lift the Wildcats' fortunes within the Southeastern Conference. He made All-America as a tight end, 1952 and 1953, while playing on teams that produced 5-4-2 and 7-2-1 records:

Coach Bryant seemed to be everywhere. That was particularly the case on the practice field. He could just walk past the offense and take a quick glance and see what was going wrong. He could do the same thing with the defense. Not only was he consumed by the job of coaching us, he knew strategy better than anybody we had seen.

I was convinced he had a photographic mind. There'd be seven of us working during a drill, the entire offensive line. He'd watch one play, stop us and give a lecture to each player. It was amazing how he could do that, tell the center what he was doing wrong and tell the tight end what he was doing wrong—all after watching one play.

Also, Coach Bryant labored tirelessly promoting the program. He was all over the state, running in high social circles, promising our supporters that we'd win big. It was an easy sell, really, but he had all of us believing in what he could do to make us winners.

◈

By his own admission, **Bryant** worked almost around the clock while at Kentucky:

I was determined to outwork every coach in the conference, including my assistants. I'd go from 4 A.M. to 8 P.M. at the office, then sit at home by myself and work on practice plans and game plans until midnight. I was possessed. I'd get in the trenches with my players, go one-on-one with them, and I pushed my assistants as far as they could go. I told people Kentucky deserved a championship in football and promised a winner in five years. I wasn't sure that'd happen, not really, but I put the load on my shoulders nonetheless.

Bryant delivered right on time. His first five Kentucky teams produced 7–3, 8–2, 5–3–2, 9–3 and 11–1 records. The 1950 team, his fifth, won a conference championship and defeated Oklahoma 13–7 in the 1951 Sugar Bowl. That victory ended a 31-game winning streak by the Sooners.

But all was not well in Lexington, Kentucky. After the Wildcats won conference championships in football and basketball, the school rewarded Bryant with a watch and rewarded Coach Adolph Rupp with a car. The football coach was livid. The basketball coach reveled in the occasion.

⟳

Paul and I got along much better than most people think. It was simply a case of basketball being the most popular sport in The Commonwealth.

—**ADOLPH RUPP,** Kentucky
basketball coach

In an interesting development, Adolph Rupp, the great basketball coach, was discussing his years working at Kentucky alongside Bryant in the press box during halftime of a football game at Commonwealth Stadium in Lexington, Kentucky, on September 22, 1973. The Wildcats were leading Alabama 14–0 at that point, but they eventually lost 28–14.

"I count Paul among my dear friends," Rupp said that afternoon. "We had our differences, yes, because he wanted what was best for football and I wanted what was best for basketball. It has been said, maybe far too much, that there was not room for both sports at Kentucky. I differ with that opinion.

"I was an admirer of what Paul did with the football program. He exceeded expectations, including mine.

"As years have passed, I think Paul and I have forgotten the bad things everybody else talked about so much."

Bryant did not talk much about his relationship with Rupp. He did have dinner with the basketball coach when Kentucky played games against Alabama after his arrival in Tuscaloosa.

"I was never sure exactly what the relationship between Coach Bryant and Coach Rupp was at the time," said **Wimp Sanderson**, the former Alabama basketball coach. "I'd say they were cordial to each other, for sure. Whether there were any ill feelings left from their years at Kentucky, I don't know."

The crowning blow at Kentucky came when Bryant was assured Rupp was about to retire as basketball coach—a promise that led to him turning down offers to coach at Alabama and Arkansas.

So after weathering two major conflicts at Maryland and Kentucky, as his superstar status grew, Bryant decided to make another career move. Immediately after accepting the challenge of coaching Texas A&M football, he found himself in the middle of another dark cloud that attracted national attention.

ॐ

When we arrived at Texas A&M, we were pretty shocked by what we saw. There wasn't much there, at least not to speak of, and Mama was really upset. She loved our time at Kentucky. She had the house of her dreams and she and Papa ran in social circles while we were in Lexington. About all we saw in College Station was a small town and military barracks on the campus. Mae Martin and I had a different opinion than Mama. My sister was at an age when she liked seeing all of the cadets. As for me, I liked seeing the cadets in uniforms and seeing an occasional tank beside a classroom building.

—PAUL BRYANT JR., son

ॐ

I've seen a lot of hard football practices in my life. We work players extremely hard at Alabama from time to time. But I haven't seen a practice that even comes close to matching what we went through at Junction, Texas.

—DEE POWELL, Texas A&M player
and Alabama assistant coach

Dee Powell, an Alabama assistant coach from 1964 through 1982, played under Bryant at Texas A&M. He was a member of the 1954 team that went to Junction, Texas, a desolate location, for preseason practice. A large squad reported that year and only twenty-seven players survived to participate in the opening game:

From the time Coach Bryant arrived at Texas A&M, it was obvious to everybody things were going to be done a little differently than in the past. His hiring created a stir, to say the least, because the newspapers reported how much success he had rebuilding fortunes at Kentucky.

Coach Bryant has always been a master motivator, and he took the state by storm. I don't recall being there, but he used to tell a story about how he rallied the troops, so to speak, just after taking the job. That included the corps of cadets.

Coach Bryant went to The Grove, an outdoor theater on campus, and there were about 5,000 Aggies there to greet him. He took off his coat and stomped on it. He took off his tie and stomped on it. He rolled up his sleeves. Then he introduced himself and said he had arrived to go to work.

More or less, Coach Bryant cast a spell on everybody.

Coach Bryant was right about the work, and it wasn't long before all of his players knew we were going to work, too. He took us to Junction for preseason practice. It was in the middle of nowhere, just a dust bowl. There were some barracks out there and there was a big fence surrounding the property. The gate was locked and only a few people had keys.

He worked our fannies off, starting early in the morning and going on through the heat of the day, when it was 100 degrees plus. The only relief we got were short dips in a lake. As you might imagine, that was an unforgettable experience for a bunch of young men who hadn't been out of high school long.

The numbers kept dwindling. The only sound we'd hear in the middle of the night was suitcases shutting, the snaps closing, and the chain rattling on the gate. People were getting out of there as fast as possible, without telling Coach Bryant they were ready to give it up.

Coach Bryant seemed unfazed. He kept preaching that the ones who made it back to College Station together would be winners.

That first Texas A&M team produced a 1–9 record. The second went 7–2–1. The third went 9–0–1 and won the Southwest Conference championship.

Bryant was the toast of Aggieland. But the next wave of trouble was already in place. Texas A&M was placed on probation for recruiting rules violations.

Bryant was embarrassed when he was told about the action during a Southwest Conference meeting, at which time he was chastised by the Texas A&M president.

"Everybody was buying players back then, left and right, and I allowed some big oil men to get out of hand," **Bryant** said on August 11, 1980. "I cried like a little baby when they put us on probation. I learned from it, too. I hit my knees and asked Our Maker to forgive me. We took a shortcut, pure and simple, and I promised to never do it again."

The 1957 regular season got off to a good start at Texas A&M. The Aggies won their first eight games and were ranked first in the nation. But word leaked that Bryant had agreed to make a move to Alabama and the team went flat, losing its final three games, including the Gator Bowl to Tennessee.

∽

I left Texas A&M for one reason. Mama called.

—PAUL "BEAR" BRYANT on his
decision to move to Alabama

When Bryant arrived at Alabama prior to spring practice in 1958, he hit the ground running. He was too wise to organize a boot camp like the one his first Texas A&M team experienced, maybe because new rules prohibited preseason practice away from campus, but worked his players hard and, more importantly, he took control of a program that had lost its discipline in three seasons under Coach J. B. "Ears" Whitworth.

∽

I watched a television news account of that first spring practice under Coach Bryant, and I looked at my dad and said, "What have I gotten myself into?" I knew the summer was going to be something like I'd never experienced.

—BILLY RICHARDSON,
Alabama player

Billy Richardson, a small running back, was among the first players Bryant recruited at Alabama. As a senior in 1961, he and his teammates won a national championship. That came after a tough beginning in Tuscaloosa:

We'd heard how tough Coach Bryant was, how demanding, and I was a little nervous when I signed an Alabama scholarship. But I wanted to be a part of something new, a fresh start, and I think most of the guys who signed with the Crimson Tide that year felt the same way.

I recall during the spring of 1958, a few months after I had signed my scholarship, sitting at home with my dad watching video clips of Alabama's spring practice. Wow, what a scene it was. You'd see eight or ten coaches on the practice field with, maybe, about thirty players. They'd pile up in blocking and tackling drills and the intensity was unbelievable. The coaches were screaming, "Get back in the huddle . . . run, run, run . . . get up, get back." They were grabbing players and throwing them this way and that way. It was something totally wild.

As a kid about to graduate from high school, it made me extremely nervous about my choice of colleges.

None of it really made much sense to me until our first team meeting with Coach Bryant. This was after the freshmen reported about a week after the varsity was on campus. He was a man who appeared totally in charge. He spoke to us as a group, but it was almost like he was talking to each one of us eye to eye. He told us his plan for success and that we would get Alabama back to a championship level again. He told us to work hard in school, that anybody who didn't wouldn't play for him. He told us to stay in touch with our parents, to write them or call them on a regular basis. He told us it wouldn't be easy becoming champions, that we'd have to work our tails off, but he assured us we could accomplish that if we'd come together as a team.

I assure you he didn't lie to us about it being hard.

There were only about thirty varsity players left by the time preseason practice started, so all of us freshmen had to scrimmage against them. By the time practice ended the first day in pads, there was only one quarterback left standing, Mal Moore, and I had lost fifteen pounds. Some people were staying and some were leaving. I guess all of us felt like going at one time or another.

But Coach Bryant remained the same. He knew what it'd take for us to get there. By the time preseason practice was over, all of us believed in him.

Alabama, which had won four games the previous three seasons, produced a 5–4–1 record in 1958. The Crimson Tide was 7–2–2 in 1959, when it lost to Penn State in the Liberty Bowl; 8–1–2 in 1960, when it tied Texas in the Bluebonnet Bowl; and 11–0 in 1961, when as national champion it defeated Arkansas in the Sugar Bowl.

ॐ

Paul Bryant is changing the way football will be played in the Southeastern Conference from this day forward with Alabama's helmet-busting, gang-tackling style of defense.

—RALPH "SHUG" JORDAN, Auburn coach

ॐ

Those first few years at Alabama were tough, no doubt about that. It was hard work and it was conducted in one way—the Paul Bryant way. Anybody who didn't buy into his plan had to go.

—JIM GOOSTREE, Alabama trainer

Jim Goostree was Alabama's trainer when Bryant arrived, having accepted the position a year earlier. A Tennessee graduate who had served as a student trainer under Coach Bob

Bryant addresses his 1958 University of Alabama team for the first time at Friedman Hall.

Neyland, he knew what demanding football was about. Still, he was surprised by what he witnessed in 1958:

First of all, Coach Bryant was a big person, tall and handsome, and he looked like he could still play football when he got to Alabama. He had a presence that made you jump when he spoke. He was as pure a leader as I've ever seen.

Coach Bryant was on a mission when he arrived in Tuscaloosa, armed with a master plan, and there were times when things got tough on the practice. In fact, I can remember days when as a trainer it was difficult to watch.

We literally had players walking off the field in the middle of drills. They'd get blocked or tackled, get up and walk away without saying a thing. Most of them didn't walk for long, though, because Coach Bryant normally chased them, kicking at them, hollering, "If you're going to quit on me, you're going to run off this practice field. You're a yellow-striped coward. I don't want . . ."

There was one instance that comes to mind that's humorous

to me, although it wasn't to the player involved. The guy quit and started running off the field. He didn't wait for a team manager to open the gate, either. Instead he just climbed over the fence and kept running toward the dressing room. All the while, Coach Bryant was hollering, "Manager, open the gate and let him out—and get his gear before he carries it off."

It's amazing how it worked out. Six national championships were the result of those hard days on the practice field.

The success at Alabama had added to the superstar status Bryant enjoyed across the nation. But it also created two more rounds of controversy, accusations that hurt the coach.

❧

Coach Bryant didn't coach dirty football and I didn't play dirty football.

—Darwin Holt, Texas A&M
and Alabama player

Darwin Holt was a Texas A&M player under Bryant who followed him to Alabama. He started for the Crimson Tide in 1960 and 1961, called defensive signals, and just after a game on November 18, 1961, he found his name in national headlines.

Alabama defeated Georgia Tech 10–0 in Birmingham. On a punt return, Holt blocked Graning, with his forearm striking the Georgia Tech player's face, and the result was a shattered jaw. It was a freak accident, although the legal hit was hard-nosed because his elbow made its way under the facemask on the helmet.

Suddenly newspapers and magazines were writing that Bryant taught his players brutal tactics. Most of the articles originated in Atlanta, the home of Georgia Tech, but the entire nation received a hearty dose of the accusation.

Bryant fretted over the exposure, defended Holt and chastised sports writers for attempting to criticize him by defaming one of his players. Ultimately, the controversy subsided, but it remains memorable in the minds of numerous people close to the Crimson Tide program at that time:

> Coach Bryant didn't coach dirty football and I didn't play dirty football. But that one play against Georgia Tech really damaged both of us in the eyes of fans because of what the Atlanta newspapers wrote about it. I don't know what those reporters had in mind, what their agendas were at the time, but I know they hurt Coach Bryant and they hurt me.
>
> To set the stage, there isn't any way I would have transferred to Alabama from Texas A&M to play for Coach Bryant unless I loved him and respected the way he taught the game. I wouldn't have loved him or respected him if he taught players to use brutal tactics, as many of his critics and my critics said.

Holt received mail from across the nation, with most of the writers criticizing him for dirty play. He received threats. He was a college student, a young man with fragile feelings, who was being, well, brutalized by a portion of the public:

> Chick Graning wasn't defending himself like he should have been. I didn't do anything illegal, outside the rules of football, but I was trashed.
>
> The thing people don't realize, the average person on the sideline or the average fan in the stands, is how quick things happen in football. You don't have time to play pretty. You react and you play, within the rules, and that's what I did.

Remember what brutal football is. The only time it's brutal is when one side is hitting and the other side ain't. You didn't play for Coach Bryant unless you were on the hitting side. If you didn't want to hit somebody or defend yourself when somebody was trying to hit you, he'd have you standing over on the sideline beside him.

—**Larry "Dude" Hennessey,**
Kentucky player and
Alabama assistant coach

ॐ

Many times over and over I heard Coach Bryant preach about playing hard within the rules. In fact, part of that standard talk he made year after year was how he wasn't the least bit interested in hurting another player. He simply wanted us to pursue the football, hit hard, gang tackle and so forth. He wasn't interested in hurting anybody. Football to him was three things: movement, sight, and contact. If you couldn't move, you didn't play. If you couldn't recognize things, you didn't play. If you couldn't hit, you didn't play.

—**Gene Stallings,** Texas A&M
player and Alabama coach

The brutal football issue continued to be a hot theme. It picked up steam when the *Saturday Evening Post* magazine wrote a pointed article about Bryant and the charges. At the urging of friends, he asked for a retraction. After he was not granted one, he sued the magazine for $500,000.

The next round of turmoil for Bryant was the strongest dose he encountered. In an article on March 23, 1963, that created another national wave of interest, the *Saturday Evening Post* accused the coach and former Georgia coach Wallace Butts of fixing the outcome of a game between the two programs.

Alabama won the game 35–0 in Birmingham on September 22, 1962. The magazine article said Butts, then Georgia's athletics director, told Bryant by long distance telephone the strategy the Bulldogs would use. The insinuation was the two coaches were able to place large bets on the outcome. The article hinted Bryant had purposely coached the Crimson Tide to a 7–6 loss to Georgia Tech on November 17, 1962, so he could win a bet on the outcome of that game.

Interestingly, the loss to Georgia Tech was the first for Alabama since October 15, 1960.

⑨

By the time those bad people at the Saturday Evening Post *wrote that second article about Paul, there had been many times through the years when I had seen him upset. But to this day, there hasn't been a time when I've seen him as mad and hurt as he was about that.*

—MARY HARMON BRYANT, wife

Mary Harmon Bryant reflected on the game fixing article at the Bryants' home in Tuscaloosa during the fall of 1981, as her husband conducted an Alabama practice five miles across town. He was a few victories away from becoming the most prolific winner in history at the college level:

I don't have any doubt that article about Paul and Wally Butts orchestrating the outcome in a game has taken some time off of [Bryant's] life. He couldn't understand why somebody would do that. He didn't know exactly how to defend himself against such a mean lie.

Even after he passed a lie detector test and told a million people he hadn't fixed any game or bet on any game, he was still tied in knots.

He'd go to bed at night like he felt fine, then toss and turn. I'd wake up and see him sitting in a chair beside the bed. His pajamas were soaking wet with sweat, and he was smoking cigarettes one after another.

I tried to help by assuring him nobody believed all of that stuff. Then he'd say the same thing. He'd say, "Mary Harmon, it isn't what they're trying to do to me that I'm upset about. I'm mad because it's unfair to my players and my assistant coaches. They're the ones winning, not me, and they don't deserve to have somebody say something like that about our football program."

Paul has always thought the lawsuit he filed after the brutal football article is the reason the game fixing article appeared. That made him madder than a hornet. On more than one occasion he'd say, "Mary Harmon, we're going to put the *Saturday Evening Post* out of business." That's what happened, too.

Bryant got a head start in what became a viciously fought battle against the *Saturday Evening Post* and Curtis Publishing Company. He received an advance copy of the article, thanks to some friends in high places. As a stroke of coincidental bad luck, the superstar was in Washington, D.C., meeting with United States Attorney General Robert Kennedy about political issues, specifically race relations in the Deep South, when word surfaced publicly. The rumor mill had it he had been called onto the carpet for betting on college football games.

⊛

That's the most ludicrous thing that happened when I was working for Coach Bryant at Alabama. We were so much better than Georgia that season it's impossible to believe anybody could accuse him of fixing the game. What was the use in us doing that? We lost one time that season, by a sin-

gle point to Georgia Tech, and Georgia had a 3-4-3 record.
It was totally unbelievable what that article said. Had we
not called off the dogs, we could've beaten Georgia 85 to zip.

—LARRY "DUDE" HENNESSEY,
Alabama assistant coach

After conferring with Dr. Frank Rose, then the University of
Alabama president, and several other individuals, including
lawyers, Bryant told his players about the forthcoming article
and, after passing a polygraph test in a hotel suite in
Birmingham on a Sunday afternoon, he went on statewide
television to tell Crimson Tide fans what they were about to
read was not true. **John Forney**, the longtime radio play-by-
play voice of Alabama football and a host on the *Bear Bryant
Show*, was in the studio when that crucial appearance was
made:

Coach Bryant looked tired when he arrived to do the television program, with good reason. He was totally drained. But
on his face I saw a cold, smoldering anger that wasn't going
to pass until he got what he wanted to say across to the public. I'm telling you, it was emanating off of him with force.

As they prepared Coach Bryant on the set, he muttered
something about the liars, only he added something uncom-
plimentary to his description of the writers of the article and
the folks at the *Saturday Evening Post*. He was as determined as I had seen him. But for good reason, he was worried what he was about to say wouldn't be taken in the right
way. He knew the enormous risk involved in a specially
arranged television show like that. He knew there would be
a lot of drama involved.

In essence, Coach Bryant was about to explain something to the Alabama public that most people in the state
didn't know about in its entirety. A lot of people had heard

about the article, but there was a multitude who hadn't. At best, only a few people had actually read it.

But that was a memorable performance. Coach Bryant rose to the occasion. He looked squarely into a camera and, without a hint of a flinch, certainly not a smile, he told the people of Alabama that he wasn't guilty of fixing a football game, as charged, that he had passed a polygraph test to prove it.

Coach Bryant had many crowning moments during his years at Alabama. However, I'm not sure he was ever any better than he was on television that Sunday afternoon.

All he did was tell the truth. But the legend grew.

୬

Acting is important to the makeup of a coach and Paul Bryant had the courtroom hushed.

—**ALF VAN HOOSE,** *Birmingham News* sports columnist

The war with Curtis Publishing Company continued. Finally, Bryant went to court in Atlanta, Georgia to testify for Wally Butts, who was seeking compensation for damages to his reputation. Among those in the courtroom as he provided meaningful testimony from the witness stand was Alf Van Hoose, the longtime sports columnist at the *Birmingham News*:

His bottled-up anger had the courtroom quiet after Coach Bryant got on the witness stand to deny the *Saturday Evening Post* allegations.

His crowning moment came after his lawyer had set him up talking about some notes he had used in the Georgia game, some hastily folded papers with a game plan on them. Bryant reached into his coat pocket, got out the wrinkled pages and fervently searched himself, as if he was looking for his eyeglasses. He reached all over, chest pockets and side pockets, looking for them, and he had the jury, made up of middle class Georgia people, on the fronts of their seats.

Bryant kept searching himself. Then in a staged whisper he said, "Damn, I left my eyeglasses on the plane."

At that moment, four jurors jumped to their feet and one of them said, "Here, Coach Bryant, try mine."

The defense attorneys, those representing Curtis Publishing, turned blue, seeming literally, and, to my way of thinking, that court case was over.

During a recess, I hurried to a pay telephone, called the editor and said, "Hold the presses. Coach Bryant just got another victory—this one a hell of a lot larger than the one his team got over Georgia."

Van Hoose was correct. In large part because of Bryant's testimony, Butts received what was at the time the largest libel suit judgment in history, $3.06 million, although a reduction was made. Curtis Publishing decided not to answer claims filed by Bryant, choosing to settle out of court for $300,000, a hefty figure in 1964.

The *Saturday Evening Post* was crippled for several years, while Bryant went on to enhance his superstar status. It reached a summit on November 28, 1981, when his Alabama defeated Auburn 28–17 for victory number 315, eclipsing Amos Along Stagg, Glenn "Pop" Warner and all others in the collegiate coaching ranks.

Bryant received a telephone call from President Ronald Reagan, who wanted to offer congratulation. The man receiving the summon answered in the victorious dressing room in this manner: "Hello, Gipper, how are you?"

A gala was staged at his house after the accomplishment. There was about as much food as there is in New Orleans, Louisiana, a city he held dear.

So what did the coach eat?

"I ate a lot, too much, cornbread, onions and milk—all in a glass," Bryant said.

I told my wife, Edith, that I didn't know what to do about Bear attending that function.

—DARRELL ROYAL,
Texas coach

When Lyndon Baines Johnson was United States president, Darrell Royal, a good friend of Bryant's, was on the board of directors of the American Football Coaches Association. The group wanted to give LBJ an award at a special event:

I was in charge of the guest list. I knew who all had to be there, like members of the board of trustees, but I wanted to make it complete and to make sure it was politically correct. So I invited Jake Gaither, the Florida A&M coach, who was black. I invited Ara Parseghian, the Notre Dame coach, to give it Catholic flavor. I told my wife, Edith, I didn't know about Bear attending that function. She was surprised to hear me say that, since Coach Bryant and I were so close, and she asked what my concern was about. I said, "Edith, I'm not sure the Oval Office is big enough to hold LBJ *and* Coach Bryant."

Well, we got to Washington, made it to the White House and got the function under way. Sure enough, it wasn't more than a quarter of an hour before I looked around and saw LBJ and Coach Bryant alone in the corner, chatting away, probably telling all kinds of fibs while they boasted.

LBJ was quite a character. But he met his match when my friend Paul showed up at the White House. Those were two men with clout.

When Paul "Bear" Bryant became the bounteous winner in college football history as a coach, with victory number 315, sports writer Mack Shoemaker of the *Birmingham Post-Herald* came up with a marvelous idea for an article. He randomly telephoned dozens of people across the United States to see how many knew about the man.

Incredulously, Shoemaker found only one who was not familiar with Bryant. He even found a man in Alaska who said, "Sure, everybody up here knows about Bear Bryant. We talk about him throughout football season."

With that in mind, consider the following portions of a column written by **Tom Cushman** for the *Philadelphia Daily News* and published on December 20, 1979:

> The signal that the long-awaited moment was upon us was the striking up of the band, a group called The Four Fashions. They opened with a chorus of "Dixie," which we can assume was not lifted from their standard repertoire, and were swinging smartly into the Alabama fight song when Paul "Bear" Bryant came shuffling through a side door and into the main arena.
>
> The assembly of 500, at $20 per plate, arose as one. Red and white shakers stirred the air and the applause was both prolonged and spirited. As "Bear" Bryant reached his seat at the rostrum, the familiar sounds of Roll Tide lifted up from the tables below, causing The Bear to smile and meditate briefly on his good fortune.
>
> Even though a certain vocal resonance was lacking in the cheerleading, the warmth of the welcoming was beyond dispute. Clearly, this was not Baton Rouge. Neither was it Birmingham, Montgomery, Selma, or Eufaula. This happened last night at the Saint Peter and Paul Ukrainian Hall,

the occasion being a testimonial dinner hosted by the Bama Booster Club of Bridgeport, Pennsylvania, population 5,630.

Never mind that The Bear usually has more people than that wanting to watch practice. A man has to eat somewhere.

Bridgeport happens to be in the suburbs of Philadelphia, some 900 miles from the campus in Tuscaloosa. There is a strong Italian flavor to the citizenry, very few Baptists, and not one member of the Bama Booster Club ever attended a class at the University of Alabama.

૭

Eight years after Paul "Bear" Bryant died, during the summer of 1991, famous comedian **Bob Hope** was asked to offer a few reflections about his longtime friend. For the sake of posterity, he sat down in front of a camera and, in his classic style, provided humorous thoughts about the coach.

Here are a few of those pearls:

I'm so happy to say a few words about a friend I sorely miss and a legend the world of sports misses, Paul "Bear" Bryant. He was truly one of the legends of football. In fact, some people believe he invented the game. Word has it, the halftime activity at games when he started featured the lions and the Christians.

Paul never knew anybody except a football player. That means he never met a man with a neck.

When Paul went to Alabama, he couldn't spell Tuscaloosa. After only one season he owned the town.

Paul had a heart as big as the outdoors. But on the outside he was tough. He once benched a player for saying have a nice day—and that was to his mother.

That houndstooth hat he wore on the sideline was lined

with real hounds' teeth. There's no doubt he was interested only in winning. How do I know? Because he once threw a player off the team for losing the coin toss.

Paul had a unique way of preparing his players for games, at the training table, where he only put out food for half of them.

My friend Bear was a tough competitor, not only when it came to football, but also golf. I had the pleasure to play several rounds with him. We had one round, eighteen holes, in which I had twelve of my tee shots blocked. What's more, he won the eighteenth hole that day by using the hidden ball trick.

Indeed, Paul "Bear" Bryant was and is a legend by all standards—as a man, a coach, and a competitor. He is a legend of strength, flair, and respect.

4

THE MOLDER OF SUPERSTARS

Coach Bryant definitely motivated players to be at their best. A strange form of fear was an interesting part of that. He was an intimidating man, size wise, and was extremely demanding.

—**LEE ROY JORDAN,** Alabama and
professional player

Paul "Bear" Bryant developed and coached numerous super-star football players during his career. He sent hundreds of students to the National Football League, some of whom were eventually considered the best at their positions. He had one Heisman Trophy winner, halfback John David Crow of Texas A&M in 1957, and a bewildering number of Southeastern Conference and Southwest Conference All Stars. Several of his former players and assistant coaches became head coaches, and as evidence of his mastery, he produced a 43–6 record in games against those individuals.

Bryant taught teamwork foremost, which is a reason many of his other players did not win the Heisman Trophy. Instead of putting one player in the spotlight, he chose to make sure the glory of winning was passed around. The 1970s at Alabama are an example of this: he often played three quarterbacks and eight running backs in games with the outcome still in doubt. He once said, "I don't treat all of my players the same way. I never have because they're all individuals who respond in different ways. But I've tried to be fair with every one I've had."

Lee Roy Jordan was a star linebacker and center for Bryant at Alabama from 1960 through 1962. He completed his college career in the 1963 Orange Bowl, a 17–0 victory over Oklahoma during which he made an astounding thirty-one tackles. He was a star with the Dallas Cowboys, an all-pro selection numerous times under Coach Tom Landry:

> The mystique of Coach Bryant, the legend formed early in his career, was in full force when he got to Alabama. Already, he had left a lot of folks in awe. I was added to that list when I went to Tuscaloosa to play for him.
>
> Coach Bryant mastered the perfect combination for success at the collegiate level—or maybe developed it. He inspired us to be the best we could be as players, students, and individuals. He did that by pushing us to the limit, to a level we didn't know existed.
>
> Fear of failing him was important in the formula. But after pushing you until you dropped, he'd come over to you, put an arm around your shoulder and say, "I just want you to be the best you can be. I know what's inside you. I know what you're capable of doing on the football field."
>
> When you got a compliment like that from Coach Bryant, or just a pat on the back, you just wanted to melt on the spot. Moments like that would overwhelm you and make you more determined to play that much harder for him.

Coach Bryant taught us to hang in there, no matter what happened in a football game. He said if we did that, we'd win in the fourth quarter because of the physical toughness and the mental toughness we had. The physical and the mental were both important to him. He always equated that to life, down times or hard times, and he said we'd understand that better after our playing days were over. I've been amazed how what he taught me has helped me through challenges in life. It's like those lessons are tucked inside my head and they come out when they're needed. What he taught his players never goes away or gets too outdated to use.

—**BILLY NEIGHBORS**, Alabama and
professional player

ஜ

When Coach Bryant had strong feelings about something, everybody else quickly developed those feelings. He had everybody on the same page, his players and his assistant coaches, and that meant everybody was going in the same direction. That's the ultimate form of teamwork.

—**RAY PERKINS**, Alabama
player and coach

Ray Perkins played split end under Bryant at Alabama from 1964 through 1966. He became a star pass receiver with the Baltimore Colts. He was head coach for the New York Giants.

In 1983 Perkins became head coach at Alabama, the man selected by the board of trustees to replace Bryant after his retirement. He coached the Crimson Tide four seasons, producing a 32–15–1 record, then returned to pro football:

There was only one Paul Bryant, and there won't be another coach like him. That's why I attempted to do things my way after following him at Alabama. It would've been foolish to try to emulate him because nobody can. In fact, he told me at the time that I should be my own man.

That doesn't mean I didn't learn a lot from him and use part of that while at Alabama.

Coach Bryant was a genuine person. He never said anything that didn't make sense. He was tough. He was a hardline guy, which I found appealing. I really appreciated the discipline he instilled in all of his players. I learned it. Others learned it. I didn't have any choice but to learn it. It was either learn it or quit and go home—and he made it clear what he thought about a quitter.

People have asked what made him such a great coach. I've studied him from top to bottom, and I believe it was a combination of a lot of things.

Coach Bryant was a great psychologist, a master at reverse psychology. He was well organized. He was a student of football and a teacher of football. He had an air about him. He had that great size and that commanding voice.

More than anything, however, there was a wonderful genuineness about the man.

᧟

I've cursed Coach Bryant, and other players have cursed him. He was so demanding and so tough. He made us do this and made us do that, at times unwillingly. Looking back, it's what I needed and what other players needed. But there were times when we all cursed him, raised hell at him, yet loved him at the same time.

—**KENNY STABLER,** Alabama
and professional player

Bryant considered his quarterbacks an extension of himself on the playing field. That is why he got closer to those players than others on his teams. He called Pat Trammell, who played for him at Alabama from 1959 through 1961, "My favorite person in life." He cried unashamedly when the young man who had just become a doctor died from cancer.

But the most famous quarterbacks Bryant had at Alabama were Joe Namath and Kenny Stabler, who became Super Bowl champions and standouts in the National Football League. Interestingly, those two students were among the more unwilling the coach had during his career. Neither tapped his potential until after suffering through disciplinary action.

⟳

Coach Bryant and Mrs. Bryant, wherever you are, thank you.

—**JOE NAMATH,** Alabama and
professional player

Namath starred for Alabama from 1962 through 1964, then went on to become "Broadway Joe" while playing for the New York Jets. He took time to thank Bryant and his wife during his acceptance speech when he was inducted into the National Football League Hall of Fame in 1986.

"I owe a great deal of what I've accomplished in football and life to Coach Bryant," Namath said in a soft voice and with misty eyes during his acceptance speech. "He was there for me when I needed discipline. He picked me up and shoved me forward when I needed to be kicked in the butt."

Namath arrived at Alabama as a ballyhooed prospect from Beaver Falls, Pennsylvania. He was a splendid athlete, "the best I ever coached," Bryant said, and he was flashy and cocky off the playing field, even as a freshman. He was the first player the coach allowed to join him on his practice field observation tower, even as he was being recruited.

Namath was a star as a sophomore and was named most outstanding offensive player in the 1963 Orange Bowl at the end of a 10–1 season. He displayed flashes of brilliance as a junior, when the record was 9–2, but he found himself in trouble with Bryant near the end of the regular season. He and a team manager, Jack "Hoot Owl" Hicks, his best friend on campus, went to a local bar, had a few drinks and wrecked a car while returning to campus. Then word surfaced he and some friends had broken training while attending a party at a women's department store.

Bryant went to the athletics dorm to talk to Namath. He asked about the team rules violations. The quarterback admitted guilt.

Bryant called a staff meeting and asked his assistant coaches for advice on how to deal with Namath. All of them except one suggested the matter be overlooked. Gene Stallings, who had played for Bryant at Texas A&M said, "If it had been me, you would've fired me."

Bryant told Namath he was being suspended from the team for a final regular season against Miami and a Sugar Bowl game against Ole Miss. He told him he could return during spring practice, if he desired, provided he would clean up his act. The quarterback asked the coach to telephone his mother with the news before it was reported in newspapers.

Steve Sloan was the Alabama quarterback during victories over Miami, 17–12, and Ole Miss, 12–7. Namath returned to lead the Crimson Tide to a national championship in 1964, when the record was 10–1, then signed what was the largest professional contract in history with the New York Jets, $400,000. In 1969 he led his pro team to a Super Bowl victory over the highly favored Baltimore Colts, a win he boldly guaranteed.

I'm thankful he grabbed me by the back of the shirt, yanked me up, shoved me back, got my shoulders straight and refused to let me throw away a great opportunity.

—**KENNY STABLER,** Alabama and
professional quarterback

Kenny "Snake" Stabler was a freshman at Alabama when Namath was a senior. That meant Bryant inherited a headache just after overcoming one.

Stabler, forever a free spirit, arrived in Tuscaloosa after starring at Foley High School in south Alabama. He turned down a baseball contract offered by the New York Yankees to play for the Crimson Tide. However, for two years, more or less, he developed a far too common routine. When he was not at football practice, he was in Mobile visiting a female friend. Obviously, he spent too much time on the highway to attend class with a degree of regularity.

Bryant heard about the lack of commitment and, after the list of team rules violations grew lengthy, suspended Stabler during spring practice before his senior season. He was dealing with a quarterback who in 1966 had led Alabama to an 11–0 record that included a 34–7 victory over Nebraska in the Sugar Bowl. The player responded positively, led the Crimson Tide to an 8–2–1 record in 1967, and became one of the truly great performers in the NFL.

"Kenny Stabler was my most productive quarterback," Bryant said. "If he had been playing quarterback when we went to the wishbone formation, they would have had to have made room for another digit on the scoreboard."

Also, on July 9, 1981, Bryant said, "I probably mishandled Kenny Stabler more than any player I've had. I could've ruined him. In many ways he went on to become a great pro quarterback with the Oakland Raiders in spite of me."

Stabler offers a contrary opinion:

Coach Bryant and I had our moments, no doubt about that, times when we didn't see eye to eye. But that was mostly my fault, not his, at least as best I can recall.

I had a chance to play football at Alabama, which is an honor, and I almost threw it away by being a nonconformist. Coach Bryant wasn't the type person to put up with that, you can bet, and he disciplined me when I needed it.

If you look back, you'll see he got me on the right path at the right time. If he hadn't, I could have thrown away what turned out to be a decent career at Alabama and in pro football.

Whatever I've accomplished, I owe a great deal of that to Coach Bryant.

Actually, I think that's true with everybody who played for Coach Bryant. It's true with teams, too.

I've always said we never really beat anybody, that he out-coached them. He outmotivated opponents. He outcommunicated opponents.

What he did was make overachievers out of a bunch of skinny kids, me included. His teams had that intangible thing he instilled in players, a will to win and the confidence that if we wanted to win badly enough, we would find a way.

ॐ

Coach Bryant was a man's man and he was a maker of men. That's what I saw through the years coaching for him and coaching against him. You couldn't be a weak person and survive long around him because he was a great judge of character, and he expected the best out of everybody he associated with.

—**PAT DYE,** Alabama assistant coach
and Auburn coach

While Bryant had several marquee players with astonishing talent, he was at his best with lesser known performers who labored intensely to be as good as they could be. Quarterback Steve Sloan is a good example. He was not particularly fast. He did not throw pretty passes. But he helped Alabama to a national championship in 1964, subbing part of the season for the injured Namath, and a national championship in 1965 that was cemented with a 39–28 victory over Nebraska in the Orange Bowl.

Bryant had superstars while leading other programs, too, like halfback Vic Turyn at Maryland, quarterbacks George Blanda and Vito "Babe" Parilli at Kentucky, and halfback John David Crow at Texas A&M. He found directing them easier because they had superb ability, were dedicated to pleasing him in all ways, and had strong leadership abilities.

༄

I'm proud our team got him started toward such a remarkable record. I'm the more fortunate man, not him, because it was a great honor playing for Coach Bryant.

—SAMMY BEHR, Maryland player

Sammy Behr played at Maryland in 1945 on the first team Bryant coached. He scored the first touchdown that season, giving him proud distinction:

> I've never met a finer gentleman or greater coach that Paul Bryant. If you gave Coach Bryant a nickel as a player, he would give you a dollar in return. He is most deserving of every victory that ever came his way. My only regret is I only got to play for him one season. I'm proud it was his first.
>
> For about an hour at our first practice, Coach Bryant did nothing other than give us a lecture and demonstration on

how to block and tackle. He took an active role, too, getting in there and mixing it up with us. He was a young man, only thirty-two, a big man, and had beautiful people working with him. Also, he could pass a mean lick.

Coach Bryant was dedicated to fundamentals. He knew what would win in football, even at that young age. We used only three plays in our first three games. We worked on them tirelessly in practice and executed them pretty well in games.

It was apparent after only that short period of time that he was a great coach with special ability. There wasn't any doubt he would become a sports superstar. Eventually, I believe he got so good at coaching that he could've swapped teams with most coaches and beat them in three weeks. The amazing thing was he had a knack for taking average players, which almost all of us were at Maryland, and making them perform like stars.

I was torn up when Coach Bryant decided to leave Maryland. I understood his position, as most of us did, and he left after a grand performance on campus. He told the student body why he was leaving. He had spoiled everybody. We won one game the season before he took over leadership of the program. We had a 6–2–1 record in 1945. The year after he left we dropped back into mediocrity. That should tell you something.

I begged Coach Bryant to take me with him to Kentucky. But he said, "Sammy, I found you here, and I have to leave you here." So I had one year with him, and I'll always be thankful.

ॐ

I'm convinced I was able to play as long as I did profes-sionally because of the discipline I learned under Coach Bryant at Kentucky. Also, the hard work he put us through made me a much stronger person. It might have been all of the running because you didn't walk at all under him. You ran to the practice field, and you ran from the practice field.

—**GEORGE BLANDA,** Kentucky and professional player

George Blanda was a Kentucky running back when Bryant arrived in 1946. He could pass, run, and kick, but the coach made him a quarterback in the Notre Dame Box offensive formation. That made him a blocker more than anything else, and he did not like the move. He sulked during practice, was demoted to the second team, and moved to linebacker. He reacted positively, becoming a terror on defense.

"I was stupid moving George Blanda to quarterback in the Notre Dame Box and more stupid for moving him to defense," Bryant said when looking back on his years at Kentucky. "He had enormous talent, and I wasted it for a year. I think he has forgiven me, but I really made a mistake with him.

"Thank goodness, George was too good and too dedicated to being great to let me mess him up."

Blanda recalled that pivotal time in a playing career that saw him still active in the NFL when he was fifty years old. He played at Chicago (1949–1958), Baltimore (1959), Houston (1960–1966), and Oakland (1967–1975).

"Playing for Coach Bryant was a lot like going to war," Blanda said. "I survived his practice sessions, but the memories have lingered for a long time. He was tough, but he was fair. I loved the challenges he presented. In fact, there were times when I wanted to stand up and applaud when he walked into the room."

❦

I was in the hospital recovering from groin surgery. Coach Bryant walked in, came to my bedside, tossed me a new offensive game plan for our game that week with LSU and said, "Learn it, Babe, because the game depends on it." I could hardly move. But he presented me with the challenge, and I accepted it.

—**VITO "BABE" PARILLI,** Kentucky
and professional player

Babe Parilli was the Kentucky quarterback under Bryant from 1949 through 1951. He was the most valuable player in the Southeastern Conference as a junior, when the record was 11–1 and the Wildcats won the SEC championship. A year earlier the record was 9–3, and a year later the record was 8–4. He passed for fifty-four touchdowns in three seasons, an unbelievable number during that era. He played professionally with the Green Bay Packers, Cleveland Browns, Oakland Raiders, Boston Patriots, and interestingly, with the New York Jets in 1968 and 1969, when he and Namath were teammates:

> The game against LSU when Coach Bryant challenged me to play came in 1950 and was the second of the season. I had suffered a groin injury in our first game—against North Texas, I believe—and they did a little surgery. To say I was shocked when Coach Bryant showed up with the offensive game plan would be a major understatement.
>
> Actually, Coach Bryant did more than that. He didn't like the way I was progressing at the hospital, so he got me discharged and took me to his house.
>
> Mrs. Bryant pampered me, and Coach Bryant and I went over the game plan he had given me. I didn't feel that great by Saturday afternoon, but I played in the game and we won 14–0 over a big and talented LSU team.

About Parilli, Bryant said, "He was the type player a coach adjusted to, built the team around instead of him just being a part of the team. He could do it all—run, fake, and pass—and as a bonus he was a great leader on the football field."

One of the players Bryant favored, no doubt, was John David Crow, his star at Texas A&M. In him he saw a prototype disciple, hardnosed and unyielding, a person who would go an extra mile on the practice field to gain an extra yard or two in a game. He was a man who had a portion of his mouth paralyzed as a four-year-old boy, but who never mentioned it or acted any differently because of it.

The two formed a small mutual admiration society. Bryant got a reminder of it when John David Crow Jr. played for him at Alabama during the 1970s. "Little John David isn't as big or as good as his daddy, but I see a lot of his daddy in that boy every day at practice and during games," the coach said. "He doesn't have his dad's speed, and he doesn't have his dad's power. But he has his dad's heart, and that's nice to see."

ॐ

A lot of people have said how much Coach Bryant meant to them. I'm one of them. In fact, it's like he got inside me and jumped up and down. He had that much influence on me.

—JOHN DAVID CROW,
Texas A&M player

I'm proud and honored to be the only Heisman Trophy winner Coach Bryant had. That's because of two things. I respected him so much because he believed in hard work, staying at it until you got it right. And, of course, he paid me a high compliment in 1957 when he said, "If John David Crow doesn't win the Heisman Trophy, they might as well quit presenting it."

Coach Bryant had such an influence on my life. In that

regard, he was a lot my father, sort of an extension of him. My father, Harry, started out pitching pulpwood at a lumber company. After two decades he became a crew superintendent. He had a grade-school education. More importantly, though, he had a commitment to hard work, staying at it. He was a truly great man. I saw a lot of those traits in Coach Bryant. After all, it's impossible to tell what might have happened to Coach Bryant if somebody hadn't gotten him out of Moro Bottom, Arkansas, and moved him a few miles up the road to Fordyce when they did.

I've been told Coach Bryant thought a lot of me. If that's true, it's easy to understand. When a person cares about another person as much as I did him, well, it's only natural for some type of mutual fondness to develop.

I can't adequately tell you how much it meant for my son Johnny to have the opportunity to play for Coach Bryant at Alabama in 1975, 1976, and 1977. I can't tell you how proud I was of my son during the recruiting process.

Johnny was an excellent high school player but was a little slow. Ohio State wanted him. So did Texas A&M, Georgia, Alabama, and some other colleges.

Johnny went to visit Alabama and found himself seated in front of Coach Bryant on that big sofa in his office that sunk down and made a person look like a midget. Coach Bryant said, "Johnny, I want you to sign a scholarship." Johnny said, "Coach Bryant, have you seen me play?" Coach Bryant said, "Well, no, but the assistant coaches have, and they think you're good enough to play for us." Johnny said, "Well, Coach Bryant, I want you to look at the films of me playing and decide if I'm good enough. If you say I am, I'll sign with Alabama."

I don't mind saying I was damn proud of Johnny for taking that approach. He came home without signing. Then the telephone rang one evening and I answered. It was Coach Bryant.

Coach Bryant said, "John David, I don't want to talk to you. I want to talk to Johnny and Carolyn." My wife talked to Coach Bryant for a while. Then Johnny got on the telephone. Coach Bryant said, "Johnny, I've watched the damn films. Get your ass down here where you belong. We want you to play football for the University of Alabama."

I was a proud father.

Bryant had a lot of less famous stars who made him feel good at every stop along the way. He had a little receiver named Donnie Gleason he loved at Maryland, a player who caught a pass to end a sixteen-game losing streak at the hands of Virginia. He had a little guard named Charley McClendon he loved at Kentucky, a player who came to the sideline in a Sugar Bowl game "with his faced torn half off" but refused to leave the combat on the playing field. He had a little quarterback named Roddy Osborne he loved at Texas A&M, a player who chased down and tackled a much faster defensive halfback from Arkansas after a pass interception to save a victory. He had a little halfback named Marlin "Scooter" Dyess he loved at Alabama, a player he inherited who stayed and helped set the foundation for more than two decades of championship glory.

Bryant had a who's who list of superstars. Dwight Stephenson was a center at Alabama during the 1970s who earned all-NFL status with the Miami Dolphins. He is considered by many the best pro in history at that position. Ozzie Newsome was a split end at Alabama during the 1970s who earned all-NFL status with the Cleveland Browns. He is considered by many people the best pro in history at tight end. John Hannah was an offensive guard at Alabama during the 1970s who earned all-NFL status with the New England Patriots. He is considered by many the best pro in history at that position.

♋

Coach Bryant always said a player could get 5 percent bet-
ter every day if he worked at it. He said the same thing was
true about anybody, like a doctor or a lawyer, and that was
his way of making sure a player didn't become complacent
and rest on his laurels. I took that to heart. I don't think
there's any doubt learning that from him at Alabama made
me a better pro player with the Cleveland Browns.

—**OZZIE NEWSOME,** Alabama
and professional player

Interestingly, Hannah is a player Bryant almost lost before he
could guide him toward greatness. The offensive guard from
Albertville, Alabama, arrived in Tuscaloosa when the coach
and the Crimson Tide seemed to be losing their winning edge.
He was a freshman in 1969, when the record was 6–5, and a
starting sophomore in 1970, when the record was 6–5–1.
Also, it was a period of student unrest on campus, with anti-
war demonstrations in the spotlight, and the distractions
caused the commitment to football to ebb a bit.

Bryant admitted he created much of that problem. After
the 1967 season, he had toyed with moving to professional
football with the Miami Dolphins. He had let success go to
his head and was moving across the nation in fast social circles. He threatened to quit after narrowly avoiding two losing
seasons.

A surprise move to the wishbone offensive formation led
to an 11–1 record in 1971 and a 10–2 record in 1972—and
helped Hannah get a chance to prove himself to pro scouts.
The importance of blocking at the point of attack was pivotal
in his development. He talked about that, plus the value of
discipline he learned at Alabama, before his induction into
the National Football Foundation Hall of Fame.

෴

Bryant had players he could not reach, if only a few, and the most painful example involved running back Linnie Patrick. He was recruited out of Jasper, Alabama, in 1980, the only other high school player at that position who was being compared to Herschel Walker, the Heisman Trophy-winning Georgia running back who started his collegiate career that season.

Patrick did not respond to discipline and did not favor the team concept. So on an afternoon during his sophomore season (1981), I watched as Bryant was moved to attempt something extreme. He lined up the first team defense and made the running back carry the football at least five consecutive times. After being hammered, he stayed on the ground with the coach standing over him screaming, "Linnie, get up and get back to the huddle. Don't you stay on the ground. Get your ass up and get ready to run the football again."

Patrick got up and started walking toward the sideline. Bryant chased after him screaming, "If you're going to quit, run off the field. Get your ass moving."

Patrick walked to the sideline and, in a fit of anger, slammed his helmet to the ground. Bryant charged toward him, sprinting as fast as a sixty-eight-year-old man could, and lectured him in no uncertain terms.

Patrick never tapped his potential, or so it seems, but during a 28–17 victory over Auburn at the end of that regular season, he made two remarkable runs as Alabama came from behind in the fourth quarter to win. Coincidentally, that was the victory that made Bryant the most prolific winner among college coaches.

During the next season, Bryant arrived at his office before dawn, as was his wont, and made the academically troubled Patrick sit on a couch in front of him and do his classwork.

"What I'd give if I could reach that young man," he said. "It's disappointing to see talent like that going to waste."

The memories of Bryant on the practice field during his last two seasons (1981 and 1982) are compelling because he remained unbelievably active although he was extremely sick.

There was a day when he literally picked up 265-pound Warren Lyles, an extraordinarily talented and totally dedicated middle guard, to show him how to tackle better. There was a day when he got in a three-point stance and pounded on a blocking sled to show Jackie Cline, a defensive tackle, the proper way to stop the charge of an offensive lineman. In essence, the coach was moving slow—until he needed to make a point.

❦

I'm convinced Coach Bryant literally willed himself through that last season in 1982. He was extremely sick. He had to take frequent long naps on the couch in his office because his circulation was so bad. There were days when Dr. Bill Hill, his cardiologist, had to give him injections to keep him going because his blood pressure was so erratic and his pulse was so low. He was a remarkable man. He wouldn't quit on his team, even when he was made aware of the consequences of continuing to push himself like that.

—LINDA KNOWLES, secretary

There was a cold afternoon in 1982 when the author witnessed Bryant walking slowly down the hallway from his office in Memorial Coliseum. He had on an oversized thick coat. His face appeared pale and drawn. He staggered as he ambled, at times bracing himself against the walls.

"Maybe this would be a good day to take a break," I said.

Bryant smiled and said, "We've got work to do because

our team seems to be going south in a hurry."

Later that afternoon, as he often did during the last three years, Bryant came down from his observation tower, got in his golf cart, drove to thick bushes at the far end of the practice field and relieved his kidneys. The blood thinners he was being forced to take were creating an uncommon fluid buildup.

When he returned to work and had taken a few steps up his observation tower, Bryant stopped and said, "You know, Alfred, I'm getting more like 'Pop' Warner every day." He was referring to an article I had written about the former coach who had to relieve his kidneys during Stanford games late in his long career, when he let his players form a shield for him on the sideline so fans in the grandstands could not see what was taking place.

"No, Coach Bryant, your record tells me you're better than 'Pop' Warner was as a coach," I said.

"Then I'm a hell of a lot better than I think," Bryant said as he continued his climb to the top of his observation tower.

I smiled, shook my head and watched the master at work, doing what he liked to do best, and I saw a genuine superstar, as well as a molder of superstars.

"You know, Coach Bryant told me one time he didn't consider himself a great coach," said Billy Varner, a friend and confidant. "He said he considered himself sort of average, really, that he just worked hard at it.

"I never did accept that statement because, as I remember, when he was on the sideline at Alabama things turned out mighty good more times than not."

5

THE MAN IN CHARGE

I don't think it would have mattered what occupation Coach Bryant had chosen. He was a pure leader, a take charge person. I'm sure he would have been a masterful military officer. At the same time, he would have been just as skillful as the chairman of the board for a huge corporation. It just so happened that football was his business, and I don't think anybody would doubt he elevated himself to the top of the ladder in that sport.

—JIM GOOSTREE, Alabama trainer
and assistant athletics director

From the day he became a head football coach, Paul "Bear" Bryant was a man in charge of the programs he led and the people he hired to assist him. There are numerous stories that point out that commonly held thought. Still, the most incredulous thing about his leadership abilities and his penchant for succeeding in a command position is the fact he was able to do that for almost four decades.

"Four decades of football at four colleges is an almost impossible feat," said Darrell Royal, the former Texas coach.

"Paul was consumed by football. He was consumed by the will to win. Nobody stays at it that long with as much success as he had. He was a great one, no doubt about it, and part of his secret was his ability to get people who worked for him and played for him to believe in him."

Bryant was at the top of his game as a no-nonsense leader throughout his time at Alabama, 1958 through 1982, as remembered by **Jim Goostree**, who served Alabama for three and a half decades after joining the staff in 1957:

Just after Coach Bryant arrived on campus in Tuscaloosa, we were walking to lunch at Friedman Hall, the athletics dorm, from the football offices. He was about a block ahead of me, and I was watching this giant man moving toward the building that housed football players. He started up the steps leading to the front door when three water bags crashed at his feet. I saw him glance up to the third floor and said, "Uh oh, somebody has bought trouble."

Coach Bryant hurried up the steps, not one by one, but about three at a time.

I was in the dining room and had gone through the chow line when he came in, got his lunch, ate and left. He didn't look upset at all. He was totally calm. I wondered what had happened after he got upstairs.

Later in the day I learned two of our players on scholarship had been asked to leave school.

ॐ

I was up there when the water balloon tossing took place. Those balloons weren't directed at Coach Bryant, rather at some people across the street.

—**Jack Rutledge,** Alabama
player and assistant coach

Jack Rutledge was an Alabama freshman when Bryant arrived in 1958:

> We had a team meeting that night, and the balloon tossing incident came up. Word was out that a couple of our players were getting kicked off the team for dropping balloons on Coach Bryant.
>
> I don't know what made me do it, unless it was coming to their defense, but I stood up and told Coach Bryant the truth. I talked fast and I stuttered at the time, so people still kid me about the black car and white car story. Basically, I said, "Coach Bryant, the black car was there, and the white car turned in. That messed up the throwing and, well, the water balloons were dropped on the steps beside you."
>
> Coach Bryant digested the explanation. He allowed the two players to stay on the team. He had gotten across his point about how discipline would be much better from that point forward, and he had gained a lot of respect by giving a couple of guys second chances.

Or, as Goostree said, "Coach Bryant had established what he expected while putting together a disciplined football program. From that day forward, our approach to the sport changed drastically."

᠌

I don't think the neckties had anything to do with the outcome that day, but that scene made Coach Bryant look like a genius.

—CLEM GRYSKA, Alabama
assistant coach

That scene from 1958 was brought to life again, sort of comically, in 1982 a few hours before Alabama played an important game in Birmingham. Clem Gryska, former Alabama player during the 1940s and a longtime assistant coach and recruiting coordinator for the Crimson Tide, recalls how the normally unpredictable Bryant scored another blow for discipline:

As people who were around Coach Bryant knew, he always had pet lines. One of his favorites was telling players to show class in all situations, to make their parents proud of them, the student body proud of them and people from across the nation who watched our program proud of them. That's why you saw so many of our players knocking down opponents during games, helping them to their feet and patting them on their butts. That's why you saw our players shaking hands with opponents after games, win or lose. That's why most of our players always looked neat, clean cut, and, for the most part, were polite to people they met.

It was easy for Coach Bryant to preach that because he always did it himself. It didn't matter what situation he was in, he acted like a gentleman—except on rare occasions, of course, when he seemed to lose control on the sideline during the heat of action in games.

As part of that discipline, or a show of class, if you will, Coach Bryant insisted our players wear ties on road trips. In fact, during the 1950s and 1960s, all of our guys wore crimson blazers and ties while traveling.

As the years passed and dress codes became more relaxed, he still insisted our players wear ties.

So comes to mind our pregame meal before we played Penn State in 1982, his last season as coach.

Coach Bryant was at the head table, and he watched as our players drifted into the hotel ballroom to eat, a few at a time, until they were all seated. It was customary for him to talk to the team after players finished eating, but he didn't wait until then that morning. He jumped to his feet and in that deep and firm voice said, "I don't want anybody eating a bite until every player in this room has on a necktie."

It looked like a fire drill the way those players were flying out of that ballroom. They ran into the lobby and started begging our fans to let them use their ties. Some of them were making ties out of napkins. My wife, Alice, and Sam Bailey's wife, Mildred, were throwing ties down from the second floor into the lobby.

Finally, everybody got back into the ballroom and every player had on a necktie. They all didn't match and some of them were tied funny, but at least they were all wearing them. In fact, I remember one of our quarterbacks looking like Captain Kangaroo with a giant yellow ribbon turned into a bow tie.

Coach Bryant surveyed the scene, got to his feet and said, without a smile, "Now you look a hell of a lot better. Maybe you'll play better because of it."

Well, we went on the playing field a few hours later and defeated a darn good Penn State team 42–21, a win that earned us a top national ranking.

Three weeks later, a junior running back on that Alabama team prompted a firm, yet humorous, response from Bryant that showed how in charge of the program he was until the end.

Joe Carter had starred at Starkville High School in Starkville, Mississippi. While there, he had worn a headband under his helmet, as many players do today. He wanted to wear one for a game against Mississippi State.

Carter asked several people what they thought. The response he got was similar: "You better ask The Man."

The softspoken and polite Carter approached Bryant on the playing field with the headband in place. He said, "Coach Bryant, when I was at Starkville High School, I was known for wearing a headband. Since we're playing Mississippi State this weekend, do you care if I wear one?"

Bryant did not hesitate before responding. He said, "Joe, I don't mind you wearing that headband. But you've got to make a choice. You can either wear the headband or the helmet."

Carter grinned, pulled off the headband and tossed it aside. Bryant chuckled as one of his favorite players, who would become a Miami Dolphins running back, trotted toward the first drill of practice that afternoon.

ॐ

I was waiting for Bob Gain and was moving toward the front door before the doorbell rang. I wasn't sure what was going to happen, how I was going to deal with an unusual situation, but I was ready to teach him a lesson.

—PAUL BRYANT,
on a strange confrontation

One of the finer players Bryant had during his career is **Bob Gain**, a Kentucky tackle who made All-America in 1949 and 1950 and played in the National Football League for the Cleveland Browns in 1952 and from 1954 through 1964:

> Coach Bryant was into intimidation and worked the hell out of us at Kentucky. I was a big ol' boy who didn't like that approach much.
>
> So I started running off at the mouth about how I was going to whip his butt. I was going to challenge him to a fight and take out my frustration on him.
>
> Fortunately, it didn't get to that point, and I learned a valuable lesson. I'm thankful for what Coach Bryant did for me while I was at Kentucky. He made me a man and a better football player.

❦

The way Coach Bryant handled Bob Gain, as well as the rest of us at Kentucky, points out one simple fact: There has never been another one like him.

—LARRY "DUDE" HENNESSEY,
Kentucky player and Alabama
assistant coach

Bob Gain, an extraordinary player and tough man, was raised in a coal mining environment. He was a seasoned person who didn't care much about the discipline Coach Bryant demanded. So after Coach Bryant got on him at practice one afternoon, he started bragging about how he was going to whip his butt.

We were at the athletics dorm when Gain started getting louder and louder. Finally, he popped off so much that we started placing bets on the impending fight. When all of the bets were going down on Coach Bryant to win, Gain got madder. Finally, we had him in such an uproar that he said he was ready to go fight The Man.

A bunch of us drove over to Coach Bryant's house to see what would happen. That was something we didn't want to miss.

Well, Gain went to the door, acting tough, and Coach Bryant answered it about as fast as he got to it. Coach Bryant said, "Gain, what in hell do you want at this hour? What brings you to my house at night?"

Gain was stunned. He started stammering. Finally, he said, "Well, Coach Bryant, uh, a bunch of us were wondering if you were going to let us go home for Christmas break."

Gain said that was all he could think of saying at that moment. He said Coach Bryant said, "I can't tell you, Gain, because I haven't made up my mind yet."

🍥

One of the many things I learned playing under Coach Bryant at Texas A&M was you better look out if he ever started singing "Jesus Loves Me." That normally meant things were about to get tough, if not unbearable.

—**Gene Stallings,** Texas A&M
player and Alabama coach

Gene Stallings was as close to Bryant as anybody during his life. He played for him, at Texas A&M, a member of the Junction Boys, coached for him at Alabama, coached against him in the 1968 Cotton Bowl and, ultimately, coached the Crimson Tide to its first national championship since 1979 in 1992:

I'm not going to say that training camp we had at Junction, Texas, at Texas A&M wasn't tough because it was hard. But after all the publicity we got down there, we came back to open the season against Texas Tech and lost 41–9. It wasn't a pretty sight.

Coach Bryant called us together after the game and said, "It's over now. I want you to go your rooms. All the Texas Tech players are going to have fun tonight. They've got the girls. You don't need to be around any girls."

The following Monday afternoon we reported to practice and discovered our game uniforms in our lockers. That was unusual because you didn't wear game gear at practice. Then our team manager, Troy Summerland, came running around telling us Coach Bryant wanted us to put on our game uniforms and report to Kyle Field. Well, you didn't practice on Kyle Field. That's where you played the games.

Anyway, we put on our game gear and, sort of like little sheep, made our way down to Kyle Field. When we got there, Coach Bryant was out there singing "Jesus Loves Me"—*Jesus of loves me, this I know* . . . geez, bad news. I thought to myself, oh boy, this is gonna be a rough one.

Coach Bryant called us up and said, "Men, there isn't any use in loosening up today. When the game ended, the ball was right there and it's still right there. We're gonna take up where we left off Saturday night."

That was one bad practice, I'm telling you, but we didn't get beat 41–9 again.

⟲

Coach Bryant plopped down in that big leather chair at the head of the table and the air flew out of it. Pooosshhh. Nobody uttered a word. We knew it was going to be an interesting staff meeting, to say the least.

—BILL "BROTHER" OLIVER, Alabama
player and assistant coach

Bill Oliver played under Bryant at Alabama from 1959 through 1962. He served as an assistant coach for the Crimson Tide numerous years, specializing in the defensive secondary, then as defensive coordinator under Coach Gene Stallings:

At some point during the 1970s, the latter part, we had become a little complacent because we had owned the Southeastern Conference and had won more than anybody else in the nation. It seems like this was in 1978.

Normally, all of us assistant coaches arrived at the office early to prepare for staff meetings. We never really knew exactly when they'd start, but Coach Bryant wasn't one to show up late in the morning.

But on this morning he wasn't there at seven, and he

wasn't there at eight. We didn't know what to think, so we just sat in our little offices and waited for him to appear.

At some point word went out that The Man had arrived. All of us hurried down to the meeting room adjacent to his office. As I looked back down the hallway, I saw him walking unsteadily and looking a little worn out. His hair was a mess, and his pace was extremely slow. Also, he had on camouflage gear, a hunting outfit, and I couldn't figure that out. I figured he might have gone turkey hunting that morning.

I remember walking into the meeting room and saying, "Gentlemen, you aren't going to believe this when you see it. Coach Bryant is in rare form this morning."

A few minutes later Coach Bryant entered the room and took a seat. I mean you could've dropped two tons of lead into that chair, and the air would have come out like it did when he sat down. Then he just sat there, for more than a minute without talking, lit an unfiltered Chesterfield and sat for another minute in stone silence.

Finally, Coach Bryant said, mumbling badly, "If you don't give a shit, then I don't give a shit."

That's all he said for six or eight minutes, three or four times. We all kept our eyes on him because we were afraid to look at each other.

Finally, Coach Bryant looked at Mal Moore and asked him something about the offense. Mal gave him an overview, at least started one, and he said, "Damn, Mal, we couldn't score on the Sisters of the Poor the way we're blocking and running."

Coach Bryant asked Ken Donahue about the defense. The same thing happened, or something like it.

After Coach Bryant asked a few more people a few more questions, it was my time. I was sitting right beside him when he asked about the defensive secondary. Actually, my guys were performing pretty good at the time, and I started telling him that. He cut me off and said, "Shit, Brother, they can't . . ."

Coach Bryant let that remark trail and got quiet again. He lit another cigarette, took about two draws and snubbed it out in an ashtray. Then he started getting out of the chair, slowly, and as he walked from the room, he said, "If you don't give a shit, then I don't give a shit."

I don't know everything that happened leading up to that performance. All I know is it was a great one, and our practice pace picked up significantly. Also, we won back to back national championships in 1978 and 1979.

ॐ

Paul, you've got to understand that our whiskey is like their marijuana.

—HENRY WAUGH, Tuscaloosa friend

There were times when Bryant had to seek help dealing with players, rare moments when he did not feel like the man in charge. One of those occasions came during the mid-1970s, when some of his Alabama players got caught smoking marijuana at an annual A-Club picnic.

Bryant was livid—and embarrassed when the misbehaving was spread by the news media. He expressed that during a fishing trip to a local lake with Tuscaloosa businessman Henry Waugh, whom he had known since his college days:

Paul and I were fishing on a pier and having a few cocktails. All of sudden he started ranting about how some of his players had been smoking marijuana and how he was going to fire all of them, including several stars. He said, "I don't know what to make of it, the way kids are today. If we'd done something like that, Coach [Frank] Thomas and Coach Hank [Crisp] would've given us hell to pay. I'm gonna run 'em off."

I listened to him for a while, then said, "Paul, times have changed. The things kids do today to get in trouble are different than the things you and I did."

He looked at me kind of funny and said, "Henry, what in hell makes you think you know anything about college kids?"

I said, "Paul, you've got to understand that our whiskey is like their marijuana. I'm not condoning what they're doing, but I'm not going to crucify them when what we did was about as bad at the time. You've got to change with the times."

Paul asked me what I knew about marijuana. He almost fell off the damn pier laughing when I told him I had tried dope a couple of times just to see what all the fuss was over.

But, you know, he didn't run off those players. He disciplined them and might have saved them. Also, I believe he changed his approach a little bit for the good.

Bryant gave the players hell to pay during conditioning drills, running them until they dropped, and he made them do scheduled community service work for several weeks at the local Veterans Administration Hospital.

The coach changed his approach a bit, too, and that might have earned him the respect of more players and, definitely, helped Alabama win at a staggering pace until he retired.

⤬

The first Black to sign with Alabama was Wilbur Jackson, a running back from Ozark, Alabama, who joined the program as a freshman in 1970 and contributed mightily to the Crimson Tide's success in 1971, 1972, and 1973. The first Black to play in a varsity game at Alabama was **John Mitchell**, a defensive end from Mobile, Alabama who transferred from a junior college. He starred for the Crimson Tide in 1971 and 1972:

> It didn't take me long to learn a valuable lesson from Coach Bryant. It came after our fourth game in 1971, a 40–6 win over Ole Miss. I played on the kicking teams that day and didn't do well at all. I disappointed myself, and I'm sure I disappointed my teammates.
>
> I went to see Coach Bryant a couple of days after that game. I started off making excuses for the way I had played. Ultimately, I told him, "Coach, I don't think I can make it at this level. I was terrible against Ole Miss. I think I should quit."
>
> Coach Bryant looked at me, took a few seconds to collect his thoughts, and said, "John, you're not going to quit this team. I'll give you two reasons. First, you're good enough to play at this level, and you'll do well after you get a little more game experience. But the most important reason is this: It's easy to quit the second time, the third time and the fourth time after you quit the first time."
>
> It was a lesson for life. It was a lesson about life.
>
> Coach Bryant had a way of accomplishing that with all of his players, not just me, and that's part of his legacy. He was so strong, so in control, that he wouldn't let you make a mistake, a bad decision, if there was any way he could keep you from it.

ॐ

I slammed the door and caught a sports writer's finger in it—almost tore the darn thing off.

—**JEFF ROUZIE,** Alabama player
and assistant coach

Jeff Rouzie, a standout linebacker at Alabama in 1970, 1971 and 1973, and an assistant coach under Bryant from 1976 through 1981, relates how Bryant was not one to hide his displeasure when things didn't go according to plan:

We were recruiting a player from over in Georgia in the late 1970s or early 1980s. The kid admired Coach Bryant, so I asked him if he would go over to a high school just south of Atlanta and visit him. He said he would, but he didn't want to fly into the Atlanta airport and he didn't want anybody to know he was coming over there except the prospect and his high school coach. He didn't want a bunch of fanfare.

I made the arrangements and away we went. Well, to my dismay, the weather was bad, and we couldn't land at a private airport, as planned, and had to go into Hartsfield International. Coach Bryant didn't like that, but he understood the circumstances.

Then it got worse. When we got to the high school, there was a mass of people waiting and cheering. Heck, they had turned out classes and had assembled the marching band, which was playing away. Also, there were about a dozen sports writers there to record what was going on.

I was sweating and melting. Coach Bryant had this look on his face that let me know he didn't approve.

Finally, we got Coach Bryant, the prospect, and the high school coach in this tiny office in the gym. There wasn't much room, but I went in there with them. In fact, I slammed the door and caught a sports writer's finger in it.

Not much was said on the flight back to Tuscaloosa. The Man was sorely upset with me, and I decided it would be best not to engage him in conversation.

But I've always thought that recruiting trip points out how admired Coach Bryant was, the respect he commanded. It also reminded me of how intimidating he could be. He wanted things his way, which was proper because his way usually worked, and it wasn't comfortable being around him when the best laid plans took an unexpected turn.

ॐ

If ever Coach Bryant showed how he could take charge and make something good happen in a trying situation, that would have been the ingenious decision he made prior to the start of the 1976 Liberty Bowl game.

—**JIM GOOSTREE,** Alabama trainer

It was brutally cold the evening we played UCLA in Memphis, Tennessee. The wind was blowing hard from the north. The wind chill was below zero. I don't think anybody really looked forward to going into action in that type weather.

That had been an off year for Alabama, 8–3 during the regular season, and UCLA was a powerhouse outfit. They were a convincing enough favorite to win.

Well, when it came time for pregame warmups, Coach Bryant instructed our young men to go on the field in short sleeved shirts. He said he wanted them to show those young men from UCLA how tough they were.

It worked like a charm. The UCLA players were all bundled up, with hoods over their heads and gloves on their hands. They looked stiff. They couldn't catch the football because they were so cold. Meanwhile, our players were running around having fun, whooping and hollering, acting like that was a normal winter night in the Deep South.

Once the game started, we took control in a hurry. We went on to a 36–6 drubbing of a powerful UCLA team.

After the game, all those UCLA players could talk about was the cold weather and how amazed they were that Alabama players could play like that in those type conditions.

Coach Bryant couldn't control the weather, obviously, but he took charge while showing our players how to deal with it.

✦

Coach Bryant was great at coaching players, coaching assistant coaches, and coaching game officials.

—CLEM GRYSKA,
Alabama assistant coach

I remember we were in the dressing room before a game with Tennessee. It was time for the officials to come in and meet the captains and check equipment, you know, to see if wraps were padded enough and everybody had on knee pads and hip pads, those type things.

Coach Bryant often introduced the game officials to our players, which made the men in stripes feel good. I think he knew that'd make them a little more kind to us.

As the officials were leaving that day, they asked if Coach Bryant had anything else they needed to know. He said, "Well, yeah, I want to tell you that Tennessee center holds on every play. It's obvious on the game films we've watched. But, well, uh, that doesn't matter because you won't have the guts to call a penalty on him in a big game like this one."

We kicked off to Tennessee. On the first play, the flags came flying. It was holding on their center. He got caught more than once that afternoon.

Then there was another game in which the flags flew against us down near the end zone on the opposite side of the field from our bench. One of the officials came running across the field to tell Coach Bryant we been caught holding.

"Who was holding?" Coach Bryant said.

The official had a blank look. He shrugged his shoulders.

"Hey, I'm paying you to officiate this game," Coach Bryant said. "I want to know which one of my players was holding."

The official turned around and took off running. I mean, he must have gone 60 yards one way. Then he came running back to the bench and, while huffing and puffing, told Coach Bryant the number of the player who had been caught holding. They were holding up the game while Coach Bryant got the information he wanted.

Coach Bryant thanked him and went back to the business at hand. But I wouldn't have been surprised if Coach Bryant had asked him to go find out which player our player was holding.

ॐ

Gene Stallings recalls a time when Bryant did a good job coaching a young assistant coach, him, and he carried the lesson with him:

Just before a game in the early 1960s, I was in the dressing room giving my defensive players some last minute instructions. They already had on their uniforms, and it was quiet in the dressing room. They were supposed to be thinking about the game they were about to play.

I ran from guy to guy. I wanted to make sure my players performed the way Coach Bryant wanted them to. I would tell one guy, "Now, if they go in motion, remember, you've got to watch the guards and tackles and see if they pull to lead a running play." I would tell one guy, "If the split end starts running a pass pattern toward the middle of the field, remember, you've got to cheat in that direction while paying attention to a halfback who might be running into the flat."

Then I heard that unmistakable voice. Coach Bryant said, "Boy, what are you doing?"

I looked his way and said, "Are you talking to me?"

He said, "Yeah, you're the guy I'm talking to."

I told Coach Bryant I was going over assignments with my defensive players.

Coach Bryant said, "Leave 'em alone, Bebes. If you can't coach 'em during the week, I don't want you messing 'em up just before a game."

❧

In many ways Bryant stayed with football until his death. He was an Alabama assistant coach from 1936 through 1939, helping the Crimson Tide produce a 29-5-3 record. During that time he spent one spring at Union College in Union, Tennessee, filling in for the head coach. He was a Vanderbilt assistant coach in 1940 and 1941. He was set to become the head coach at Arkansas the next year, but instead found himself serving in the United States Navy during World War II.

In 1946, because of the influence of George Preston Marshall, the at times controversial owner of the Washington Redskins, Bryant started his head coaching career at Maryland.

On September 15, 1980, as he was nearing his 300th victory, **Bryant** recounted conversations he had with Marshall and Dr. Curly Byrd, the Maryland president:

I was fresh out of the U.S. Navy and in Chicago for the College All-Star Game. I was at the Chicago Tribune's party at a hotel when George Marshall showed up. I told him I was looking for a coaching job and had already turned down a couple of offers from Alabama and Georgia Tech.

Marshall said, "Damn, what do you want—a head coaching job?" I told him that was exactly what I had in mind. I was thirty-two years old, young and brash.

Marshall left me on the hotel mezzanine. I thought I had

Photo by Barry Fikes

Paul "Bear" Bryant, the man in charge, with three of his favorite assistant coaches: (left to right) John David Crow, Richard Williamson, and Pat Dye.

blown the chance. Then he came back and told me to get up to my room and call Curly Byrd, the president of the University of Maryland.

I contacted Curly Byrd, who said, "Are you interested in being my football coach?" I told him yes. He asked how soon I could get there to talk to him. This was on a Thursday night, so I suggested Saturday night. He said, "Young man, if you want this job, be in my office tomorrow morning at eight."

It took some doing, a scramble, but I was there at eight o'clock the next morning. All of a sudden, I had a job that launched me to whatever I've accomplished.

Bryant never had another occupation because he knew how to coach football better than he knew how to do anything else.

101

〜

There are numerous stories about football staff meetings when Paul "Bear" Bryant coached the Crimson Tide. Most of them relate to how he sometimes kept assistant coaches on "hot seats" while going over practice plans and game plans.

Bryant gave his staff flexibility. **Clem Gryska**, Alabama's recruiting coordinator, says Bryant made it clear that his stamp of approval was to be added to whatever they developed.

Coach Bryant kept us on the ball, without question. He had a way of making everybody feel like part of the team, too, every assistant coach.

As most people know, Coach Bryant would put certain assistant coaches in charge of certain opponents and let them sort of manage the game plan. That worked well because each assistant coach had a chance to direct things for a week, with Coach Bryant approving, of course.

We had a game once against Tennessee and played masterfully. The headlines in newspapers talked about the great game plan so and so put together. Then after we beat Auburn, the headlines in newspapers talked about the great game plan so and so put together.

I don't know if it was jealousy or what, but as the recruiting coordinator I didn't ever see my name in the headlines, and that sort of bothered me. So I went to Coach Bryant one day and said, "Coach Bryant, I'd really like to be more of the team, you know, contribute a little more to what we're doing in games."

Coach Bryant looked at me and said, "Clem, you're a hell of a recruiter. I can go to Birmingham and find a few dozen coaches who can handle the Xs and Os. There are thousands of them across the country who can do that. But there aren't many people who can recruit winning football players."

Coach Bryant didn't say anything else. He didn't have to. I felt a dozen feet tall when I went back to my office—and he made everybody feel that way at one point.

But he could cut you to the quick, too, in a second, such as he often did in staff meetings.

What Coach Bryant did was go around the table and ask for opinions on certain areas. He might not get to everybody in a single day, but eventually everybody got to go under the gun. Most of us wanted to avoid that. But my buddy "Dude" Hennessey seem to always to take the bait.

Coach Bryant would say, "So how did that second period at practice go yesterday, when we were working on defense?"

Dude would say, "Oh, it was great, Coach Bryant. Our linebackers were really hitting some folks, and the defensive ends were fantastic."

That's when Coach Bryant would take a hard draw off of a cigarette, exhale smoke everywhere, let the assistant coach answering the question sweat for about a minute and say, "Damn, you know that's not right—or you should know. Ol' so and so didn't hit a damn person, and ol' so and so was so far out of position on most plays he couldn't have gotten close enough to a runner to even attempt a tackle. Damn, how can they learn anything if you can't see that well enough to correct their mistakes?"

Understand, it wasn't just "Dude" who caught the devil. We all got it at one point. In fact, "Dude" used to keep a running list on who got chewed out by Coach Bryant on a given day. Then he'd have a lot of fun with it.

I'm telling you, Coach Bryant didn't miss a thing. He saw it all from that observation tower.

But I'll tell you what was most impressive about Coach Bryant to me, at least when it came to the football staff. It was his willingness to take the blame publicly after a loss or after we didn't play particularly well in a game. You never heard him criticize a player. You never heard him criticize an assistant coach. You always heard him say something like, "I just didn't do a good job telling the offense what to do in a certain situation" or "I just didn't have our defense prepared for this or that."

Then when we got together for our next staff meeting, he would say, "We didn't do a good job teaching this or teaching that." The defense and kicking might have been great, and the offense might have stunk. But he didn't embarrass the offensive assistant coaches or the offensive players. He simply said, "We didn't do a good job."

It was never "I" or "you" with Coach Bryant. It was *we*, the Alabama team as a whole.

✤

I don't know how he found the time to be as organized as he was. He had it all planned to the letter.

—**JACK RUTLEDGE,**
Alabama assistant coach

Coach Bryant never showed up at a staff meeting when he wasn't totally prepared. He was particularly masterful at planning practices so there wouldn't be any wasted time. He'd come in the morning staff meeting with every minute written on a tan folder. He'd go over it and we'd make notes, our own practice schedule to follow.

The fire came out when somebody failed to follow his practice schedule, like when one of the assistant coaches would spend a few minutes working on something else.

The next morning he'd say, "I noticed yesterday that we spent a couple of minutes during period four working on the option play. I don't remember having that on my practice schedule. In fact, I know I didn't have it on there. So I'd like to know why we decided to work on the option play."

That's when the squirming started.

That brings to mind something that happened on the sideline during a game in the late 1960s or early 1970s.

We had a linebacker go down with an injury, and quickly there was another linebacker running onto the field to take his place. Coach Bryant saw that and started racing up and down the sideline screaming, "Who put that linebacker in the game?"

Pat Dye was on the staff then and hurried over to Coach Bryant and said, "I made the substitution."

Coach Bryant took that rolled up folder he always had with him during games, jammed that thing into Pat's belly, hard enough to almost knock him over, and said, "Let me tell you something, Pat, I make the substitutions for this team. Don't you ever send anybody out there without talking to me."

Pat got the point.

At the same time, Pat was the assistant coach who talked Coach Bryant into kicking an extra point to tie our game with Tennessee 10–10 in Knoxville in 1972. That was late in the game, with less than four minutes to go. We scored again in a matter of seconds and got out of there with a 17–10 victory, although it looked like a tie was about all we could get.

That's how Coach Bryant was. He'd listen to your input, welcome it, and make a decision about it. But you didn't go the other way on your own after he had a plan in place, either at practice or during a game.

6

THE MOTIVATOR

Paul "Bear" Bryant had a knack for saying the right thing at the right time while motivating his football teams. Most of the time he downplayed their abilities in public, particularly in the news media, and talked in more confident terminology to them in private. He seemed to be at his best during the darker moments, when games seemed to be out of reach, or during pivotal moments, when the outcomes of games were hanging in the balance.

Coach Bryant came into the dressing room at halftime and started walking back and forth. He was clapping his hands and smiling. He kept saying something like, 'This is great . . . This is great . . . We've got 'em right where we want them. I couldn't believe what I was hearing because Tennessee had killed us during the first half.

—**STEVE WHITMAN,** Alabama player

The date was October 20, 1979, and undefeated and untied Alabama trailed Tennessee 17–7 at halftime at Legion Field in Birmingham, Alabama. At one point it had been 17–0, a score that had not been lost on Crimson Tide fullback Steve Whitman:

I don't recall how the statistics stacked up that day, but I knew what the scoreboard said. Let's just say we weren't on top, not by a long shot, but Coach Bryant didn't sound that way when he talked to us at halftime.

Coach Bryant was totally calm while we were more than a little concerned. He just walked and clapped and kept talking about us having Tennessee right where we wanted them. I thought he had lost his mind. I thought he thought we were ahead.

Then he started talking about how we had a chance to show what we were made of, a chance to show class. He gave us his patented talk about how we could come back because our parents had raised us right. He told us we had a chance to show a national audience what we were about.

I don't think we talked that much about strategy, other than Coach Bryant telling us our game plan was solid, that we just had to execute better.

Near the end of the talk, maybe as a parting shot, Coach Bryant said, "If you come back and win this game, nobody in the nation will question whether you're the best team in the nation. If you win in the second half, I won't have any doubt you have what it takes to win a national championship."

Coach Bryant said he wanted us to sit for a few minutes and think about that. After he left, Don McNeal, our great defensive halfback, jumped up and screamed, "Coach Bryant is right. I'm not going to quit and nobody on this team is going to quit." We had people talking and people praying. We broke down the doors trying to get out of the dressing room and get the second half started.

Alabama won the game 27–17 in stunning fashion. The Crimson Tide gained 235 yards in the third and fourth quarters, after gaining 161 during the first half. Tennessee gained 81 yards in the second half, only three running the football, after gaining 119 in the first half.

There's a difference between a football player and an Alabama football player.

—PAUL "BEAR" BRYANT,
on the practice field

The 1979 Alabama team is considered by many observers the best in Crimson Tide history. It won coming from behind. It won with offense. It won with defense. But that team did not respond in the early stages of preseason practice, not until Bryant gave a wonderful pep talk from his observation tower.

I was present on that miserable afternoon on Thomas Field in Tuscaloosa, Alabama. The temperature was about 100 degrees, and the humidity was at least 90. The heat index was out of sight, and consequently, the Crimson Tide players were dragging.

Bryant ordered a team manager to blow a whistle for a short timeout. Through a megaphone he commanded his players to line up in front of him for a water break. Then after a few minutes he said:

> These are the type days that should tell you why you're at the University of Alabama. You were invited to join this program because you've got what it takes to survive in this type weather.
>
> I know you're hot and miserable. I'm hot and miserable, too. I know you're tired in this heat. I'm tired, too.
>
> But it's days like this that let you know the difference between a player and a football player. There's a major difference. A player goes through the motions. A football player works at it and enjoys the challenge.
>
> There's a difference between a football player and an Alabama football player. You're here because you're a cut

above. It isn't supposed to be easy, not with the rewards so high. You're here because you've got something inside you that'll make you give a little more when you think you're totally spent.

Bryant blew a whistle and said, "Now let's get back to work and get something done."

The remainder of the practice was spirited. The entire season was triumphant, 12–0, including a victory over Arkansas in the Sugar Bowl that capped a national championship.

༄

We went to Miami thinking we were going to beat Nebraska. I attribute that feeling to Coach Bryant because when he had faith in you, it sort of grew on you.

—JOHN CALVERT, Alabama player

Alabama arrived in Miami for a January 1, 1966, Orange Bowl game against Nebraska with an 8–1–1 record and ranked fourth in the nation. The Crimson Tide was a decided underdog to the much larger Cornhuskers, who were ranked third in the nation behind Michigan State and Arkansas:

Coach Bryant drew up the scenario that would make us Number 1 on a chalkboard the night before our game with Nebraska. He wrote that Arkansas would lose to LSU in the Cotton Bowl. He wrote that Michigan State would lose to UCLA in the Rose Bowl. He wrote that Nebraska would lose to Alabama in the Orange Bowl. He wrote that after all of that happened, we would be named national champion.

That was a longshot, no doubt, but he had us believing it could happen. Then, by golly, it happened just like he wrote it. We were given a challenge, and we made it happen because he motivated us.

Actually, he challenged us after we lost our first game of the season, 18–17, to Georgia. He told us we could come back and get in the national championship chase. He refused to let us lose sight of that goal. He was the master of motivation.

⟋⟍

I never doubted anything Coach Bryant said because he was usually right. But that was a shocking thing that happened on January 1, 1966.

—DENNIS HOMAN, Alabama player

Dennis Homan, an Alabama sophomore wide receiver during 1965, recalls the twists and turns that led Alabama to a glorious victory:

During the afternoon, not long before we went to the Orange Bowl from the hotel, we learned LSU had defeated Arkansas. That gave us a little more lift before our game with Nebraska, particularly since Coach Bryant had put together that checklist for us.

Then we jumped out to a 24–7 halftime lead in the Orange Bowl and found out that UCLA had defeated Michigan State in the Rose Bowl. It was an unbelievable feeling. Suddenly we were two quarters away from a win over Nebraska and, in all likelihood, a second straight national championship.

When we finished off Nebraska, 39–28, I don't think anybody was prouder of us than Coach Bryant. That meant a lot to us, seeing him as happy as he was that night. We were even prouder when he said, "I don't have a vote for Number 1, but if I did, Alabama would be my choice."

A few days later, after the votes were counted, Coach Bryant arrived at the athletics dorm before daylight and put a note up for all of us to read. He congratulated us for being the national champion and he challenged us to go back to work to make it three in a row.

We won every game in 1966, the only unbeaten and untied team, but got beat out at the ballot box by Notre Dame and Michigan State.

❀

Coach Bryant stepped back about six feet, told everybody to get out the way and charged through the dressing room door. He knocked it off of its hinges.

—**JIM GOOSTREE**, Alabama trainer
and assistant athletics director

We had two unfortunate things happen during the 1965 regular season, a controversial loss to Georgia on opening day and a heartbreaking tie with Tennessee on the third Saturday in October. So maybe the good fortune we had on January 1, 1966, was in order.

The tie, 7–7, came when it looked like our team was going to bounce back in total from the loss, 18–17. Also, it provided all of us with the opportunity to see Coach Bryant at his maddest and his motivational best.

We had the football at the Tennessee goal line with inside of a minute to play when one of our quarterbacks [Kenny Stabler] threw the football out of bounds on fourth down to stop the clock. That happened as our field goal unit was running onto the field to attempt a chip shot that would have won the contest.

After shaking hands with Tennessee Coach Doug Dickey, Coach Bryant arrived at our dressing room and found the door locked. There was chain on it with a padlock in place. Our players were milling around, not knowing what to do.

Coach Bryant started screaming, "Manager, get over here and open that door." But for some reason one of the managers didn't have a key, as was normally the case.

Coach Bryant turned to Captain Joe Smalley of the Alabama State Troopers, who traveled with the team, and shouted, "Captain Smalley, shoot the damn lock off." When Captain Smalley just stood there, rightfully weighing the danger involved with using a pistol, Coach Bryant said, "Then damn it, I'll knock the damn door in." He charged it like a bull, raised up one of his big feet and kicked the door open. Wood went everywhere and the door was on the ground. He literally ripped the chain and padlock out of the frame. I'm talking about a lock that was about as thick as a little finger.

I couldn't say that display led our team to the national championship at the end of the season. But I'm certain that team played with a little more purpose from that day forward. There seemed to be a sense of urgency about everything that team did, right on through the victory over Nebraska in the Orange Bowl.

⟡

We got to the practice field at 5 A.M. and saw this solitary figure out there in the dark. Coach Bryant was already there waiting for us.

—JERRY DUNCAN, Alabama player

At some point during the 1965 regular season, Coach Bryant had seen enough of our bad performances. So he called a practice session before dawn and before classes. We arrived to see this tall dark figure waiting for us, standing there in street clothes and a pair of work boots.

When we got to him, he put the football on the 20–yard line and said, "Here's what we're going to go. We're going to see if the offense can knock it in." We clicked right off the bat. We scored three touchdowns, just like that, and he said, "That's much better. Now let's see if the defense can stop the offense." He put the football on the 3-yard line and, boom, the defense stopped the offense on three consecutive series.

We weren't out there a half hour, but he made his point. He got the offense focused and the defense focused. But he wasn't finished because that practice on Wednesday morning, followed by one on Wednesday afternoon, was designed to set us up for a hell of a speech.

Coach Bryant had heard rumblings that we were complaining about being tired because he had worked us so hard from the start of practice right on into the regular season. That was true, too, because we were physically and mentally whipped. We had no speed, which was our forte.

Coach Bryant got us together Thursday night and said, "One of the coaches told me you guys are whipped, that you don't know if you can practice another day. He said you're wondering if you can take any more. Well, I want you to know I'm tired, too, tired of putting up with you players who are reading in the newspapers how good you are when, in reality, you aren't good at all. I'm trying to make you good, and you're talking about being too tired to work.

"What I want you to know, though, is there'll be times later in your lives when you won't want to work. You might have a wife and three kids. Your wife might be sick and your kids might be sick. You might have hospital bills to pay, and you might think you're too tired to go to work. But you'll have to go to work at that time just to make it."

Coach Bryant had that tired football team thinking about the future. Suddenly, none of us were as tired as we thought.

That national championship didn't come easy, but we won one because he was that kind of leader.

༄

Coach Bryant yanked the packet from the man's hand, threw it down on the floor and said, "Fella, we didn't come up here for a damn tour of the Smoky Mountains."

—JERRY DUNCAN, Alabama player

Bryant tended to get worked up, so to speak, for Alabama games against Tennessee and Auburn. He told his players to "be brave" before those encounters. He felt that way about those rivals because of the lack of success he had against the Volunteers while coaching at Kentucky and the lack of success the Crimson Tide had against the Tigers in the 1950s, just before he arrived to steady the sinking ship:

When we went to Knoxville to play Tennessee in 1966, it was a major game for us as we attempted to win a third consecutive national championship. Coach Bryant was extremely uptight about that game, as he usually was, and the tie we had with them in '65 added to his anxiety. He was determined to make amends for that screwup. You could see he was a little more fired up than usual.

I think most of our players were tied in knots, too, because it wasn't easy playing Tennessee up there, or any place, because those Volunteers would hit you for four full quarters. They hadn't beat us since 1960 and Coach Bryant wanted to continue that streak of dominance.

When we arrived at the airport in Knoxville, they had a greeting party for us, some chamber of commerce folks dressed in orange. As we departed the plane, they started handing us pamphlets, or sightseeing tour sheets, that pointed out the local attractions. I think they even had a key chain for all of us. We knew we were only going to be there for one night, and there wasn't going to be any time for looking over the area, but we took the pamphlets and thanked them. We were trying to be polite, as Coach Bryant always told us to be. But it was a strange scene, a greeting party on the afternoon before a game with a rival.

Well, when the president of the chamber of commerce handed a pamphlet and key chain to Coach Bryant, he took a quick glance, slammed the packet to the floor and said, "Fella, we didn't come up here for a damn tour of the Smoky Mountains. We came up here to play a damn football game."

If that had happened any place other than Tennessee, it would have been humorous. But after seeing Coach Bryant react like that, everybody on our team realized the seriousness of the football game we were about to play.

It rained like crazy during the game. Tennessee went ahead, 10–0, and we came back to take an 11–10 lead late in the fourth quarter. They missed a short field goal at the end, barely, by an inch, and we got out of there with a slim victory.

Obviously, Bryant was gifted at seizing the moment when it came to motivating his teams. During the 1960s, he took an Alabama team to Grant Field in Atlanta, Georgia, to play Georgia Tech. There was a lot of hostility between the programs, the result of the Darwin Holt and Chick Graning incident, and the Yellow Jackets' fans hurled whiskey bottles at Crimson Tide coaches and players as they took a pregame stroll around the playing field. The coach reacted by putting on a helmet, which inspired his team before a convincing victory.

I ran off at the mouth and got those Auburn folks riled up.

—PAUL "BEAR" BRYANT,
on a bad choice of words

There were two strong rallying cries among Auburn fans during the 1970s when it came to games against Alabama. One was "Punt, Bama, Punt" and the other was "Plow, Bear, Plow"— and the latter was the result of an ill advised statement by Bryant.

In 1972 Auburn won a game 17–16 by blocking two Alabama punts for touchdowns in the fourth quarter after being badly outplayed. Hence, "Punt, Bama, Punt" became a rallying cry that still surfaces on occasion.

After Bryant described Auburn as a "Cow College" before that game, fired-up Auburn students chanted "Plow, Bear, Plow" as Alabama players and coaches made pregame strolls at Legion Field in Birmingham. The coach disarmed the rivals with the help of sports information director Charley Thornton.

Bryant asked his longtime aide and confidant to get in front of him and act like a plow. Thornton did that, extending his arms behind him as if they were handles. The coach grabbed his hands and acted like he was churning dirt in a field. The Auburn students cheered mightily and, from that moment, the home field advantage in an equally split stadium belonged to the Crimson Tide and its fastidious leader.

Alabama players responded with a convincing victory.

※

I hobbled in and Coach Bryant was at the blackboard. I could see the fire in his eyes right away, and I knew I was in trouble.

—LAURIEN STAPP, Alabama player

Laurien Stapp, an Alabama quarterback and placekicker from 1958 through 1960, told an interesting story to Mike Fleming of the *Memphis Commercial Appeal* newspaper just before Bryant coached his last game on December 29, 1982. It points out the at times intriguing ways the coach motivated players. The setting was a team meeting room in Tuscaloosa just before the Crimson Tide was to make a trip to Philadelphia, Pennsylvania, to play Penn State in the Liberty Bowl:

> I had a broken leg and didn't figure in the game plan for the Liberty Bowl. So I went hunting one afternoon, got back in town a little late and was a few minutes late for a team meeting.
>
> Coach Bryant looked at me and the first words out of his mouth were, "Stapp, that's going to cost you two Liberty Bowl tickets." Each player got six, so that left me with four.
>
> Coach Bryant got back into what he was doing, but he wasn't finished with me. He paused, looked in my direction and said, "Stapp, that won't cost you two tickets, rather four."
>
> Coach Bryant started drawing plays again. Then, to my dismay, he looked at me again and said, "No, Stapp, that's going to cost you six tickets, and it might cost you the trip to Philadelphia for the Liberty Bowl."
>
> I didn't realize it, but Coach Bryant was using me to motivate our team. It was the first of twenty-four straight bowl games for Alabama under Coach Bryant, but some of our guys weren't excited about going to Philadelphia to play in snow and ice. He was using me to get to the others. He was using me to make playing in the Liberty Bowl look like the chance of a lifetime.
>
> I learned that day that Coach Bryant was ahead of his time when it came to motivation. He seemed to always come up with a different type twist.

☙

When I quit the team as a sophomore, I went with my father to have a meeting with Coach Bryant. I expected him to be glad to see me, to talk to me about the problem, you know, to welcome me back with open arms. Instead, I got a real shock.

—BOB BAUMHOWER, Alabama
and professional player

Not only was Bryant gifted when it came to motivating teams before and during games, he was equally skillful managing the small parts, individual players. Bob Baumhower, who became a Pro Bowl nose tackle for the Miami Dolphins, discovered that in 1974, his sophomore season at Alabama:

Coach Bryant had demoted me to the scout team when I thought I was good enough to be a starter on defense. So I quit.

Fortunately, a meeting was arranged that straightened out things, only not the way I figured it would happen.

When his secretary escorted my father and me to his office, Coach Bryant said, "Hello, Mr. Baumhower, it's good to see you again." Then he looked at me and said, "What in hell are you doing here?" I told him I thought he wanted to talk to me about rejoining the team. He said, in that deep voice, "Talk to you? Hell, I don't want to see a quitter around here."

Just like that Coach Bryant had turned it around. I was there expecting him to ask me to come back, and he was asking me what in hell I was doing in his office. Then he said, "Since you're here, I'll take the time to talk to you, although I'm more interested in visiting with your father."

What Coach Bryant did was give me a quick and complete

attitude adjustment. Up until that point, I didn't have any direction as a football player. I was happy just to be one, to be on the Alabama team, and I didn't really care about being a good player or the best I could be.

Basically, through that conversation he let me know he didn't care how good I thought I was, who I was and what type ability I might have. All he wanted was for me to show him I was willing to make the necessary sacrifices to be the best I could be. He told me the only way he would let me come back is if I was willing to work at tapping my potential instead of wanting a starting job handed to me without the effort.

By the time the meeting was over, the guy who had quit and walked out, me, was begging for the opportunity to rejoin the team, pleading for a second chance.

I took what I learned that day and put it to good use. It was a turning point in my life. It got me focused. It made me dedicated. It helped me at Alabama, it helped me in Miami, and it has helped me in my professional life after football.

The point is Coach Bryant knew what was best for me, how to motivate me to become a winning player. He seemed to know how to do that with almost everybody.

ॐ

I've never been more motivated for a football game than I was for Coach Bryant's last one. I don't think there was a person on that playing field that night who even considered letting him go out as a loser.

—Jeremiah Castille,
Alabama player

Bryant had nothing but willing combatants when he coached his last game in the 1982 Liberty Bowl. His Alabama players were on a mission, although the master motivator attempted to downplay one of the grand moments in sports history. Jeremiah Castille, a defensive halfback who earned Liberty Bowl most outstanding player honors, remembers how what Bryant said prior to the 21–15 victory over Illinois was pure vanilla, at least when it came to his words, yet dynamite at the end of a short fuse when it came to the effect:

> Coach Bryant was extremely quiet that night, and there was a mist in his eyes when he talked to us. It wasn't a rousing speech, to say the least, more like a straightforward chat.
>
> I don't remember everything he said. It's impossible to recall it word for word. But it was something along the lines of the Liberty Bowl being a game we should play for ourselves, not for him. He apologized for the fanfare, all of the attention, and he apologized for the pressure his retirement had put on us.
>
> Basically, Coach Bryant said we should forget about him and all of the last game business. He said we should play for Alabama and for ourselves. He said we should try to win it because people would remember us for the outcome a long time after he was dead and buried. He said that was unfair, something he should apologize for, but it was a fact of life.
>
> We were going to win it for him, anyway, but it was one of the more inspirational pregame talks he gave us. He spoke from his heart, and that really got us ready to play.

ॐ

If anybody wanted to learn something about life, all he or she had to do was attend one of our Wednesday night team meetings at the athletics dorm. It was during that hour that Coach Bryant was at his absolute best as a teacher and motivator.

—CLEM GRYSKA,
Alabama recruiting coordinator

"A lot has been said, with good reason, about Coach Bryant's motivational talks before games, either at the team breakfast or in the dressing room," said Clem Gryska, an Alabama assistant coach who served as recruiting coordinator. "But the times he really reached those young men were at team meetings on Wednesday nights at Paul Bryant Hall. He had more time then, about an hour, and he talked about life in general."

Jack Rutledge, another assistant coach, recalls one of those occasions, the best he can remember:

Coach Bryant always talked about the spiritual, the mental, and the physical with players. He'd have the same theme, almost always, but he'd say it a little differently each time.

His sense of timing was amazing.

During his last decade he incorporated love a lot, told players how important it was to love people. He was more philosophical then, a great teacher and a great motivator.

One Wednesday night he had a chalkboard full of information when the players arrived for the meeting. He had a big chart up there, too. He had a wall full of things he wanted them to grasp. Obviously, it had taken a lot of his time to prepare.

Coach Bryant said, in part, "Let's talk about ages zero to six. That's a time when you didn't choose to be here in life, rather your mothers and fathers made the decision for you. Your life was just starting, when your parents, your doctor, your grandparents and others were forming it for you.

"Then you're ages six to twelve. That's when you were meeting other children, making young friends. You wanted to take their toys, and they wanted to take your toys. You were sent to school, and you had to decide if you were going to study or you weren't going to study. That's also when you were deciding if you were going to be the type person another person respected or if you were going to go the other route. Some of you probably thought you knew everything at that point, that your parents, your grandparents and other people didn't know a thing. Those of you who felt that way were wrong.

"Let's talk about ages twelve to eighteen. That was your high school years, your most important time, when you had teachers who could teach you something. Some of you probably thought you knew more than your parents then, that they didn't know anything about life and what was good for you. You were wrong if you thought anybody who had lived longer than you didn't know anything about life. By all means, that was a time when you either earned respect or didn't or respected other people or didn't.

"Now here you are, in college, out on your own. Now you're really learning what we just talked about. You're learning that your parents knew best. You're learning about the importance of earning respect and giving respect. You're learning your teachers have something worthwhile to say. You're learning about a love for our country. You're learning that it isn't all that easy to be on your own, that you have to make the right decisions when it comes to everything you attempt. You're learning the value of teamwork. You're learning more about the value of prayer and being thankful for what you've had and what you have.

"It's now that you're preparing more for the future. It's what you do with these years that'll set up what's to come in your life.

"When you're forty years old, no matter what you're doing, whether you're a doctor or a lawyer or a common laborer, or how much money you're making, you'll know if you're respected because of your actions and if you respect other people. That's the measuring stick of success. It doesn't matter what you become professionally. It's what you are morally and spiritually, whether other people respect you and you respect them.

"You'll be expected to carry out the letter of the law, no

matter what you're doing. If you don't, if you don't take responsibility, you'll end up in the streets as a drug addict or some other form of riffraff.

"The most important thing is love. You need to learn how to love other people. Chances are, they'll love you in return. The same with respect.

"You'll have a family, or most of you will, and when you're in your forties, you're going to learn something really important about yourself. If at that time your children are about as old as you are now, if they're off on their own for the first time, at college or wherever, and they come home on a regular basis to see you, then you'll know you've been a success."

I wish I had that entire talk on tape or had gotten it typed. But I think you see the point. Coach Bryant didn't always say things in the normal way, rather his way, and he had a way of getting people to listen and then think about what he said. He put it to them with the good on one side and the bad on one side. Usually, it was about making choices.

Coach Bryant felt an obligation to teach players—and not just about football.

7

THE COMPETITOR

Paul grinned and said, "Well, ma'am, don't you folks take your football seriously?"

—RED BLOUNT, Alabama Board
of Trustees member

It was early in the morning during the 1970s, not much later than six o'clock, and Paul "Bear" Bryant was in his office with successful businessman and friend Red Blount. It was the week of a contest against intrastate rival Auburn, and the coach wanted to talk to Ralph "Shug" Jordan, his counterpart across the state, about game management for the annual battle that at the time was staged each year at Legion Field in Birmingham:

Paul and I were discussing an assortment of matters when he excused himself to place a telephone call. He said he needed to talk to the folks at Auburn about logistical plans for the Iron Bowl game.

After letting the telephone ring several times, Paul hung up. Then he tried again, with the same result. Finally, somebody answered in the Auburn Athletics Department.

"This is Paul Bryant at the University of Alabama," Paul said. "I'd like to talk to Coach Jordan."

There was a pause, at which time a cleaning lady told Paul it was too early in the morning for the coaches to arrive and she was the only person in the building. At that point, Paul said, "Well, ma'am, don't you folks take your football seriously."

Paul was joking with the lady, of course, just having a little fun, and he really got a chuckle out of that conversation.

Auburn has always taken football seriously, by all means, but it is doubtful anybody has coached the game with a passion comparable to Bryant. That was particularly the case when it came to the intrastate rival, which he defeated nineteen times in twenty-five attempts, including nine victories in a row from 1973 through 1981. He despised losing to the Tigers so much he attempted to resign after back-to-back defeats in 1969 and 1970, 49–26 and 33–28, respectively. The other losses were by narrow margins: 14–8 in 1958, his first season; 10–8 in 1963; 17–16 in 1972; and 23–22 in 1982. He and Jordan matched wits eighteen times, and he had a 13–5 record, which could be considered a compliment to the man with whom he teamed to develop one of the more memorable series in the nation.

☙

It's over . . . It's over . . . It's finally over.

—David Housel,
Auburn Athletics Director

David Housel, now the athletics director, was sports information director at Auburn on November 27, 1982, when Auburn defeated Alabama 23–22 in its last game against Bryant. That ended a streak of nine consecutive Crimson Tide victories in the series. Hence, the relief he felt watching the Tigers win that afternoon:

> In those days Auburn was under the yoke of Alabama. It didn't matter what we did, how many other games we won, to be successful and to be free, we had to break the yoke Coach Bryant had on us. We were under the tyrant's boot, yeah, true, because he had that boot on our throat.
>
> It was a period in which Auburn had to throw off the yoke of dominance if we were going to rise to prominence. At last, after nine losses in a row, that's what happened that afternoon.

Housel was a friend and confidant for Jordan and was instrumental in planning his funeral. He remembers Bryant arriving at a small and filled chapel in Auburn and standing in the rear of the room during the service after being invited by Evelyn Jordan, the grieving widow, to take a seat with her family.

"I remember seeing Coach Bryant at Coach Jordan's funeral," Housel said. "He seemed to be walking slower, more deliberate, and had a somber, almost ashen, expression on his face.

"I think when he saw Coach Jordan's casket, he realized his own mortality. I think it put some of those competitive juices both men had through the years in perspective."

ॐ

I don't think it's any secret Coach Bryant advised me not to accept the Auburn job. In fact, he was pretty adamant about it. He said, "Pat, we'll beat you and ruin you." I told him I appreciated his concern, but I knew he wasn't going to be at Alabama forever.

—Pat Dye, Alabama assistant coach and Auburn coach

The last two Auburn teams Bryant faced were coached by Pat Dye, one of his assistant coaches at Alabama from 1965 through 1973. He did not like the idea of one of his pupils and friends leading the rival program. But he had a soft spot in his heart for the man he introduced to coaching in 1965:

The most vivid memory I've got of Coach Bryant was when I interviewed for a job on his staff. I was excited about him and excited about the chance to become a coach. But I hadn't coached at all, not then, and I was extremely nervous when I went to Tuscaloosa for an interview with him.

I had on a new suit, and I hadn't cut off the tags. Richard Williamson, Jimmy Sharpe, and "Dude" Hennessey, who were on the Alabama staff, took off the tags after we had been to the Alabama student center and had coffee, which gave them time to have a big laugh over a country boy with a new suit.

Finally, I got in the interview with Coach Bryant. One of the first things I said was, "Coach Bryant, I don't know anything about coaching football because I've never coached. All I know is what I've learned playing at Georgia. But I'll work if you'll hire me. I've got a chance to play some more at the pro level, but I'll give that up if you'll give me a chance to work for you at Alabama."

Coach Bryant said they couldn't pay me much if they hired me. I told him I just had to feed my family, a wife and two kids. I'll never forget what he said next. He said, "Now, Pat, if we couldn't feed you we wouldn't hire you."

I'm not sure Coach Bryant realized what it took to take care of a wife and two children because I made $6,000 starting out at Alabama. Graduate assistant coaches make more than that now. But on the first of June in 1965, he put me on the payroll.

Actually, Coach Bryant said he needed to talk to Dr. [Frank] Rose, the university president, to make sure it was okay to hire me. What he was doing, I learned later, was buying some time so he could tell the other applicants he was going the other way.

When the deal was finally made and I was on board, Coach Bryant said, "Pat, we're going to let you watch the linebackers." You'll notice he didn't say coach the linebackers. He was just going to let me watch them.

But that's Coach Bryant for you. He had an unknown commodity as an assistant coach, which wasn't lost on him, and he was gonna let me learn before he let me coach. We talked about that a lot in later years, how he was only going to let me watch the linebackers, and we laughed about it.

But, you know, that was Coach Bryant. He didn't always act like he knew everything going on around him, but he sure as hell did. In fact, he was in control of almost all of it.

Dye was on the Auburn sideline as a loser the afternoon Bryant became the most prolific winner in college football history. He was on the sideline as a winner the afternoon Bryant coached the Crimson Tide a last time against Auburn. He was one of the first to arrive at First United Methodist Church for the funeral service the day Bryant was buried:

Not long before Coach Bryant died, I was able to go on a hunting trip with him and some other folks at a lodge in West Alabama. It was more like a gathering of good friends, a down home kind of thing, and we played a lot of cards, did a little fibbing around the camp fire, did a lot of talking and did a little hunting. In fact, there's a picture circulating of Coach Bryant and me seated around a camphouse table talking and having fun.

We stayed up sort of late and morning came early. When we went out hunting rabbits, everybody except Coach Bryant wanted to go down to the left side of the lodge, where the guide said the best chances of success were. He said he wanted to go down to the right side, even when everybody knew a rabbit hunter went where the dogs went. He was insistent about it, so we finally gave in and told him to have at it.

But before I let him go off by himself, I said, "Coach Bryant, let me see that fine gun you have." He handed me his shotgun and I emptied the shells out of it without him knowing about it.

Well, the hunt went on for a while and when somebody went to check on Coach Bryant, they found him sound asleep.

<hr>

Nobody wants to believe it, and few ever will, but Paul Bryant and Bobby Dodd were allies, not enemies.

—BOBBY DODD,
Georgia Tech coach

Bryant had fierce battles with several named opponents during his years at Maryland, Kentucky, Texas A&M, and Alabama. He won head-to-head battles with superb coaches, such as Bob Devaney and Tom Osborne at Nebraska, John McKay at Southern Cal, Bobby Dodd at Georgia Tech, Joe Paterno at Penn State, Bud Wilkinson at Oklahoma, Woody Hayes at Ohio State, and Johnny Vaught at Ole Miss. He had trouble beating some others, such as Ara Parseghian and Dan Devine at Notre Dame, Darrell Royal at Texas and General Bob Neyland at Tennessee.

All told, Bryant had a 4–2 record against Nebraska, a 2–2 record against Southern Cal, a 10–3 record against Georgia Tech, a 4–1 record against Penn State, a 2–0–1 record against Oklahoma, a 1–0 record against Ohio State and a 14–7–1 record against Ole Miss.

Bryant never beat Notre Dame, posting a 0–4 record, defeated Texas once, posting a 1–7–1 record, and never defeated Neyland during his years at Kentucky, posting a 0–5–2 record. However, he posted a 16–14–4 record against Tennessee, with all the victories coming while he was at Alabama.

So comes to mind a story many people have told about Bryant through the years.

When Bryant attempted to quit at Alabama, Dr. David Matthews, the youthful school president, refused to accept his resignation. In fact, he tore up the first one. Then when the coach tried again at the end of the 1970 regular season, the chief executive officer and Blount, the board of trustees member, told him he could leave if he could find a skilled leader as good as him to move into the position.

Bryant developed a short list of names. He called at least one of them, John McKay at Southern Cal, to see if he was willing to make such a move. He checked out several candidates. Then at about six o'clock one morning, he telephoned Matthews and asked if it was too early to have a cup of coffee and a discussion. The school president told the coach he was already up, fretting over a coaching change.

When Bryant arrived at the president's mansion on campus, he said, "You're right, Dr. Matthews, I can't find anybody as good as me to replace me."

Thus ended an ordeal.

A remarkable decade of winning continued, 103 games during the 1970s, even after only six wins the first year. There were only eleven defeats from 1971 through 1979—three to Notre Dame, two to Nebraska, one to Auburn, one to Texas, one to Missouri, one to Ole Miss, one to Georgia and one to Southern California.

Bryant lost forty-six games in twenty-five seasons at Alabama, with eighteen of those defeats coming during four seasons—four in his first, four in his last, five in 1969 and five in 1970. That means he lost twenty-eight games during the remaining twenty-one seasons. What is more, while leading the Crimson Tide he had twenty-nine defeats by seven or fewer points, including ten by three or fewer and six by one.

Bryant lost eighty-five games in thirty-eight seasons. His average record per season was 8.6–2.2–0.4. He had forty-five defeats by seven or fewer points, including fourteen by three or fewer and ten by one. What is more, Notre Dame won its four games by one point, two points, three points, and seven points, and Texas won five of its seven games by one point, two points, two points, four points, and four points. Four of the five losses to Neyland and Tennessee were by seven points, seven points, six points, and seven points.

❧

Every place I went in South Bend, Indiana, people wanted to talk about Coach Bryant. I don't guess I should have been, but I was amazed by the respect the Notre Dame people had for him and for Alabama football.

—**MAL MOORE,** Alabama player,
assistant coach and athletics director

Outwardly, Bryant never appeared troubled about his lack of success against Notre Dame. Instead, he was complimentary of that program and termed it something special. His Alabama teams lost to the Fighting Irish 24–23 in the 1973 Sugar Bowl, 13–11 in the 1974 Orange Bowl, 21–18 during the 1976 regular season and 7–0 during the 1980 regular season.

Mal Moore was offensive coordinator for the Crimson Tide during all of those games. He later served as assistant head coach at Notre Dame. He is the athletics director at Alabama:

The people at Notre Dame constantly expressed love for Coach Bryant. That was from the top to the bottom, from Father Hesburgh and Father Joyce all way down to fans on the street. I don't think a day passed that I wasn't asked about Coach Bryant. People wanted to learn all they could about him. The same was true after I left Notre Dame and coached in St. Louis. He was a powerful man, an influential man across the nation, and the brand of football he taught at Alabama was unique. Fans across the nation identified with it. It was popular among the masses.

At Notre Dame they have a picture of Coach Bryant in the football museum. Also, there's a framed letter he sent to Father Joyce after the 1973 Sugar Bowl. It's a tribute to his greatness, as well as evidence of how they feel about Coach Bryant in South Bend, that he has a place in the hall of honor with all those famous Notre Dame coaches and players.

We beat Southern Cal in South Bend when I was there and Father Hesburgh, the school president, came to the dressing room to congratulate everybody. I quickly noticed he had on a houndstooth hat like Coach Bryant used to wear. When he shook my hand, I said, "Father Hesburgh, you look mighty handsome in that hat." He smiled and said, "Thank you, Mal, my good friend Paul gave it to me."

I was fortunate to cover the Notre Dame dressing room after the battle of unbeatens in the 1973 Sugar Bowl. Players were exchanging hand slaps, high fives, even with priests, and the mood was joyous.

Suddenly, a hush fell over the room. Bryant had entered enemy quarters to congratulate the victors. He did not ask for Notre Dame Coach Ara Parseghian, at least not first, rather for the Fighting Irish's quarterback.

"Where's Mike Clements?" Bryant said, calling Notre Dame quarterback Tom Clements by the name of an Alabama defensive halfback in the other dressing room. "I'd like to shake his hand."

Nobody corrected the mistake. Bryant shook hands with Tom Clements, plus several other players who stepped forward to meet him, then congratulated Parseghian.

It was a display of class, Bryant style, and it was a scene that was repeated after other games Alabama lost under his direction, albeit a limited number. Another that comes to mind was a 6–3 loss to Mississippi State on November 1, 1980 in Jackson, Mississippi, a defeat that ended a twenty-eight-game winning streak. Like the loss to Notre Dame in New Orleans, that was painful because the Crimson Tide lost a fumble at the Bulldogs' 2-yard line in the final minute. But that did not keep the losing coach from paying tribute to the victors.

Interestingly, Bryant said he learned to do that from Bud Wilkinson, the Oklahoma coach when his Kentucky team defeated the Sooners 13–7 in the 1951 Sugar Bowl. "That made a lasting impression on me," Bryant said.

⚆

I rank Coach Bryant at the top of the profession and I'm qualified to do that because I competed against him, got to know him, and observed his teams through the years.

—**Ara Parseghian,** Notre Dame coach

Ara Parseghian completed his Notre Dame career when the Fighting Irish defeated Alabama in the 1975 Orange Bowl. He remembers Bryant as a fierce competitor who coached with a great deal of style:

I wrote Coach Bryant after our first game, the 1973 Sugar Bowl, and told him there were no losers that night. I told him it was great that Alabama and Notre Dame finally got together on the football field because, historically, both had been powerhouses.

With everything at stake in that game, the first meeting and both teams unbeaten, there was a potentially explosive situation. Instead, both programs developed a profound respect for each other, including the players, the alumni, the assistant coaches, Coach Bryant, and me. That happened, in part, because of the class he brought to the game.

I regret Coach Bryant died so quickly after his last game because he richly deserved to have more accolades than time gave him. On the other hand, I have no doubt he would have continued as a living legend had he lived longer and coached longer. He made college football much richer.

෪

Coach Bryant was a man with many different sides to him. But more than anything, he was a heck of a football coach and, to me, he was a dear friend.

—DARRELL ROYAL, Texas coach

One of the better friends Bryant had in the coaching profession was Darrell Royal, who led Texas to victories over his Alabama teams. They were an interesting duo, for sure, because the man who led the Longhorns shunned the spotlight and the man who led the Crimson Tide loved an admiring public.

"I won't tell you my ol' padre Darrell Royal wasn't a good coach because he was damn fine one," Bryant said on December 30, 1981, two days before a Texas team coached by Fred Akers defeated Alabama 14–12 in the Cotton Bowl. "But he has to be one of the luckiest son of a guns who ever coached. He tied us in the 1960 Bluebonnet Bowl because we had to play in the Lone Star State. He beat us in the 1966 Orange Bowl because Joe Namath could barely walk—and the officials were kind to Texas. He beat us in the 1973 Cotton Bowl because the officials didn't see his quarterback step out of bounds on a touchdown run—that plus my team was deflated after Auburn beat us with two blocked punts about a month earlier. We didn't have time to recover from something like that.

"I'd imagine Darrell has another story to tell. But what I just said is the absolute truth."

Royal chuckled after digesting that statement. Then he offered his take on the coach from Alabama:

I could definitely see how Coach Bryant could say that, as well as how he would have said that. But if he had won those games, I'd be calling my ol' buddy lucky.

Every one of the victories Texas had over his Alabama teams was razor thin. It was hoss against hoss every time, too, some good football. I would guess we won a couple of times when we weren't supposed to, and I'm sure if we had played more than four times, he would have stuck some losses in our craw.

You're talking about a man I admired and liked very much. Coach Bryant was a man with many different sides to him. A few people saw and a lot of people heard about the rough and tough side. He had that, without doubt. But not many people saw the smooth and political side, the mover and the shaker, nor the compassionate side.

I've said it before, so why not again? Paul Bryant was just tougher than the rest of us. That, plus his ability to make everybody believe in him made his teams hard to beat.

Winning was important to him. He gave everything he had to give to the profession. I don't know what else could be asked of a person, a coach or anything else.

Coach Bryant was the same way as a friend—and, by

golly, that counts a whole lot more with me.

Not many people know it, but Coach Bryant and I met in 1949, just after I had graduated at Oklahoma. I had just taken a job at a high school. He was at Kentucky then and he came to Norman, Oklahoma, to see what Coach Bud Wilkinson was doing with his offense and his defense. They were having spring practice, and Coach Wilkinson told me to take care of Coach Bryant, to show him around and to make sure he was comfortable. Also, he told him I knew everything about the offense and defense and could answer any questions he might have.

I don't know of anybody who could have been more lucky. Can you imagine graduating from college, after playing football, and being put in charge as a host for Coach Bryant, who already had made quite a name for himself?

Coach Bryant was full of questions, too. He wanted to know how Oklahoma did this and how Oklahoma did that.

One thing I know. Coach Bryant didn't forget that introduction. The man said a lot of nice things about me when I was an assistant coach, like in 1956, when I was at Mississippi State and we played Kentucky. He really helped along my career, for which I was always grateful.

Royal was asked how two old warriors, both great coaches, became such good friends.

"Let's remember that Coach Bryant was a heck of a lot older than me, by fifteen years," Royal said, reacting to the "old warriors" part of the question. "I just had the good sense to get out of coaching faster than he did. I wanted to leave on my own terms. I didn't want for somebody to shoo me out at Texas. Of course, I don't remember anybody shooing him out at Alabama, either."

ॐ

I've borrowed, or stole, more football coaching philosophy from Bob Neyland than anybody. He taught kicking and defense, the backbone of any good program. That plus minimizing penalties and fumbles. I learned the hard way, through some agonizing losses to The General, but at least I learned it.

—PAUL "BEAR" BRYANT,
on lessons learned from the enemy

ॐ

Paul Bryant and General Bob Neyland are two men I respected more than all other football coaches. Earl Blaik of Army was another. But Paul "Bear" Bryant and General Robert Reese Neyland were so much alike in the way they coached it is almost a miracle they were once rivals.

—LINDSEY NELSON,
hall of fame sportscaster

Nelson, the voice of the Cotton Bowl to so many people, was speaking on December 29, 1979, three days before Alabama defeated Baylor, 30–2, in Dallas, Texas. He had interviewed Bryant for a special pregame report. Then on a cold, blustery afternoon in 1984 in Knoxville, Tennessee, his chosen home by Neyland Stadium and the river that flowed across four lanes of pavement and a median from it, he talked about two of the more famous men in the history of Deep South college football:

> I was at Tennessee as a student when The General began solidifying the Volunteers as a national power. Even back then he said the way to measure the abilities of a player was the way he performed against Alabama.
>
> I watched in amazement as emphasis shifted to

Kentucky, not that Alabama was ever considered something other than the ultimate. The reason was a young coach named Paul Bryant had assumed the leadership role in Lexington, Kentucky, which set the stage for some monumental confrontations.

The General won almost all of them, but not by much, and it was obvious to me another coaching star was being developed. From that beginning Paul Bryant became a coaching legend. His was an upbringing of hard knocks. But his was an upbringing that survived the test of time.

৩

The passing of Paul "Bear" Bryant brings to an end a great era in college football. He was bigger than the game at times. He was a master at motivating his players for battle. He competed hard. I hope people think the same thing about me because I am honored to have counted him among my friends.

—WOODY HAYES, Ohio State coach

Woody Hayes, the former Ohio State coach, was not a young man when Bryant died. But he mustered the strength to travel to Tuscaloosa for the funeral. He was the most famous coach in attendance.

Hayes and Bryant battled only once on the football field, when Alabama won the 1978 Sugar Bowl game, 35–6. The Crimson Tide was favored by one point but dominated the contest from start to finish. This came after several weeks of hype during which the coaches had a lot of fun.

At a joint press conference in New Orleans two days before the game, Bryant said, "I'll agree to stay at the hotel and watch the game on television if Woody will do the same thing."

To which Hayes said, "Oh no, not for a minute. I'll be on the sideline because I want to see it up close."

After the victory, Bryant was leaving a press conference when he was followed closely by a few sports writers. He was asked the significance of winning over such a storied coach.

Bryant said, "This isn't about Woody and me. This doesn't mean Woody isn't a great coach. In fact, Woody is a great coach—and I ain't bad myself."

ᔕ

Coach Bryant always seemed to be indestructible. He was a monumental figure in intercollegiate athletics, a man who set standards not easily attainable by men. He was a giant in our profession and a giant among men.

—JOE PATERNO,
Penn State coach

Joe Paterno entered the 2001 college football season an almost cinch to become the most prolific winner among coaches at the Division I level of competition, pushing Bryant into second place. The Penn State leader admits to being humbled by the accomplishment.

Paterno recalls having never defeated Alabama in four memorable meetings when Bryant coached the Crimson Tide. The results were 13–6 in the 1975 Sugar Bowl, 14–7 in the 1979 Sugar Bowl, 31–16 during the 1981 regular season and 42–21 during the 1982 regular season.

ᔕ

We wanted unbeaten Alabama and unbeaten Penn State for the national championship in the Sugar Bowl. For some reason, Joe Paterno was reluctant. So I went to Tuscaloosa, visited Coach Bryant at his house and said, "Paul, you've got to call the guy and issue a challenge."

—**ARUNS CALLERY,** Sugar Bowl
committee member

I don't recall why Joe Paterno wasn't interested in coming to New Orleans and playing Alabama in the 1979 Sugar Bowl. It seems he wanted to take his team to the Orange Bowl, maybe because of the warm weather, which is something I'm sure Penn State fans favored.

Anyway, it was a natural, two unbeaten teams, and I went to visit Coach Bryant, who at the time had the reputation of being a master matchmaker for bowl games. We sat with Mary Harmon for a while, just visiting, and part of the conversation centered around the matchup we wanted.

Paul said he thought the game would be a good one, too, so I prodded him into telephoning Joe Paterno. I'll never forget the conversation. Paul told Joe that they had played a great game in New Orleans in 1975, that both programs were national names, and that maybe it was time for them to get together again. Then he offered the clincher. He said, "Joe, it's only right that one of us win the national championship this season, so let's get the players together on the field and let them settle the issue."

After a few minutes, Paul hung up the telephone, smiled, and said, "Aruns, ol' boy, you've got your match."

We got more than we bargained for, really—one of the classic confrontations in history.

Billy Varner, Bryant's friend and confidant, was at the house when the Sugar Bowl deal was struck. He remembers it taking a little coaxing to convince Paterno to take his team to New Orleans.

"What Mr. Callery didn't say is it took about five calls to

Joe Paterno to get the game arranged," Varner said. "I think the final convincing statement by Coach Bryant came when he said, 'You know, Joe, we aren't worth a hoot, really, and somebody is going to beat us. I'd like for it to be a good team like yours to do that when it happens.' Joe Paterno bit the bait."

Alabama preserved the 14–7 victory over Penn State in a remarkable manner, with a stunning goal line stand. The Nittany Lions appeared to be driving for a tying touchdown with a shade more than six minutes remaining. A tackle on a pass receiver at the one-yard stopped the first thrust. A running play on third down gained a little more than two feet. A running play on fourth down, from about a foot from the end zone, gained nothing.

Alabama fans refer to the goal line stand as The Gut Check, phraseology Bryant favored. "To see our players win like that was the ultimate for an old coach," he said.

೧

I was at Paul Bryant's funeral for a good reason. We were friends and had been for decades.

—Bobby Dodd,
Georgia Tech coach

Bobby Dodd was seated in a Holiday Inn motel room in Knoxville, Tennessee, in the mid-1980s. He was an elderly man, yet in grand physical condition because of a homemade regimen: "I try to take a little exercise, play a little tennis, and drink a little bourbon every day." The former Tennessee quarterback who coached Georgia Tech through a tumultuous era against Bryant and Alabama was willing to talk about bad blood.

Lord knows, Alabama and Georgia Tech spilled a lot of it

when Bryant coached the former and Dodd coached the latter. There was the Darwin Holt-Chick Graning incident that received national attention. There were whiskey bottles thrown at Grant Field in Atlanta. There were whiskey bottles thrown at Legion Field in Birmingham, although that incident did not receive as much media attention.

Mostly, though, there were Alabama victories, nine in eleven games against Georgia Tech when Bryant led the Crimson Tide, only one loss, 7–6 in 1962, when Dodd coached the Yellow Jackets. This happened when the two programs were fierce rivals, both in the top five of Deep South football. Previously, there was a 1–1 split when Kentucky and Georgia Tech battled:

> People don't want to hear why we left the Southeastern Conference. Likewise, people don't want to hear that Paul Bryant and I were allies. It's better, it seems, for everybody to portray us as two coaches who hated each other. That's not close to the truth.
>
> Paul and I were friends for a long time. We used to exchange telephone calls and letters after victories. As an example, one of his slow quarterbacks from Texas A&M chased down a defensive halfback who had intercepted a pass, stopped a touchdown, and I called him to ask how that slow guy chased down the fast guy. Paul told me the reason was his quarterback was running for his life and the defensive halfback was running for a touchdown. He used to call me, too, just to talk. It isn't good gossip, I guess, so nobody ever talked about those times.
>
> People said Paul and I were at odds about academics. Well, I'll tell you it was harder for a player to stay in school at Georgia Tech than at Alabama. But Alabama wasn't low on the Southeastern Conference totem poll, about five rungs down, maybe, somewhere below us, Vanderbilt and a few others, which meant there were worse cases.

So we used to go the SEC Meeting every year and fight it out with some others as allies.

But the bottom line related to us leaving the SEC wasn't academics or the Darwin Holt-Chick Graning incident. It was scheduling and the fact we had trouble beating Alabama.

Every year, it seemed, we'd produce a good record and get the bowl games people excited. Then we'd have to play Alabama and Georgia, usually back to back. Well, Alabama would beat us more times than not, sometimes barely, and the bowl games people would lose a lot of interest in Georgia Tech because there weren't many bowl games at the time.

So we had to do something. It might not have been the wisest decision in the world, but we decided we should become an independent, leave the SEC.

It wasn't bad blood that led to that. It was economics. It wasn't Paul Bryant and Bobby Dodd fighting. It was what appeared best for Georgia Tech at that time.

⟲

You never saw defeat in him.

—Mal Moore, Alabama player
and assistant coach

Nobody was closer to Bryant on the sideline than Moore, an Alabama assistant coach from 1964 through 1982 who was offensive coordinator for most of those years. He stood beside the coach during games where he witnessed a competitive fire:

Even when we got in trouble, got behind in a game, you could see strength in Coach Bryant's face. You never saw defeat in him. You could look at his eyes and see a will to win. Of course, these are things players notice, too, which was important to our success at Alabama.

During a game, players expect the head coach to be a leader, and Coach Bryant was definitely that. The fight was there all the time. That was something Coach Bryant had that a lot of people don't have. He was such a competitor, a pillar of strength from whom the players drew strength. The man had it, the whole package, and competitiveness was a major portion of it.

8
THE GAME DAY WARRIOR

Coach Bryant had everything planned for a game. He left nothing uncharted. It was a routine. He even had the way he wanted a game to go written down in sequence. He had a plan for those times when his plan for the game got messed up.

—CLEM GRYSKA,
Alabama assistant coach

Paul "Bear" Bryant left nothing to chance when it came to attempting to win a football game. He had a timeline for everything his teams did, all the way down to when, by police escort, the team would arrive at the stadium and exactly how long it would take to get there from the motel.

This game day routine came after a disciplined week of preparation.

Coaches would "break down" the film from the previous game, position by position, on Sunday morning and provide Bryant with grades for each player. He used their opinions while making comments on his weekly game review show on television.

The game plan for the next opponent started taking shape

Sunday afternoon, with a coach in charge leading the process. That person had viewed game films of the next opponent for several months, searching for offensive and defensive trends, and had updated his information week by week during the season.

Bryant always believed getting his team ready to play at its best was more important than game plans. But the scouting reports were valuable, to say the least. He asked numerous questions during staff meetings. He maintained total confidence in his assistant coaches.

The team worked extensively on its offensive game plan and defensive game plan on Tuesday and Wednesday, put in a few "new wrinkles" or "gimmick plays" on Thursday and had a loosening up practice on Friday.

Bryant called the game "show time," and he told his staff and his players he wanted every performance to be grandiose. He told them a game was a reward for all of the hard work they had put in on the practice field. In turn, most of them said games were easy because of the labor they had experienced preparing.

"I can tell you from experience that playing Tennessee in Knoxville, Georgia Tech in Atlanta, and Auburn in Birmingham wasn't hard compared to what we went through on the practice field under Coach Bryant," said Jack Rutledge, an Alabama offensive guard in 1959, 1960 and 1961. "It wasn't always easy winning, but it was much easier than practicing under him. He taught us to always be humble, but, yeah, we had an air of confidence about us because of what we had been through getting ready for a season."

Clem Gryska, an Alabama assistant coach, said that Bryant made sure that when game day arrived, everybody was on the same page, so to speak:

> Goodness, everything was programmed.
>
> I guess a good example would be my game day responsibilities. As recruiting coordinator, I also worked with the

kicking game. He had me put a stopwatch to everything we did, checking the time it took for us to snap the football on a punt until the punter kicked the football. I had to check the hang time on a punt. I had to check how long it took our coverage team to make the tackle on a punt. It was that tedious.

Then there was the weather. I was in charge of monitoring it, the temperature and the wind.

We were playing somebody in Birmingham, and the wind was brisk. I watched it like a hawk during pregame warmups. Then it was time for our captains to go to the coin toss. Normally, I went with them to make sure they knew which goal to defend if the other team was going to get the football first.

Bryant, the game day warrior, could somehow turn even a sub-zero wind chill to his team's advantage.

Photo by Barry Fikes

On that day, Coach Bryant caught up to me as we were leaving the dressing room. He said, "Clem, I'm not a meteorologist, but that wind looks mighty unpredictable today. Stay on top of it. It might be the difference in winning or losing."

I can tell you it isn't all that entertaining watching a football game when all you watch is the flags at the top of the grandstands to see which way the wind is blowing.

But Coach Bryant was that precise.

Also, Coach Bryant was a tiger to deal with when something went wrong during a game. It was those times when his anger, or disappointment, to put it kindly, was aimed at the assistant coaches in the press box.

We were playing somebody—I don't recall who—when the defense got burned for a touchdown. Coach Bryant hurried to the sideline telephone, which at that time was somewhere behind the bench with a short cord on it. He wanted to call the press box and let our coaches up there know how he felt.

Coach Bryant grabbed the telephone and screamed, "Hey, what in hell is going on out there? I want this defense to . . ."

Coach Bryant slammed down the telephone. All he could hear was static-like noise—shhh-ca-poosh, shhh—and he hurried back to where I was standing and said, "We need to get that damn telephone fixed. Hell, I can't hear anything except static."

I wasn't a telephone technician, but I went to check it out. I picked up the receiver and said something like, "Test . . . one, two, three, four . . . test."

The next thing I heard was "Dude" Hennessey, one of our assistant coaches in the press box saying, "Clem, don't let him get back on that telephone. I was making static noises as loud as I could up here. But he's going to catch on sooner or later."

Bryant had several comical moments like that. He literally fired assistant coaches on the sideline, then hired them back after games, win or lose. **Ken Donahue**, the famous defensive coordinator was no exception:

I got fired five or six times after our game with Ole Miss in 1969. That was the night Archie Manning of Ole Miss picked apart our defense. Every time we scored, he would lead them to a touchdown. Every time that happened, Coach Bryant was in my face screaming, "Donahue, you're fired. Get your stuff out of your office and get out."

Finally, we won the game, 33–32, and Coach Bryant caught me walking off the field and said, "Ken, I want you stay with us. I'm taking back that firing notice."

ॐ

I've never seen a pregame talk quite like the one Coach Bryant gave before the 1972 game with Tennessee. It was surprising because it was so unexpected.

—JACK RUTLEDGE,
Alabama assistant coach

Coach Bryant was normally soft-spoken and to the point in his pregame talks with players. I think it was his opinion that the hay was already in the barn, as he put it, and it wasn't a time for a lot of emotion.

In fact, he would do the same thing less than a half hour before the opening kickoff. At that point he would scream in a loud voice, "Twenty minutes . . . okay . . . twenty minutes." That was a time for quietness, thinking about the game plan. There would be no more coaching and no more chatter. That was the time to get ready.

Then just a few minutes before we went on the playing

field, he would scream, "Check your chin straps. . . . Check your shoelaces." Everybody would follow those commands. His thinking was he didn't want to have to waste a time-out or have a foul-up because of a loose chin strap or a loose shoestring. He had everybody reacting as one.

But he broke with all of that just before we played Tennessee in Knoxville in 1972. Coach Bryant decided to make a little talk that day.

He said, "Gentlemen, when Steve Bisceglia is running with the football today, *we* will be running with the football. When John Hannah is blocking, *we* will be blocking. When Terry Davis is passing, *we* will be passing.

"It's the day when we're going to come together as ONE.

"I want you to give everything you have to that, because when you come off the playing field and go in there to shower, you're going to look in the mirror, and that face looking back at you will tell you whether you've done your best.

"Then I want you to go outside and hug your mother when you see her and shake hands with your father when you see him. He'll be able to look into your eyes and, like that face in the mirror, tell you if you've done your best.

"This is the day we're coming together as ONE. I want you to make sure you do your part so that face in the mirror won't remind you that you didn't do your best."

Alabama was outplayed most of that game. The Crimson Tide trailed 10–3 late in the fourth quarter. But when it looked like it was whipped, Alabama scored two touchdowns and kicked two extra points to win 17–10.

As Bryant was leaving Neyland Stadium that afternoon, walking toward a bus, an angry Tennessee fan approached him, got right up to his face and said, "Bear, you're the luckiest son of a bitch in history."

Bryant doffed his houndstooth hat, said "thank you" and kept strolling.

9

THE RESPECTED RIVAL GENERAL

In my early years as a sports journalist, I saw in Paul "Bear" Bryant and Ralph "Shug" Jordan two men with strikingly different personalities. This was during the 1970s, as the former produced havoc in the Southeastern Conference because Alabama was almost unbeatable, and the latter moved toward retirement after producing as much misery for the Crimson Tide and its coach as anybody.

Bryant lost five times to Auburn, which Jordan coached, from 1958 through 1972. He won the next nine games.

The intrastate rivalry, Alabama versus Auburn, was special when Bryant and Jordan were in command of the programs. They fought like rabid dogs at times, but carried on for the most part by playing a cat and mouse game. They were up in age, and they grew softer as years passed.

Bryant liked to talk about the "college across the state." Jordan liked to talk about "the doctors, lawyers and politicians from the school in West Alabama."

When it came to recruiting, they both sported red faces. When it came to game days, they frothed at the mouth. When it came to the other weeks of the year, they had fun with a rivalry that made the fans from both sides see double.

But let us get back to the 1970s.

Bryant had a hard edge. He was on a mission. He thought every word spoken and every step taken could make the difference between victory and defeat. He talked about football more than anything else.

Jordan was tough, also, maybe an equal to the rival general, but a person visiting with him never got that impression. He was quick with a joke. He wanted to know about the background of the person visiting with him, either in person or by telephone, and he loved to talk about history. He was from Selma, Alabama, a country boy, too, and was about as grandfatherly as the real thing. He was as perfect for Auburn as Bryant was for Alabama.

Jordan gave Auburn its only national championship in 1957, not to mention five consecutive wins over Alabama. Bryant took most of that glamour away, not to speak of the nine consecutive wins he recorded over the intrastate rival during the last decade he coached the Crimson Tide.

There were times when Bryant and Jordan met socially, usually at Lake Martin near Alexander City, Alabama. On the other hand, their wives, Mary Harmon and Evelyn, respectively, were closer. They played bridge together and visited by telephone much more frequently than their husbands did.

There is a Bryant-Jordan Scholar Athlete Fund that annually provides college tuition for athletes of both genders who excel in the classroom. It is an impressive program.

There is an equal, yet not quite as powerful, testimonial heard each year, annual chatter about "Shug" and "Bear" at the start of and throughout football season.

The late 1950s, the 1960s, and a part of the 1970s were great times for both programs.

So now we get to an interview conducted by former Associated Press Sports Editor Will Grimsley with Jordan at some point between his retirement in 1975 and his death in 1980. The subject was an old rival and, maybe, dear friend.

During that interview, Jordan predicted Bryant would become the winningest college coach in history. Or, as he put it in his homespun manner, "I think The Bear will overtake Stagg's record." Also, he said, "Personally, I think Bryant is the best coach in the country."

Jordan coached Auburn to 175 victories in twenty-five seasons, including participation in twelve bowl games. He talked about the difficulties of competing in the same state with a living legend:

> It's true Alabama has a big advantage over everyone in the South in recruiting. When you find a fine high school prospect, he often as not will say, "I want to go to Alabama." You ask why. He will say, "Because I want to play on a national championship team and go to a big bowl game."
>
> It's hard to overtake that kind of prestige and historical significance. It's the same with teams like Southern Cal, Michigan, Notre Dame, Oklahoma, Texas, and Ohio State.
>
> Success breeds success.
>
> You might as well drag out the cat and look at it. Just look at the number he's lost. It ain't many.

Jordan viewed and scouted Bryant up close. Although many people saw him as an innovator, including myself, Jordan saw him as a serious student of the sport.

"The Bear is not an innovator, but he will find something good in the wishbone formation, for instance," Jordan said. "He will embellish it, enlarge on it, and recruit for it.

"But we've got some things even The Bear hasn't got. We've got a Heisman Trophy winner, Pat Sullivan, an Outland Trophy winner, Zeke Smith. We built a hospitality house for our team. The Bear copied it. We enlarged our press box, and he did the same. They put my name on our stadium, and Bryant got his name put on his stadium.

"I still kid him about stealing us blind."

Those were classic moments, on the local level, as Bryant and Jordan swapped wits.

🌀

Coach Bryant and Coach Jordan, because of the intensity of the rivalry, couldn't be close friends.

—David Housel, Auburn
athletics director

The rivalry was too great for Coach Jordan and Coach Bryant to be close friends. But I always had the impression there was civility to their relationship. Others can speak about that, but I had the feeling they got along about as well as they could.

I'm sure they enjoyed the stature of the rivalry during those years. But I'm sure Coach Bryant enjoyed it more because Alabama was winning so much.

Coach Jordan won five times between 1958 and 1975. I think the greatest tribute that can be paid to him was he was able to survive, even prosper, in the same state with Coach Bryant during an era when there were no scholarship restrictions. Nobody beat Coach Bryant much. That made it all the sweeter to him when he did win.

I know how Coach Jordan felt. I became an Auburn fan in 1955. I saw my first Auburn game in 1956. Auburn won in 1955, 1956, and 1957. Coach Bryant returned to Alabama in 1958. We won that game. From that point, I went from the seventh grade in junior high school to my sophomore year in college and beat them one time.

In summary, I think for all of our suffering, Auburn people had a great respect for Paul "Bear" Bryant and what he did.

Then he got his 315th victory, to unseat Amos Alonzo Stagg, and he did it at Auburn's expense. He beat us. It was

As was the case in this picture from the late 1970s, Paul "Bear" Bryant kept his game plan on several sheets of rolled paper with him at all times.

Courtesy of Paul Bryant Museum

a truly magnificent accomplishment.

From a personal standpoint, I'm honored to have handled the postgame media conference as Auburn's sports information director. From a real nature, what's good for Alabama isn't good for Auburn. But I think Auburn displayed a growth and maturity that day that has enabled us to grow in stature.

I don't know if Coach Bryant was a great Xs and Os coach. They're mighty plentiful. But, looking back, he was a successful coach in the 1940s, 1950s, 1960s, 1970s, and 1980s.

The thing that made him great in my book was his communicative skills. He could communicate with young men who came out of World War II, young men who came out of the Korean War, young men who came out of the opulence of the 1950s, young men who came through the hippie movement and the civil rights movement, all the changes that went through our society and our culture, young men who came through the Vietnam War era. He was able to communicate. As Coach Jordan used to say, you can look into the heart and soul of a football player and that was what you were recruiting.

Both men could do that. But it was amazing how Coach Bryant could communicate to young men. He did that for a lot of years that transcend our society, the incredible things that our nation, particularly the Deep South, were going through between the 1940s and the 1980s.

Paul "Bear" Bryant could do that, especially in this state.

But Bryant's fame spread to distant boundaries, as if there were any to hold him, and that brings to mind his warm relationship with **John McKay**, the former Southern Cal coach who became the leader of the Tampa Bay Buccaneers of the National Football League:

Mmmm, first off let me say Paul and I never discussed football, or not much. Way back I guess we did some, but not much. We used to run a three-man defensive front at Southern Cal, and he wondered about my ideas on that. I guess he wanted to know the positives in case he played against something like that or decided he wanted his team to utilize it.

Normally, our discussions were philosophical. I recall one such occasion when we talked about giving players second chances. Paul did that a lot, gave second chances, but he said a guy who had knowingly messed up, a player who had violated team rules, was a lousy gamble. I don't think that's true, not always, but I had free agent training camps in which a couple of them came in out of shape. They were begging me to give them second chances. They started making excuses, and I said, "No, you're out of here. It's over." Somebody else can have those guys. I learned that from Paul.

I think Paul made his strongest impact with his personnel decisions. I respect what he did and what he accomplished.

One of his great moves was going to the wishbone formation in 1971, after we had whipped his team the year before. It surprised us. They got ahead of us in Los Angeles and we couldn't catch up.

The year before we showed his team something in Birmingham. We beat Alabama good, 42–21, and I think he knew he was overmatched.

The next year, 1971, he brought a team out to the West Coast and beat probably the most talented USC team I had. That was the year he went to the wishbone formation. He changed his entire approach to match his personnel.

But that's not the Paul Bryant I remember best. I recall a guy who was loyal to his former players, a guy who was compassionate and gave more than he received.

Also, I remember a great friend and fierce golf competitor. I loved playing with him because Paul always thought he was better than he was, and I felt the same way about my golf game. That made for some interesting rounds, fun afternoons.

But no matter how we lied on the golf course about our abilities, it's true we had some grand times together. We were friends first and football coaches second.

10
THE RECRUITER

Coach Bryant had a way of reaching a prospect, also the prospect's parents. It didn't matter what the background was, the social or economic standing, he knew how to push the right buttons at the right times.

—CLEM GRYSKA, Alabama
recruiting coordinator

First of all, Coach Bryant didn't place talent as the only criteria for a prospect during his years at Alabama. He wanted character, too, because he figured a good citizen with ability could become a great football player.

After reviewing game films, we did serious background checks on prospects. We'd talk with his parents, of course, but also to high school principals, high school guidance counselors, neighbors, friends and so forth. Then if we were convinced a prospect was who we were looking for, the assistant coaches and Coach Bryant got involved in the recruiting.

Once we got prospects in front of him, Coach Bryant, we would get about 90 percent of them. He had a way of communicating with them. He would tell them what he would do for them and the University of Alabama would do for them. He would tell what he expected from them in return. He would tell them what was expected from their mothers and fathers. He challenged them, too, told them they would get every chance to compete for playing time and, if they were good enough, they would play in games.

His honesty was a major part of that.

🌀

Condredge Holloway, the great Tennessee quarterback, wanted to come to Alabama. His mother wanted him to come to Alabama. But Coach Bryant told him the truth, which kept him from coming to Alabama.

—**JACK RUTLEDGE,**
Alabama assistant coach

I recruited Condredge Holloway out of Huntsville, Alabama in the late 1960s, actually became a part of their family, it seems. In fact, I spent so much time with him and his mother that we started looking like a family when we'd go out to dinner.

Condredge was a great athlete. He had speed. He had ability. He had good sense. He was a superb baseball player, too, a pro prospect. He was a player I wanted us to sign in a big way.

Condredge has told this story several times for several years, and it bears repeating.

When Condredge visited with Coach Bryant late in the recruiting process—we had gone after fourteen players, had signed thirteen and were holding the last scholarship for him—they had an interesting conversation. Coach Bryant told him the timing wasn't right for a black player to be the quarterback at Alabama, that it was still a little early for that.

Condredge weighed that statement and signed with Tennessee.

You would think that conversation would have left Condredge with a bad feeling. But that's not the case. What it left him with was great respect for Coach Bryant, who could have told him something different and signed him. In fact, to this day Condredge talks about that respect any time Coach Bryant's name comes up.

Obviously, I wish we had signed Condredge. But while Coach Bryant normally accepted recommendations from the assistant coaches when it came to prospects, he made an honest decision in that case that kept us from getting a fine player.

We didn't get everybody we wanted. We didn't make the right decision on some other stars. For instance, the assistant coach recruiting the Birmingham area in the early 1980s didn't think Bo Jackson was good enough to play running back in the Southeastern Conference. He won the Heisman Trophy at Auburn and helped them to two wins over us.

§

Sometimes we made mistakes with the players we signed. That's when Coach Bryant really got more involved in the evaluation process.

—**CLEM GRYSKA,** Alabama
recruiting coordinator

We didn't make many mistakes recruiting players, or else we wouldn't have won so much. But one comes to mind, a player I'll leave unnamed.

We had a lineman the entire staff thought would be a super player. We signed him. But by his sophomore season Coach Bryant realized we had made an error in judgment.

I'll never forget a staff meeting when Coach Bryant said, "I knew ol' so and so wouldn't amount to much as a player. He can't bend his ankles and he keeps getting his knees locked. There's no way a guy can play football locked up like that."

Well, he was exactly right about that, which shows how good he was at paying attention to details. In fact, after hearing him say that one of the first things we looked at when evaluating a prospect was whether or not he had flexibility in his ankles. That sounds strange, but Coach Bryant had it right.

Coach Bryant knew the proper techniques for football, whether they were related to blocking, tackling, running, or whatever. He'd get enthusiastic about it, too, particularly in staff meetings. We used to laugh at him saying "boom" and pushing his hand upward, like under an opponent's chin. He literally loved getting involved like that.

In the early years, at Maryland, Kentucky, and Texas A&M, he got in the trenches with his players, literally showed them how to block and tackle. He did that at Alabama, too, at least early on. Then he backed off a little bit. He'd put somebody else in charge of a certain area and let him coach. He did that with total trust, too, which was important because nobody ever wanted to let him down in any way.

In summary, if he saw a prospect on film, he could quickly pick up on strengths and weaknesses.

ও

Coach Bryant had a way about him that allowed him to blend in to any situation. He was charming when visiting in homes. He knew how to talk to people.

—**Clem Gryska,** Alabama
recruiting coordinator

The recruitment of Mike Stock, a fine young man from South Bend, Indiana, comes to mind. He was right there in the back yard of Notre Dame, but he had an interest in Alabama. He was a fine running back.

Mike's dad was in the construction business, and they had all they needed. He was a millionaire, I was told, and that meant Mike could have gone to any school he wanted if his parents were willing to pay his way. We wanted him at Alabama, on scholarship, and he came down for a visit.

Mike lettered for us in 1973, 1974, and 1975, ironically on two teams that lost to Notre Dame, by one point in the Sugar Bowl and by two points in the Orange Bowl.

When Mike and his parents came for a visit, it was unseasonably cold in Tuscaloosa. They came to a practice, and it was a miserable afternoon.

So what did Coach Bryant do?

He saw Mr. and Mrs. Stock shivering as they watched practice. He came down from his observation tower and instructed a student manager to go inside Memorial Coliseum and get them something warmer to wear. He delivered the warm clothing to them, a couple of ponchos and blankets, maybe a couple of sweatshirts.

The point is the Stock family, including Mike, was probably there because of Coach Bryant. But being the gentleman he was, he wanted to make sure they were comfortable.

That was a closed case because of him.

That was the case, also, with the recruitment of Rich Wingo, a linebacker from Elkhart, Indiana. He was from Notre Dame country, too. The magical line Coach Bryant had was, "Rich, I just got finished talking to your grandmother in Anniston [Alabama]." He had done that out of courtesy and the fact he genuinely enjoyed talking to the lady.

That sealed the deal.

Coach Bryant was masterful in the Joe Kelly deal in the mid-1960s, although it was a little different.

Joe was an excellent quarterback from Ozark, Alabama. Now, he's an ultrasuccessful businessman in Nashville, Tennessee.

To advance the story, there was a house full of coaches in Ozark during the recruiting process. "Shug" Jordan was there representing Auburn. Duffy Daugherty was there representing Michigan State. Bob Devaney was there representing Nebraska. There were a couple of others there.

Pat Dye was working the recruitment for us. He took Coach Bryant down there, and they arrived as all of the others were inside talking. You can imagine what that was like, coaches pitching their programs at the same time.

As was the case at most of those gatherings, there was food everywhere, as well as family friends and other people.

Well, Coach Bryant arrived and said hello to everybody. Then, Mrs. Kelly, Joe's mother, said something about there being some snacks in the kitchen for everybody to eat.

Pat told me Coach Bryant said immediately, "Mrs. Kelly, you just keep your seat. Can I get you something to eat? I'll get you a cookie and cup of coffee—and anything else you might want."

Coach Bryant went into the kitchen, hollered to ask Mrs. Kelly how she liked her coffee, and returned to the den or living room with what she wanted.

Pat said those other coaches looked at Coach Bryant like they could kill him. I think they knew he had won that recruiting battle.

That was a master at work. He didn't feel above anybody or below anybody. He was in his element, talking to a prospect from the Deep South, a small town, which is where he was reared. It was like he was talking to an old friend on the corner of Main Street.

The beauty is he wasn't phony at all. He was talking to his type people.

෯

I think the problems we had at Alabama in 1969 and 1970, the 6–5 and 6–5–1 records, can be attributed to us getting away from our basic philosophy. I think Coach Bryant said he was shopping his talents some, thinking about moving to Southern California or Miami, Florida. Maybe he wasn't as focused as he should have been. He said that. Regardless, we got greedy recruiting. We went nationwide, trying to get this guy or that guy, and that went against what we had done best.

—JACK RUTLEDGE,
Alabama assistant coach

The thoughts Rutledge advanced eighteen years after the death of Bryant, to the day and almost to the hour, at the Paul Bryant Museum, mirrored the statements the coach made on August 18, 1981. He said, "I was looking to move during 1967, 1968, and 1969. I was too full of myself. I should have known Alabama was the place for me."

So after admitting to mistakes, Bryant embarked on the recruitment of quarterback and placekicker Danny Ridgeway in 1971 out of tiny Fyffe, Alabama. For the most part, says Rutledge, he kicked points after touchdown and a few field goals for the Crimson Tide.

Danny Ridgeway is a class example of the way Coach Bryant recruited and handled players and other people. He was from a small town in Alabama, a tiny place, and he signed a scholarship to play for us.

Danny is known mostly as an extra points kicker, in fact is listed that way in the media guide. But he made numerous contributions to our teams. He was a smart player. He loved being a part of Alabama football.

167

When Danny completed his playing career at Alabama, they had a day for him in Fyffe. Coach Bryant was there, taking part in the parade and the banquet that night.

The point is he made a decision about a high school senior and signed him to an Alabama scholarship. He was there when Danny had a proud day in front of the home folks.

Coach Bryant was gifted choosing his kind of people. Danny is a good example of that.

11

THE COMICAL MAN

We've got to get that coffee maker repaired.

—PAUL "BEAR" BRYANT,
on a perplexing problem

Linda Knowles, a longtime secretary, tells one on Coach Bryant:

> One of the more humorous things that happened while we were working for Coach Bryant involved his inability to get a pot of coffee brewed. Amazingly, to this day nobody ever got up enough courage to tell him what the problem was all along.
>
> Several times Coach Bryant would walk down the hall and put on a fresh pot of coffee. He was constantly annoyed because he never got one made. He just kept saying, "We've got to get that coffee maker repaired or buy a new one."
>
> So what was the problem? Coach Bryant got the coffee in the maker, but he didn't know you had to put water in there, too.

☙

Oh, my God, they've killed one of us.

—PAUL "BEAR" BRYANT,
on an injured player

Jim Goostree, longtime Alabama trainer and assistant athletics director, recalled:

We were playing Tennessee in Knoxville when they had a big kick returner named Jim Cartwright. We had a fullback named Buddy Wesley, who also covered kicks.

It was 1960, at some point during a 20–7 Tennessee victory, when Cartwright caught a punt and started running up the sideline in front of our bench. Ol' Buddy, who was small but so tough he had guts running out of him, lit into Cartwright and hit him squarely on the thigh with his head. When he did, it knocked him as cold as a wedge.

It happened near our bench, so I went running out there with the doctors to check on Buddy. After a minute or two, I felt this presence hovering over me. I looked back and there was Coach Bryant peering over my shoulder.

Of course, with Buddy unconscious we didn't want to move him. We were taking every precaution. Then all of a sudden we saw a little trickle of blood on his cheek. When that appeared, Coach Bryant said, "Oh, my God, they've killed one of us."

Coach Bryant was as relieved as anybody I've seen when he learned Buddy was okay, that he just had a slight concussion. But you wouldn't have thought that after we got back to Tuscaloosa and got our players settled in the athletics dorm.

Coach Bryant got the players together and said, "Gentlemen, I want you to know one of your teammates, Buddy Wesley, might be about to die in the hospital after making a hard tackle in that game this afternoon. I want you to think about that tonight while you're sitting around thinking about how Tennessee whipped us."

You could see a look of horror on the faces of those young men as Coach Bryant left the room.

Well, Buddy Wesley was back in action quickly, the following week, as I recall, and the final record that year was 8–1–2.

⟲

I don't ask you what you and your wife talk about in the morning when you're taking a crap and she's putting on makeup, do I?

—**PAUL "BEAR" BRYANT,**
on a question a sports
writer asked

Alabama had just come from behind in the second half to win over Washington 20–17 in Seattle on October 7, 1978. Bryant was drained as he was led to a Greyhound bus to conduct a postgame press conference because the dressing room at the stadium was so cramped.

The bus was packed, with many of the sports writers on board from the West Coast. Most of them had seated themselves near the rear while those from the Deep South huddled around the coach in the front because we knew he was often difficult to hear when he spoke in a deep and mumbling drawl.

Bryant opened his remarks in typical fashion—"Needless to say, we're happy to win over a fine Washington team"—and he was whispering more than he was talking.

"Speak up, Coach Bryant, we can't hear you," said one of the sports writers in the rear of the bus.

Bryant continued his spiel—"I'm proud of our players for coming back and winning"—and his voice grew softer as he spoke.

"We can't hear a thing you're saying," said a sports writer.

"Can you please talk up?" said another writer in the back.

Bryant was growing a bit exasperated. Suddenly, he reached for the bus driver's speakerphone.

After some more rambling, most of it inaudible over the crackling sound system, Bryant opened up the press conference for questions and answers.

"Bear, what did you tell your players at halftime to make them come back and win?" said a sports writer in the rear of the bus.

Bryant paused before answering, then said, "I don't ask you what you and your wife talk about in the morning when you're taking a crap and she's putting on makeup, do I?"

The audience laughed. The stunned sports writer attempted to save face. He said, "No, I don't guess so. But we're talking about football players, not my wife."

"It's the same thing," Bryant said, his voice louder. "Some things are private. What goes on at your house in the bathroom is private. What goes on between me and my players in the dressing room is private."

ॐ

Coach Bryant didn't crack a smile. He just said, "Boy, I believe you really need an automobile."

—**Jim Goostree,** Alabama trainer and
assistant athletics director

Not long after Coach Bryant arrived on the Alabama campus, he asked me to accompany him to Druid Drug Store for a cup of coffee. That was in keeping with an afternoon ritual, sort of a pick-me-up when practice wasn't going on.

I didn't have any money, and I had an old car, a 1950 Chevrolet I had bought the year before for $75. The left front door wouldn't open. I had to use a wire to keep the right front door closed. The car had been painted with a hand brush. Needless to say, it wasn't a pretty sight.

When we got outside to start our walk to the drug store, it was raining and Coach Bryant said, "How about me riding with you?" Well, I wasn't planning on driving that old car. I was just going to walk in the rain. But I agreed to give him a ride, as if I had much of a choice.

We started to get in the car and I said, "Coach Bryant, if you don't mind, I need to get in first." I got in the passenger side and crawled behind the steering wheel. He got in behind me. He was in pretty good shape, even as scrunched up as he was, being a big man, and we got to Druid Drug.

When he started to get out of the car, he stepped down on my floorboard, which was covered with cardboard, and his foot and a lot of leg went through all the way to the ground. When he brought it out, it drew blood that was running down his shin. It was sort of funny, at least to me, but it wasn't funny to him.

We went inside and had our coffee. Then we walked outside to make the return trip to the athletics department, and it was pouring down rain. Coach Bryant looked at the car, then at the sky, and said, "I believe I'll walk back to the office."

There I was trying to keep a job with a new coach on the scene, and there he was walking in the rain with blood on his pants. It was funny then, funnier now, but not so funny that I felt like laughing at the time.

Later that day, back at the office, Coach Bryant said, "Boy, I really believe you need an automobile." I said, "Yes sir, I suppose I do need something better than I've got."

About three weeks later, Coach Bryant called me into his office and said, "Boy, I want you to go down to see so-and-so at so-and-so dealership." I went down there and the man got me in a relatively new car.

I don't know how I made it through that episode, but it got me off to a pretty successful start with Coach Bryant.

✺

I wish I had a picture of Coach Bryant's face when he saw all of those tickets.

—**Linda Knowles,** secretary

When Coach Bryant broke Amos Alonzo Stagg's record as the winningest coach in collegiate history against Auburn in 1981, we received telephone call after telephone call from friends, relatives and acquaintances wondering how they could get a ticket to the game. In all my years in the Athletics Department, I never saw such a demand as that week.

Coach Bryant was doing the best he could to take care of everybody, and he really became frustrated. He said, "Linda, what happened to all of those tickets I had? There's no way I've given all of them away."

But it was obvious there weren't enough tickets to go around, not even close, so we had to apologize to people, tell them we were out, that there weren't any more to be found.

Toward the end of January, a couple of months later, I was in his office taking dictation. For some reason, he opened the top right drawer on his desk. At that moment, everything in the back flew forward, and there was a stack of those tickets about two inches tall.

Coach Bryant looked at them and didn't say a word. He just closed the drawer—left them in there.

✺

I don't give a damn if he has graduated, I want him in the game.

—PAUL "BEAR" BRYANT,
on an impossible substitution

Sam Bailey, an Alabama assistant coach who in 1969 became associate athletics director in charge of all sports other than football, remembers a neck-to-neck game with Florida State where Bryant was grasping at straws:

> We were playing Florida State on opening night in 1967 after going unbeaten and untied in 1966. It was a back and forth game, hellaciously wild from the start, and it ended in a 37–37 tie.
>
> In 1963 and 1964 we had a pretty stout tackle from Memphis named Ron Durby. He could play offense and defense and was damn good rushing the quarterback on pass plays.
>
> Well, Florida State had a hell of a passing offense and they were matching us touchdown for touchdown. At some point in the second half, Coach Bryant had seen enough and he started screaming, "Get Ron Durby in the game . . . I want Ron Durby on the field . . . Somebody get Ron Durby out there."
>
> Everybody on the sideline knew Ron Durby had graduated, or wasn't available, but Pat Dye, one of our assistant coaches at the time, was running through the bench area screaming, "Get Ron Durby in the game." Finally, one of the other assistant coaches, maybe "Dude" Hennessey, said, "Pat, Ron Durby graduated three years ago."
>
> So Pat ran over to Coach Bryant and told him Ron Durby wasn't on the team. That's when Coach Bryant said, "I don't give a damn if he has graduated, I want him in the game."

Paul Bryant was such a showman. I'm not sure we would have gotten the Liberty Bowl off the ground without him.

—Bud Dudley, Liberty Bowl founder

First of all, I'm indebted to my friend Paul Bryant for helping us get the Liberty Bowl started on a snowy and frigid day in Philadelphia, Pennsylvania, in 1959 and for the contributions he made to the event. We were fortunate to have his final game on a windy and frigid night in Memphis, Tennessee, in 1982, a tremendous honor and forever a feather in our hat.

I'll never forget the ingenuity and humor he displayed in Philadelphia. This happened after we met the Alabama team at the Thirtieth Street Train Station and he asked me what kind of publicity the game with Penn State was getting. I told him it was just fair, that the Philadelphia Eagles were grabbing almost all of the newspaper headlines. He said, "That's fine. We'll have some fun with the news media, and maybe it'll help."

I told Paul I was open to any ideas. He said, "Good. For starters, get me twenty-two folding chairs on the practice field when we have our first workout up here." I asked him what he had in mind. He said, "Bud, just get me the chairs and I'll show you."

So we put the chairs out there for him at Municipal Stadium, which is JFK Stadium now, and he arranged them—eleven on offense and eleven on defense. Then he put his players in them and called signal drills. The players would motion with their feet in the direction they were supposed to go.

The Philadelphia press was astounded by the display. The sports writers were going nuts, asking Paul what that drill was about. He told them it was a lazy man's way of preparing for a bowl game.

Well, out came the cameras and the newspapers were filled with pictures of Alabama getting ready to play Penn State.

That was so quick on his part. He came up with a promotion that created interest in our game. He didn't let me forget it, either, because throughout our friendship he reminded me that he came up with the idea to launch the Liberty Bowl the right way.

❧

I don't know why you're so scared of that cat.

—PAUL "BEAR" BRYANT,
on a feared mascot

Bryant knew how to put his team at ease and get them focused on the game, recalls Jerry Duncan, Alabama junior tackle:

In 1965, the same year Coach Bryant was such a master motivator while leading us to a national championship, we went to Baton Rouge, Louisiana, to play LSU. At the time, Tiger Stadium was a loud and riotous place to play, hard on the visiting team.

One of the things they did down there was parade Mike The Tiger, a genuine bengal, around the playing field before the game. The crowd went crazy. Then they put the caged tiger outside our dressing room and poked him to make him growl loud enough for us to hear him.

Not long after we got to the stadium, Coach Bryant led us on a stroll around the playing field in our street clothes. Mike The Tiger was already on the scene, growling away outside our dressing room. So when we started back inside the dressing room to put on our uniforms for pregame warmups, Coach Bryant stopped by the tiger cage and said, "I don't know why you're so scared of that cat. That thing must be forty years old."

Just like that, he loosened us up with a little homespun humor. Also, he probably helped some of our players who were scared of Mike The Tiger to gain a little confidence.

ॐ

I couldn't believe what was happening. But Ruth Ann said, "Coach Bryant told me to walk back to the clubhouse, and that's what I'm going to do."

—GENE STALLINGS,
Texas A&M player and coach

Gene Stallings knew Bryant for many years, having played for him, coached under him, and coached against him:

Coach Bryant and I were teamed in a televised golf match with Steve Sloan and Joe Namath. This was when I was coaching at Texas A&M after coaching on Coach Bryant's staff at Alabama.

I was playing pretty good that day and, out of respect, asked Coach Bryant what I should hit on my second shot on a par five hole. He said it didn't matter because I couldn't make it to the green from that far out. But I did make it to the green, and the ball came to rest several yards from the hole.

Ruth Ann, my wife, had walked the previous hole with us, and she was tagging along, really enjoying herself, and she watched me make three putts to salvage a par on a hole I should have birdied and, with a lot of luck, could have eagled.

When I got back to the golf cart, I saw Ruth Ann leaving. I said, "Where are you going?" She said, "Coach Bryant is sending me back to the clubhouse." I couldn't believe what

I was hearing. I said, "Honey, I don't work for Coach Bryant any more."

Ruth Ann was adamant. She said, "Gene, Coach Bryant said you were playing good until I showed up to watch. He's sending me back to the clubhouse."

I said, "Ruth Ann, you don't have to do that. You've come all the way out here to watch us play." She said, "Yes, I have. But Coach Bryant told me to walk back to the clubhouse, and that's what I'm going to do."

✺

Bingo, there's a winner.

—PAUL "BEAR" BRYANT,
on a greyhound

Bryant enjoyed making small wagers on greyhounds and thoroughbreds. One evening he was at Greenetrack near Eutaw, Alabama, an establishment in which his son, Paul Bryant Jr., owned an abundance of stock. He was excited. He was seated with patrons in the general clubhouse section with a pile of bettor tickets on a table in front of him.

"Bingo, there's a winner," Bryant said, his voice loud, as he slapped the table. "Ol' Number 4. Yeah. Bingo, bingo, bingo."

Bryant jumped from his seat and hurried to the cashier as people seated around him chuckled and enjoyed being in his jubilant presence. A few minutes later, he returned with a hint of a frown on his face.

"How much did you get for the win?" I said.

"Nothing," Bryant said, in a mumble.

"Then you ought to talk to the management," I said.

"I don't have a claim," Bryant said with a grin. "I had the right dog, four to win on the ticket, but it was from an earlier race."

Another brush with a loser hit Bryant at Greenetrack when he made a trip with Jim Bates of Tuscaloosa, a man who was a fine handicapper.

Bates suggested the Number 2 greyhound in a Big Q race. Bryant objected, wanting to go with Number 8 because he had seen a car tag with three 8s on it as they were driving to the track.

They argued the point. The bets were placed on Number 2.

"The race went like I expected, with Number 8 at the back of the pack and Number 2 running up front," Bates said. "But when they turned for home, there was a big wreck up front. Number 2 went down, as did several others, and Number 8 got around the mess to win.

"I've never seen a madder loser in my life than Coach Bryant was that night."

❧

There's ol' Big Chunk making another good play.

—PAUL "BEAR" BRYANT,
on a hard to pronounce name

There seem to be a million stories about comical moments Bryant had while hosting *The Bear Bryant Show* on Sunday afternoon. That was his televised review show of the Alabama game played the afternoon or evening previous.

It was not a polished production, to say the least, which added to its charm. At the opening, Bryant usually opened a bag of Golden Flake potato chips, spilling them all over the desk in front of him, and took a huge swig of Coca-Cola. After commercial breaks it was not uncommon to see him waving his hands trying to get billowing cigarette smoke off the screen. Then there was his inability to correctly pronounce the name of some of his players.

Buddy Aydelette (Adda-let) was Aud-letie.

Steve Bisceglia (Bah-shell-yah) was Bee-siglah.

David Chatwood was Chipwood.

And, by all means, Bryant struggled with offensive guard David Gerasimchuk, who was called just about everything imaginable until one afternoon when the coach said, "There's ol' Gera . . . Gara . . . Gerrio . . . There's ol' Big Chunk making another good play."

༺༻

That gingerbread house must have been six feet wide. I made him take it back to the store.

—MARY HARMON BRYANT, wife

It was not long before Christmas Day in 1981, and Bryant wanted to do some shopping. He asked Billy Varner, his driver, to take him to McFarland Mall in Tuscaloosa, Alabama. They were taking a stroll when the coach spotted something he liked.

"Coach Bryant spotted this huge gingerbread house in one of the stores and said he wanted to get it for his grandchildren," Varner said. "It was extremely big and I wondered about it. Also, I wondered about getting it in the car.

"Well, he had his mind made up and we bought it. He was talking about how they were going to love it because it was so big and decorated with all kinds of candy.

"Things changed when we got to his house."

"I had never seen a cookie house so large," said Mary Harmon Bryant, his wife. "I'll admit it was pretty, but I knew the grandchildren didn't need something like that. Goodness, if they had eaten a tenth of it they would have been sick for months.

"So I told Paul he needed to return it. He objected, of

course, and after a few minutes of discussion, he suggested I take it back. I said, 'No, Paul, you've got to take it back. You bought it and you've got to return it. It's a wonderful house and the kids would love it, but it'll make them sick.'

"That gingerbread house was massive, like something you'd buy for an entire party of children. It wasn't the kind of thing you'd give a couple of little girls.

"But the beautiful part about it was Paul acted like a child when he came through the door with it. You would have thought the world was coming to an end the way he and Billy acted carrying that gingerbread house back to the car."

❧

I told Coach Bryant to get in the middle because the guy would recognize him and be thrilled.

—**SAM BAILEY,** Alabama
associate athletics director

Sam Bailey coached under Bryant at Texas A&M and Alabama, then served an associate athletics director in charge of every Crimson Tide sport except football. He and his boss were dear friends for more than three decades:

Coach Bryant and I enjoyed hunting, particularly turkey, and one day we decided to go deep in the woods. We left our truck by the highway and took a long hike. When we started back to the truck, we got hopelessly lost. We knew the highway was nearby, but we didn't have a clue how far we were from the truck. We figured it'd be at least three miles.

As we walked along the highway, we decided we better flag down somebody because we didn't know how far we'd have to go. Coach Bryant said, "Don't worry, partner, somebody will recognize me and get us out of here."

It wasn't long before an old man came along in an old pickup truck. He pulled over and I told Coach Bryant to get in the middle because the old man would recognize him and be thrilled.

Then the damndest thing happened.

The old man didn't say a word for at least a couple of miles. I decided to help along the conversation. I said, "Sir, do you know who this man is seated next to you?"

I was looking at Coach Bryant, who was smiling, and the old man was looking at him, too. Then the old man said, "Oh sure, I know you. You work down at the mill."

I thought I was going to pop my pants laughing. Coach Bryant was laughing, too, and he gave the man a $10 tip when we got to the truck.

As we were leaving, I said, "Coach Bryant, why did you give that guy ten bucks when he didn't even know who you are?" He said, "Sam, 'cause I would have given him a twenty if he had recognized me."

ॐ

Alabama comes out and Bryant has on a long-sleeved shirt—you can see the cuffs.

—**BILL CONNORS,** sports writer
(From the book *Bud Wilkinson*)

Jay Wilkinson, the son of legendary Oklahoma Coach Bud Wilkinson, wrote a book with Gretchen Hirsch in 1994 entitled *Bud Wilkinson: An Intimate Portrait of an American Legend*. It was published by Sagamore Publishing. Included in the text is a story related to the 1963 Orange Bowl, when Alabama, coached by Bryant, defeated Oklahoma, coached by Wilkinson.

The story relates how Bryant was impressed with the way

Wilkinson dressed. Or as he said to sports writer Bill Connors, "He always looks like he just came out of the barber shop."

Bryant was worried that he would not look so good, and his concern was amplified because President John F. Kennedy was going to attend the game. So he said to Connors, "I don't want to look bad in front of the president. Do you think you could find out what Bud's going to wear?"

Connors asked Wilkinson how he planned to dress for the game, told him Bryant wanted to know. The Oklahoma coach chuckled and refused to answer the question.

Bryant asked Connors if he found out anything about the wardrobe Wilkinson had planned. He was told no. So he said, "I'll just send Mama [Mary Harmon Bryant] down to one of those Palm Beach stores and let her try to guess what kind of Florida clothes Bud would wear."

Correctly, Connors recalled that Bryant had been wearing a lucky blue sleeveless sweater on the sideline, with a sport coat over it.

In the book, Connors said, "It was game day and it was hot. When Bud comes out he has on a white short-sleeved shirt with a tie and, as Bear said, he looked fresh and cool. Alabama comes out and Bryant has on a long-sleeved shirt— you can see the cuffs. He still has on his light blue sweater and he's got him a new Palm Beach sport coat. He just looked like he was burning up."

12

THE COMPASSIONATE MAN

As Bob Hope said, Paul "Bear" Bryant had a big heart. That was particularly the case when it came to people experiencing problems, large and small, from former players he knew well to total strangers.

I witnessed a lot of that during the 1970s and early 1980s. I saw a philosophical coach at times, evidence that a hard life coming up had left a soft spot going down, and I saw a tender man at times.

One of those latter times came on September 12, 1982, when the telephone rang in Bryant's office as we were talking. Bryant answered it and had a relatively short conversation. When it ended, he excused himself and instructed Linda Knowles, his secretary, to write a Western Union check made payable to an unannounced party and to send it to a hotel in New York City. He looked troubled when he returned to his desk.

Bryant shook his head, grimaced and said, "One of my former players has overextended himself at a hotel in New York. It isn't the first time, either. But what else can I do, other than hope he'll straighten out in time?"

It was suggested the former player would repay the loan.

Bryant smiled, shook his head and said, "If that's the case, fine. But the track record so far doesn't indicate that'll happen. I'm betting I'll never see that money again.

"But that's okay. He can't get out of that fancy hotel without it. If he can't get out of the hotel because of a big tab, the next stop won't be that comfortable."

✿

Coach Bryant said we needed to ride up to Birmingham. I was wondering if he knew it was Christmas Eve.

—**Billy Varner,**
friend and confidant

Billy Varner was ready to go home and spend Christmas Eve with his wife, Susie, when Bryant suggested they make a drive of about an hour each way.

We were about ready to leave his office when Coach Bryant said, "Billy, do you think we could ride up to Birmingham before we go home?" By then I'd learned not to ask questions, just to do what The Man wanted, but it did come to mind that it was Christmas Eve. I couldn't imagine what he had in mind.

I think this was in 1979, maybe 1980. Anyway, I know the football team was going to assemble on campus the next day and go to either New Orleans for the Sugar Bowl or Dallas for the Cotton Bowl.

Also, I remember it was cold, and the roads were hazardous. There was even some sleet spitting at the time.

When we got near Birmingham, I asked Coach Bryant where he wanted to go. He reached into his coat pocket and pulled out an address. There were a few names on the sheet—a wife, a husband, and a little girl. I didn't recognize them, and I don't recall who they were to this day.

Anyway, we drove around, found the address and stopped in front of the house. When Coach Bryant started to get out of the car, I asked him if he wanted me to come along. He told me that wasn't necessary, that he'd only be a few minutes.

It wasn't long before he was back in the car, maybe fifteen or twenty minutes, and we were rolling back toward Tuscaloosa.

Coach Bryant didn't say anything about that visit for several days, maybe a couple of weeks. Then he told he had gotten some letters from some super Alabama fans, the mother and the father, talking about how their daughter loved Alabama and had some kind of serious illness.

I didn't question that trip to Birmingham any more.

Man . . . I saw a lot of that through the years.

Bryant received a multitude of letters, obviously, and he had a fondness for those from children—many written, of course, by their parents. It was a tradition for pictures of little ones to find a spot on bulletin boards or the side of file cabinets in the area near his office. He chuckled when he saw infants and toddlers dressed in crimson with footballs at their sides.

Part of my duties as an administrative assistant was to monitor correspondence and to make sure every letter sent was answered. So comes to mind one received from a youngster from San Francisco who said his nickname was "Bear" and he despised hearing his classmates call him that.

"I hate that nickname," the youngster wrote on widely spaced paper. "What can I do about it?"

Bryant got a kick out of the letter, but was serious with his response. He told the child, "It doesn't matter what people call you, what your nickname is. It only matters what you do, how you behave. If you're a good boy and do the best you can at everything you try, you'll make your mother, your father, and another 'Bear' real proud of you."

There was a letter from a man in Mississippi who was in a hospital recovering after attempting suicide. He explained his rural upbringing and poor lifestyle and said he had failed to end his life because it was a weak effort on his part after he considered how Bryant had overcome a humble beginning and long odds to become successful.

Bryant was troubled by that letter. He wrote in his response that the man "could be a winner in life and become a champion if he worked hard."

ᔡ

I never really understood what Coach Bryant meant when he said football is a lot like life. Then it dawned on me after he had died what he meant by that.

—LINDA KNOWLES, secretary

Coach Bryant always said the game of football is like the game of life. He'd talk about starting on one goal line and moving toward the other goal line.

What he was saying was the 20- and 30-yard lines were your age, that you sort of reached a peak in life at the fifty. He talked about the unpredictable bounces of the football being like what happens in your life, that the blocks and tackles were part of it, too. He always said there were five or six plays that made the difference in who won and lost games. He was talking about the decisions you make in life, like your mate, your career decisions, your faith, and other important ones.

From the fifty in was the ultimate. When you score that touchdown, well, that's the end of life.

Another thing Coach Bryant always said was to expect the unexpected. How wise that man was.

༺

Our eyes locked and both of us were thinking the same thing, wondering if we should run up the score.

—**MAL MOORE,** Alabama player
and assistant coach

I'm convinced Coach Bryant always tried to do the right thing when dealing with people, including opponents on the football field. That was certainly the case during the 1978 Sugar Bowl, our easy victory over Ohio State.

During the latter part of the third quarter, they announced on the public address system that Notre Dame was leading Texas by a large margin, something like 40–14, in the Cotton Bowl. We knew the significance of that game because we were ranked third in the nation, in the national championship hunt, and Notre Dame was ranked fifth.

Immediately after hearing that score, our eyes locked and both of us were thinking the same thing, wondering if we should run up the score. It was obvious by then that we could pretty much have our way against Ohio State, at least on that day.

Coach Bryant said, "Mal, I don't know whether to run up the score and get the votes we need for the national championship or play everybody we brought down here." We kept looking at each other for several seconds, as he was thinking. Then he said, "I'm going to play them all."

We won the United Press International championship, and Notre Dame jumped from fifth to first to win the Associated Press championship. Coach Bryant and I talked about his decision later, particularly in light of that disappointment. He told me there wasn't any way he was going to humiliate Woody Hayes, the famous Ohio State coach, and he said it was only right that our down the line players got a chance to play in the Sugar Bowl after working as hard as they did during practice all year.

I don't know if you'd term that compassion, but you'd certainly call it a show of class.

⟲

Eddy Arnold said, "Mr. Bryant always worked for his beloved Alabama."

—MAL MOORE,
Alabama athletics director

I remember in the early 1990s watching a television show in which Eddy Arnold, the great country musician, was talking about his life. He was telling a story about his son, who had gone to school at Alabama and had been severely injured in an automobile accident during that time. I'm not sure about the extent of the injuries, but it was obvious to me that they were bad and had lingering effects.

Mr. Arnold said Coach Bryant frequently visited his son, that, to his knowledge, he never made a trip to Nashville without stopping by to see how he was doing or telephoning to check on him. He said, "Mr. Bryant always worked for his beloved Alabama."

I would never question that conclusion.

⟲

Paul gave away a lot of checks to help people.

—BERT BANK,
radio and television producer

Tuscaloosa businessman Bert Bank had a long relationship with Bryant. He was producer for the Alabama Football

Radio Network and, for a while, the producer of *The Bear Bryant Show* for television:

> As part of his deal at Alabama, Paul Bryant got a lot of money from endorsements, appearances, and television and radio commercials. Some of them were small and some of them were large.
>
> I don't know exactly how many times it happened, but on several occasions through the years I'd hand him a check and he'd say: Bert, just give my check to so and so, a former player, or to so and so, a person or organization in dire need of help.
>
> It'd be staggering to calculate how much money Paul Bryant gave away like that. He truly cared about the welfare of his players and a lot of other people.

John Forney, the radio voice of the Crimson Tide for more than two decades, was present when some of that giving took place:

> I understand that a person who wanted to criticize Paul Bryant could find a lot of ammunition. Several people did through the years because he wasn't perfect, nor did he pretend to be.
>
> Similarly, people who were close to him saw good points about him that the masses never did. I'm talking about a man who was quick to help somebody in need. He was a tough and hard taskmaster, but he had a heart of gold. He was a soft touch at times because he had so much compassion.
>
> If Paul Bryant was for you, really liked you, you had one staunch ally at your side.

Coach Bryant was blessed with an ability to make people feel good, or important, and I was amazed until he died how he could remember faces and names.

—**JACK RUTLEDGE,** Alabama
player and assistant coach

Late in Coach Bryant's career, maybe as late as 1980, there was a longtime English teacher at the University of Alabama who was retiring. It had to have been that late in his career because she had been one of his classmates in the 1930s. For some reason, she wanted to come by his office for a visit.

Normally, there were a lot of people who wanted to do that, for no good reason, and we'd either discourage them or find a way to get them in and out of there in a hurry.

Well, this lady came by, and I sort of thought she might fall in that category of the welcomed, but only to a point.

That nice lady said, "Paul, I'm retiring, and I just wanted to come by and say goodbye and see if you remember me."

Coach Bryant quickly said, "Sarah, do you remember Woods Hall and History 102 class? I was sitting on the second row and you came in wearing one of those big ol' hats with the needles sticking out of the top. Just as you came by, you dropped your book. I reached down to pick it up for you, and one of those stickers almost hit me in an eye."

She said, "Paul, I believe you do remember me."

Coach Bryant laughed, and they had a good long visit, probably longer than he needed to spend that day.

ॐ

There was no reason in the world for him to help me. But Coach Bryant had the ability to care about other people.

—**LARRY LACEWELL,**
Arkansas State coach

Bryant did not have a stronger ally when he died than Larry Lacewell, the second most famous football coach to come out of Fordyce, Arkansas.

Lacewell's father played high school football with Bryant, which led to him becoming a graduate assistant coach at Alabama after he graduated from college.

"I stayed in the athletic dorm and went to graduate school," Lacewell said. "It didn't cost me a dime and I've been told Coach Bryant paid my way. He took care of a poor ol' country boy."

But it was in 1978 that Lacewell found out even more about the compassionate man. He had lost his job as defensive coordinator at Oklahoma, and his life was in shambles:

> I was down and out. My marriage was over. I was drunk. Basically, I was in a whirl, traveling across the country and landing where I could.
>
> Coach Bryant heard about it and started tracking me down. I think he called my mother in Fordyce. Ultimately, he found me at a friend's house in Dallas. I still don't know how he found me. It had to have taken a lot of his time.
>
> Coach Bryant said, "Larry, I need for you to come babysit me through this season. Then I'll get you the kind of job you need. You need to be in coaching. We'll find one for you."
>
> Coach Bryant, Mrs. Bryant, and the Alabama football family took me in. After that year, I was back on my feet.
>
> Nobody from Fordyce, Arkansas, asked Coach Bryant to take me under his wing. He didn't have to do a thing. He could have ignored the problem I was having. Instead, he did something about it, literally saved me.

Only a couple of years before he died, Paul told me he had never felt so contented as he did watching that young boy on the Alabama sideline during a football game.

—LOUISE GOOLSBY, sister

My brother was the type person who would give somebody anything as long as that person was trying to help himself. I think that's something he learned when we were young, when people helped us get by with some generous gifts, like old clothes and the like.

On the other hand, if somebody wanted a handout and was unwilling to work to help himself, Paul wouldn't have anything to do with that person. He believed in people as long as they were committed to accomplishing something. Also, if somebody wronged him, or took advantage of him, that was it. He wouldn't give that person the time of day.

That brings to mind a television commercial he did for South Central Bell late in his career. That's the one where he did the great ad lib. The script was supposed to end with Paul saying, "Have you called your mother today?" When they taped the commercial, Paul said, "Have you called your mother today? I sure wish I could call mine."

At first, the producer of the commercial thought it would be a big loser. He hated that extra line. But when all was said and done, it was that last line—"I wish I could call mine"— that made everybody talk about the commercial. With that heartfelt added line, prompted by the genuine overwhelming love he had for our mother, he gave South Central Bell much more than just another television commercial.

But the point is not that. The point is Paul didn't keep any of the money he earned from that commercial. Instead, he used it to advance a college education fund for people who couldn't afford to pay tuition. He asked others to join him.

Mary Harmon, Paul's wife, told me that commercial raised a bunch of money for that college education fund. She said she received letters after that commercial ran from people all over the world, not just from every state in our nation.

Paul had a soft heart. He knew how to use his fame to help people. I believe he cared about children in need more than anything else.

Normally, Paul didn't talk about his generosity or his caring. He kept it private. But he told me a story one time that warmed my heart and made me proud of him.

There was youngster in Alabama who was dying with leukemia. It was a little boy who loved the Crimson Tide. So after hearing about him, Paul contacted his parents and invited the little boy to be his guest on the sideline at a game.

I wish people could have seen and heard my brother when he told me about that afternoon. He said he had never seen such joy on a face in his life. Paul told me he had never felt so contented as he did watching that young boy on the Alabama sideline during a football game.

⤫

Coach Bryant was always interested in helping those people who had helped him through the years. He had a tremendous sense of loyalty to the people he worked with and the young men he coached.

> **—JIM GOOSTREE,** Alabama trainer
> and assistant athletics director

For several years before Coach Bryant died, he put in place something extremely important to him. The Paul Bryant Endowed Scholarship Fund at the University of Alabama is for the children of his former players, both male and female.

It has been a great assistance to many young men and young women who might not have been able to get their college educations any other way.

A lot of people set up funds like that, endowed scholarships included, and make a big deal about it. Not everybody, but at least some, are interested in receiving publicity. It wasn't like that with Coach Bryant. He did it quietly. To this day there aren't many people who know about that endowed scholarship.

The same thing can be said about a First And Ten organization he helped develop. It's set up to help his former players get started in the professional world. At times, it helps his former players get fresh starts after things go bad for them.

I don't think there is any question Paul Bryant genuinely cared about the young men who played for him. Anybody who doubts that should take a trip to the Paul Bryant Museum on the University of Alabama campus. One of the first things a person sees is a complete listing of every player who played for him at Alabama, Texas A&M, Kentucky and Maryland. He insisted that be a shrine for them, not him, and that's consistent with the way he lived his life as a coach.

13

THE MAN AT HOME

During the fall of 1980, Paul "Bear" Bryant and Mary Harmon Bryant sat at home on a Sunday afternoon watching a National Football League game on television. They occupied straight-back leather chairs and watched the action unfold. Interestingly, one of the teams featured was the Miami Dolphins, which at the time had three former Alabama stars on their roster: nose tackle Bob Baumhower, center Dwight Stephenson and defensive halfback Don McNeal.

The Miami team was coached by Don Shula, who had gotten the job because Bryant had turned it down.

The husband and the wife were comical, without meaning to be. In essence they were like most husbands and wives when it comes to watching football on television.

"Hey, that's a good tackle by Bumhower," Bryant said.

"Baumhower," Mrs. Bryant said.

Bryant remained fixed on the game.

"It looks like Bumhower was offsides on the play."

"Baumhower," Mrs. Bryant said.

Bryant sort of grunted, sipped on a Coca-Cola and said, "Mary Harmon, I'll call him what I want."

"It's Baumhower, not Bumhower," Mrs. Bryant said.

"Well, Bumhower wasn't offsides," Bryant said. "Their offensive line drew him offsides."

Bryant talked about Baumhower. He said, "He's a good person, a fine player, too, and he has helped us recruiting in South Florida for several years."

"Who?" Mrs. Bryant said.

"Bumhower."

Some scores of other NFL games in progress flashed across the screen. The Indianapolis Colts were involved in one, prompting Bryant to remember linebacker Barry Krauss.

"You know, Krauss isn't starting for Indianapolis," Bryant said. "At least that's what Marty Lyons told me the other day."

"Well, he ought to be," Mrs. Bryant said.

Bryant almost choked on the swallow of cola he was trying to take from a bottle. He said, "Well, Mary Harmon, that might not be true. Do you think a coach ought to play a person who isn't as good as somebody else just because you like him?"

"You told me yesterday you had a dad calling wondering why his son isn't playing more for us," Mrs. Bryant said.

"What did I tell him?" Bryant said. "I told him the same thing I've said to every recruit. I said I'll give him every chance in the world to prove himself, that if he didn't believe that, he shouldn't send him to Alabama."

There was silence until Shula appeared on the television screen.

"How old is Don Shula?" Mrs. Bryant said.

"I don't know," Bryant said. "I guess he's fifty or fifty-two."

"He looks like he's about fifty," Mrs. Bryant said.

"I'd guess he's fifty-two or fifty-three," Bryant said. "One thing I do know is they're glad they don't have me coaching down there after the success he has had."

Mrs. Bryant explained that flirtation by the Miami Dolphins.

She said, "I went to see what penthouse the man was giving us and all the clubs down on the Florida Keys. I saw these big houses and all of that other stuff. But I like a small town."

"I wouldn't live in a city," Bryant said.

"I don't just like a small town like Tuscaloosa, I love it," Mrs. Bryant said.

"I wouldn't live in a city unless I could live like Sonny Werblin or George Steinbrenner," Bryant said. "I'm talking about flying in for a couple of days and taking care of business, then leaving and going back to something more comfortable. I just couldn't live in the city day after day.

"Like living here, I can go down to Greene County to my son's farm and relax."

Before Bryant could complete that thought, Mrs. Bryant said, "I believe most folks would rather do that, really."

14

THE YEAR AT MARYLAND

I was with him at his first game, in which I played, and I was with him at his last game, which I watched from the grandstands. I can tell you Coach Bryant had everything. He fit every hole, every aspect of football and life.

—JOE DRACH, Maryland player

The University of Maryland football team Paul "Bear" Bryant coached in 1945 had one week to prepare for its first game. Hastily, he blended returning players with a dozen or so war veterans he had coached the year earlier at Navy Pre-Flight.

The Terrapins defeated Guilford 60–6 and went on to produce a 6–2–1 record. Maryland, a doormat for several seasons prior to that, was invited to play in the Gator Bowl, but could not accept because Bryant had left the program for Kentucky after a dispute with the school president.

That was an incredible debut for Bryant as a coach, a bewildering start to a triumphant career.

"I can't talk about that first year at Maryland without talking a little about the year at Navy Pre-Flight," said Joe Drach, an offensive tackle and defensive end for Bryant during the one year at Maryland. "Let me start with my introduction to Coach Bryant:"

I was a wrestler and had separated a shoulder. I mean it was a bad one, and the doctor told me I couldn't play football at Navy Pre-Flight until it healed. I wanted to play, so I went out on the practice field and started doing calisthenics with the other guys, only I didn't have on a full uniform, just a sweatsuit. I was waving one arm while doing side straddle hops.

Coach Bryant came up to me and said, "Are you a football player?" I told him I was. He said, "You're not a football player because a football player wears full gear." I went inside and put on my uniform, shoulder pads and all, and reported back to practice—hurting like the devil, I might add.

Navy Pre-Flight was a place where a lot of war veterans were sent until they were discharged. That's what most of the guys on that football team were, veterans waiting to go home. That's what Coach Bryant was, too, one of us, really, except he was our coach because of the experience he had playing at Alabama.

Late in the summer of 1945, Coach Bryant had a meeting with us and said he had a few coaching offers to consider. He said he could go to Alabama as an assistant coach, maybe to Vanderbilt as the head coach and to Maryland as the head coach. He said wherever he went, we all should go because we could be a good team after playing together at Navy Pre-Flight.

Ultimately, we hired him, or you could say, because a little more than a dozen of us told him Maryland was the best place for us to be.

Coach Bryant made his deal at Maryland, and a bunch of us were summoned at Navy Pre-Flight. We saw a Greyhound bus with the University of Maryland on its front. They hurried us through discharge, even forgot to give us our $100 each for travel money, and off we went from Chapel Hill, North Carolina, to College Park, Maryland. We arrived after dark, but they hurried us to the registrar's office, and we enrolled for classes. They took us to a dorm for some sleep. The next afternoon, we reported to football practice.

The rest of it was a blur. All of us vets, seasoned men, tried to blend in with the other players, the college boys, and most of them became great friends and fine teammates. There were some good players in that group, too, although not an abundance.

I'll never forget what I did to earn a place in the starting lineup. I went to practice an hour early, showed up on the field and worked on my game. That impressed Coach Bryant. I was the starter when we played Guilford.

We practiced a week and played the game. That was the first victory Coach Bryant got as a college coach.

I'm not sure Coach Bryant was a good coach that first year. He definitely wasn't exceptional when it came to strategy. But he was a leader and a motivator, which is what we needed.

—JOE DRACH, Maryland player

Maryland defeated Richmond and Merchant Marine in its second game and third game, respectively, then lost to Virginia Tech in its fourth game, tied West Virginia in its fifth game, lost to William and Mary in its sixth game, and finished the season with victories over Virginia Military, Virginia and South Carolina:

The win over Virginia was the biggest Coach Bryant ever had because it created national attention. That was a team that had already been selected to play in the Orange Bowl. It had been several years since Maryland won a game like that. The win attracted all kinds of attention for Coach Bryant.

Again, Coach Bryant wasn't a great coach, not then, but he was a master psychologist. He was so good motivating that he could have taken a 120-pound cheerleader and made her believe she could run fifty yards through a mean defense.

And, of course, as everybody knows, Coach Bryant was a tough person and a demanding person.

I discovered how demanding he was and how much he wanted to win at halftime of the West Virginia game. The score was tied, and I had broken my hand late in the second quarter. It was doubled back and the bones were sticking out. It was hurting like the devil, and he noticed me bent over in pain while talking to us in the dressing room.

Coach Bryant walked over to me, took a look at my hand and said, "That looks like it's broken."

I told him it looked that way because it was broken.

Coach Bryant grimaced and said, "Manager, get some tape and get over here."

I said, "Coach Bryant, you can't tape that hand. Look how it's all bent backwards."

Coach Bryant and Carney Laslie, a coach and trainer, put my hand down on a bench and pressed the bones back into place, like a doctor would before putting on a cast.

I don't guess it says much for my intelligence, but I played the second half of that game and the rest of that season with that broken hand. The son of a gun still kills me.

But that's what Coach Bryant could get a person to do, play in pain and play hard.

❧

We were mad as hell when Coach Bryant left. I've forgiven him now, but it wasn't easy then.

—**Joe Drach,** Maryland player

When Bryant left Maryland, abruptly, after a dispute with

school president Curly Byrd, students on campus and other fans were mad. They had tasted uncanny success for the first time in what seemed like ages.

Oh yeah, sure, it's all true what you've heard about students rioting in protest of Curly Byrd and how he had made Coach Bryant mad enough to leave Maryland. Students were burning chairs and tables in classrooms and dorms. They put chains on the doors of the classrooms and refused to go to class. It was a mess on campus until Coach Bryant addressed students and told them to go back to class and to settle down.

As for us players, we were mad as hell when Coach Bryant left. He got the Kentucky job, and he was gone in a flash. We got a Gator Bowl invitation and couldn't accept it because we didn't have anybody to coach us.

I can't tell you how many times through the years Coach Bryant apologized to me and most of the others players for leaving like that. He felt like he bailed out on us. He had his reason to leave, a good one, but I don't think he was ever comfortable thinking he had reneged on a commitment.

I had breakfast with Coach Bryant on the morning of the game in which he broke Amos Alonzo Stagg's record for wins. Harry Bonk, a fullback on our Maryland team was there, too, as was Danny Ford, the former Alabama player and Clemson coach. He was still apologizing then.

Then I saw Coach Bryant on the afternoon before his last game, the 1982 Liberty Bowl. We chatted a few minutes in the hotel lobby, which was packed with people. He said, "Joe, I want you to get in touch with all of those vets from Navy Pre-Flight that played at Maryland, as well as some of the other players, too. Because when all this craziness ends and I get settled down, I want us to get together for a reunion and talk about life."

Obviously, we never got the chance to do that. I really regret us not getting together again in that type setting.

15

THE KENTUCKY YEARS

What I want to tell you old men, the Kentucky boys of autumn, is I love you and I respect you.

—PAUL "BEAR" BRYANT, at a reunion
in 1981 with Kentucky players

It had been more than a quarter of a century since some of the University of Kentucky football players who labored under Paul "Bear" Bryant had seen their coach. They were gathered at reunion in Louisville, Kentucky.

Earl Cox from the *Louisville Courier-Journal* was at the event that included Kentucky players from 1946 through 1953. He recorded the remarks of the Alabama coach as he addressed the Wildcats who produced for him a 60–23–5 record in eight years.

Bryant told them, "When we play Penn State on national television this year, it won't be any more important than that North Dakota game you won 83-to-nothing." He talked about his pursuit of Amos Alonzo Stagg's record and said, "When the record is broken—it will be broken, if the Good Lord lets me live to do it—I want you to know you had as much to do with it as anybody else. It won't be just the Alabama players on the field at the time. It'll be the boys of autumn from Kentucky out there, too."

Bryant told them there was talk about the construction of a museum on the Alabama campus. He said, "If they can get something big enough for me to get the name of every player who played for me on it, I'll pay for it. Also, all the other important names should go up there, too, the assistant coaches, the mamas, the papas, and the sweethearts.

"If something like that is built, I can assure you Kentucky will be honored by it alongside Alabama, Texas A&M and Maryland. It'll be built in honor of my players, all of you, and not me."

Ermal Allen, a Kentucky quarterback under Bryant in 1946 who returned to Lexington to coach under him, was at that reunion. He recalls an interesting chat he had with his mentor and boss:

In those years Coach Bryant had a most unusual way of coming up with our starting lineups. But I think it points out the value he placed on commitment.

Coach Bryant used to get me in a meeting room. He said, "Ermal, get your skinny butt up to that chalkboard. Now, here's the situation. You've got to go into combat, and your life is on the line. I want you to think of eleven guys on our team you want in the trenches fighting for you. Put their names on the chalkboard."

That was how he determined starters. But during a few of those years he paused, then said, "Of course, Ermal, Babe Parilli is our quarterback. You can take it from there."

ᔕ

My motor home is blue, but I'm all red this week. My loyalty to Coach Bryant is too deep. I've got a red hat with a white 'A' on it that I'll wear proudly tomorrow afternoon. I'm one of the Kentucky boys. But I'm backing ol' 'Bear' in this game.

—BEN ZARANKA, Kentucky end

Ben Zaranka played on the 1950 Kentucky team that produced an 11–1 record and defeated Oklahoma in the Sugar Bowl. He made the above statement on September 18, 1981, the evening before Alabama played against the Wildcats at Commonwealth Stadium in Lexington. The Crimson Tide won the game 19–10 but only after a hard struggle. Zaranka continues:

> I can't help but feel that way about Coach Bryant because he took us up the ladder, put Kentucky at the top in the Southeastern Conference. He took young boys, none of us real superstars, to a mountain peak. Believe you me, he had the entire state enthralled with Big Blue football, and that was a historic accomplishment.
>
> I'll tell you how our stature improved. The governor of our state once helped me get out of my uniform after a game.
>
> As a high school senior, I had just played on two state championship teams, so when somebody mentioned me going to Kentucky, I said, "You expect me to go play with a bunch of losers after being a winner?"
>
> Kentucky had just produced 3–6 and 2–8 records the two previous seasons. I wasn't the least bit interested.
>
> But guess who the next coach at Kentucky was at the time?
>
> When "Bear" came to my high school for a visit, he shook my hand and immediately convinced me Kentucky was the place for me. He was young and dedicated. He said he wanted people with pride and loyalty, that I shouldn't

consider Kentucky if I didn't have that in me. He said he was going to build a football empire at Kentucky, that there could be a grand day for Kentucky football if people like me went there and went to work.

Well, boy did he work us. He got every ounce of football out of us, on the practice field and during games.

The first thing he did with the freshmen is sit down and talk about life with us. He didn't say much about football, just what it takes to be successful in life. He insisted we set goals for ourselves, and he told us we could win only if we gave everything we had to being winners.

We agreed to it. By golly, it happened.

There were times I got angry at Bryant for pushing us so hard, probably harder than any team in the nation. I never hated him for it, though, rather grew to love him for it.

The reason we felt that way, I believe, is he never asked us to do a thing he wouldn't do.

Coach Bryant had something magical about him. He was one step ahead of everybody. I was in awe of him. There were days on campus when I'd walk a full circle to keep from meeting him face to face on a sidewalk or in a parking lot. He commanded that type respect.

Coach Bryant had interesting ways to motivate people.

One afternoon we were putting the finishing touches on a game plan, and everybody was pretty sluggish. He stopped practice and said, "If you guys want to have a picnic, then we'll have a picnic." He knew about a vendor who sold apples and oranges outside the stadium. He gave a manager twenty dollars and told him to go buy some fruit. It wasn't long before the manager returned without any apples and oranges. Somehow, I believe Coach Bryant knew that vendor had gone for the day and that was the way he wanted to make his point.

That was the day I knew the man had greatness on his side.

Ultimately, we got to the Sugar Bowl and that famous game against unbeaten and untied Oklahoma, which hadn't lost in more than three years.

During practice for the Sugar Bowl, Coach Bryant got upset with us because we couldn't grasp a new and unusual defense he had come up with. We'd screw up and he'd blow his stack. He said, "You guys just don't understand what I'm trying to do with this defense." Then he sent us in from practice.

It was a defense like none of us had ever seen. It was weird. It didn't make sense to us. But when we got the playing field with Oklahoma, the lights came on in our heads. They hadn't seen anything like it, either, and we shut them down.

We won the game 13–7 when nobody thought we could. We stopped their offense when nobody thought we could.

That was the day I knew Bear Bryant is an absolute genius when it comes to football.

16
THE TEXAS A&M YEARS

By the time Paul "Bear" Bryant arrived at Texas A&M as its football coach, he had created a monster with three heads. The success he had at Maryland and Kentucky had the attention of a national audience. He was expected to do the same with the Aggies.

Interestingly, Bryant had turned down the chance to coach at Arkansas and Alabama during his time at Kentucky, on the assurance basketball coach Adolph Rupp was about to retire, and those lost chances added to his determination to win at Texas A&M. There was a sense of desperation. The program had won only a dozen games in three years under Coach Raymond George, and expectations were much greater than that.

Bryant was about to learn a lesson he had taught, that a person who has given what he perceives to be his all is capable of giving a little more.

Two big busses showed up. Coach Bryant said, "Ya'll get a pillow and a change of clothes or two. We're going to take a trip."

—**GENE STALLINGS,** Texas A&M player and
Alabama coach

Gene Stallings was a six-foot-two, 165-pound sophomore end at Texas A&M when Bryant uttered those words, signaling the beginning of a training camp for his football team at Junction, Texas. Seventy players embarked on that journey. Twenty-seven survived its rigors.

"We had no idea where we were going," Stallings said.

The answer became clear, after some doing. The Aggies were on their way up.

The "Junction Boys" have become sports icons because of what they went through and what they accomplished.

"I was a senior that year, and I was determined not to let Coach Bryant run me off," said Marvin Tate, who later became Texas A&M athletics director. "I'm sure if we had, we wouldn't be where we are in life. We're better for having stuck it out during that week and a half at Junction."

How tough was that first preseason training camp under Bryant? Well, for starters, five centers quit the team in a single day. Troy Summerlin was a student manager when that round of practices began. He became a player at that position because there was nobody else available.

At one point during the ten days of hell, the *Houston Post* newspaper sent a reporter to the training camp.

"My editor heard there's dissension up here, with people leaving the team, and he wanted me to check it out," said the reporter to Bryant.

Bryant said, "You can go tell your editor that there isn't any dissension, not yet, but there's going to be because I'm about to create some."

Later, word surfaced that the following season, Bryant called together some offensive linemen during early summer to find a center. He held auditions, to use a term, in the press box at Kyle Field because it was against rules to practice that early in the year. It was hot, and the concrete floor and walls were punishing. Sweat and blood poured. He had a center within a week.

The "Junction Boys" had a reunion in the desolate area on May 18, 1979. Twenty-three survivors showed up. So did the coach, who said to the group, "Over the years when I've thought about Junction, I haven't been sure I did the right thing. But now that I've come back and seen how it all worked out, I want you to do something for me. I want you to get the names of all of the players who stayed with us, gutted it out, and I want you to write down what they're all doing now. I'm going to frame it and hang it on my den wall at home. Then when people ask about the 'Junction Boys' all I'll have to do is point at that picture frame."

Bryant arrived at Texas A&M on February 8, 1954. There was a large crowd at the airport to greet him. Then he went on campus and produced the theatrics mentioned earlier by Dee Powell when he addressed the corps of cadets.

ॐ

When I was coaching under Coach Bryant at Alabama from 1969 through 1971, we had an interesting conversation one afternoon after practice. He said, "John David, you know, if I had moved you to fullback, left Richard Gay at center and had done this or that, we would've won a national championship at Texas A&M in 1956." I quickly said, "Coach Bryant, if you had just kicked two damn field goals we would've done that with the same lineup we had on the field." He picked up pace and walked away. But I'm sure he was smiling.

—JOHN DAVID CROW, Texas A&M player

Bryant had one losing season as a coach. His first Texas A&M team posted a 1–9 record in 1954. The victory came in the third game, over Georgia 6–0 but the Aggies never were blown away by an opponent.

The record improved to 7–2–1 in 1955, after a 21–0 loss to UCLA in the first game.

That was the year **John David Crow**, the Heisman Trophy winner in 1957, had a bewildering experience under a coach he grew to love and respect:

It was hot on Kyle Field, smoldering, and we were practicing in front of some of our supporters, boosters, I guess. We had been out there for about three hours, and Coach Bryant concluded we were having a horse shit practice, as he would term it. He sent us inside, told us that was it.

We hit the showers. Coach Bryant cleared out the boosters. I was in the shower sitting in a chair, enjoying getting drenched, when a team manager came in and said, "Put back on the gear. We're not finished. Coach Bryant wants you back on the practice field."

We were out there for about two hours. He kept running me with the football. I was afraid to take a knee because I didn't think I could get back up. I'll be honest. I was looking at him and looking at the gate on the fence around the practice field. I was trying to decide if it wouldn't be better to leave. He made some comment, something about quitters and losers, and that was the end of my thoughts about leaving.

Ultimately, I passed out. They took me inside and packed me in ice. I was that far gone. They took me to the hospital. I was out for more than three hours.

When I came around, the first person I saw was Carolyn, my wife. She was beside the bed. Then I saw Coach Bryant standing at the foot of the bed. He had been there through it all, even dumped ice on me in the dressing room.

When I focused on him, he said, "John David, why didn't you tell me you were that tired?"

I tried to tell him, "Hell, Coach Bryant, we were on the practice field for more than five hours."

I didn't understand until later. But that was Coach

Bryant. He believed if a guy could go another step after thinking he couldn't take another step, then he'd be able to take several extra steps the next day.

I don't know that what we went through under Coach Bryant was his toughest act. I remember my son, Johnny, calling me during the 1970s, when he was playing at Alabama. He said, "Dad, if what you people went through is tougher than what we're going through, it must have been unbearable."

Honestly, I think anybody who put on a helmet and played under Coach Bryant paid a price for success.

But I'll tell you something else about him. He was tough as hell, but underneath was one of the most tender men I've known. You don't find that combination very much.

In 1956, Texas A&M won the Southwest Conference championship and posted a 9-0-1 record. The tie was with Houston, 14-14, and the team could not play in a bowl game because the program was on probation.

In 1957, the Aggies posted an 8-3 record. The regular season losses were to Rice, 7-6, and Texas, 9-7, when field goals would have made the difference in a perfect record and one with two losses. Texas A&M lost in the Gator Bowl to Tennessee 3-0, after word had leaked about Bryant making a move.

Actually, Alabama had solidified a deal with Bryant three months before Texas A&M played in the Gator Bowl. That developed after Dr. Frank Rose, school president, and Fred Sington, a star on the 1930 Crimson Tide team, flew to Houston, Texas with a contract in their hands.

❦

We had Paul Bryant ready to sign the contract, but we couldn't find it.

—FRED SINGTON, Alabama
player and representative

We got to the hotel suite in Houston, and Coach Bryant had agreed to our terms. Coach Bryant was anxious. It was a secretive meeting. We were there to hire him as Alabama's next coach, and he was worried the Texas A&M folks would get wind of it.

Dr. Rose and I arrived at the hotel and went to his suite. We shook hands and had idle chatter. Then he said, "Do you have the contract?" Dr. Rose said, "Of course, we've got the contract." But we couldn't find it.

We looked here and there. Finally, we called the front desk, asking if they could check the lobby, we called the airport, asking if they could check the terminal, and we called the taxi company, asking if they could check the cab.

All the while, Coach Bryant was getting on edge. He was mad. He wanted to get back to campus and go to work.

I was nervous, too, and I walked to the window, drew the curtain and looked outside. Lo and behold, there it was, the briefcase with the contract. It was behind the curtain.

We pulled it out, Dr. Rose went over the terms, and we shook hands to make a deal. Paul Bryant, who had most of a season to go at Texas A&M, was our coach for the next season.

If it hadn't been Alabama, his school, I don't think it would have ever materialized. He loved those Aggies, through and through.

17

THE BUILDER OF CHAMPIONS

I've heard a lot about the Junction Boys at Texas A&M.
But what we went through at Alabama until we won that
first national championship in 1961 was just as tough. It
just happened on our campus, on the practice field, not at
some far away location in the middle of nowhere.

—**JACK RUTLEDGE,** Alabama
player and assistant coach

Jack Rutledge was a star fullback at Woodlawn High School
in Birmingham, Alabama. He signed with the University of
Alabama when J. B. "Ears" Whitworth was the coach. He
completed his freshman season and heard that Paul "Bear"
Bryant was about to return to Tuscaloosa.

Bryant had a following at the time, but mostly in coaching and news media circles. Few people in Alabama remembered him as a Crimson Tide player. But word spread quickly,
says Rutledge, who would star for Alabama as an offensive
guard and, eventually, coach under Bryant from 1966 until his
retirement in 1982:

> The program was down and the alumni wanted it restored to
> what it had been. When they announced that Coach Bryant

Paul "Bear" Bryant was like The Pied Piper when it came to leading his players and developing them into champions.

was coming home, a wave of enthusiasm swept through the state. Everybody was hungry for a winner, at least Alabama folks, and I think people were finding hope in the fact a successful coach at Maryland, Kentucky, and Texas A&M was coming to make things better.

My father had steered me to Alabama. He said that was the place to be. I had been recruited by numerous programs, including Auburn, which was winning at the time, but he pointed me toward Tuscaloosa.

I was a leftover from the Coach Whitworth era. There weren't many of us around when that national championship came in 1961. The roster started thinning quickly, even during winter workouts in 1958, about a month after

Coach Bryant arrived.

It didn't take long to understand things were going to be done differently. I didn't know much about Coach Bryant. But it didn't take long for all of us to learn about him.

When they arrived, Coach Jerry Claiborne moved into Friedman Hall, and they started the off-season program in the old gym on top of the athletics department offices. They had us broken down into three groups, and the workouts lasted for forty-five minutes, without a break. You just kept going from station to station without pause.

They had mats where we would wrestle. You wrestled for your life. They had big weighted bags hanging from the ceiling. They'd pull them back and throw them at you, and you had to stop them with your arms behind your back. That canvass would tear apart your face, drawing blood. We'd do pushups and situps 150 at a time, then start again. Your butt would get raw, even start bleeding.

There were two doors in and out of that gym with trash cans beside them. There weren't many days when anybody got out without throwing up in one of those trash cans.

It was forty-five minutes, without stopping, in that hot gym. Then, after a while, weightlifting was added.

The thing about it was you almost never saw Coach Bryant—unless you had a problem. The exceptions were team meetings he'd call to talk about what we were going to accomplish.

During the first spring practice, Coach Bryant was working us to find out who was going to stay. There were a bunch who left, crawled over the fence during practice. It was hard. It was tough. It was wild out there.

There were some exceptions among those who chose to leave. Buck Burns, my best friend, was one of them.

Coach Bryant gave out weights for people to get to before spring practice started. Buck worked at it, but was about four pounds over. So he had to run and go and do, and he lost way on down, now underweight.

Buck went to Coach Bryant and told him he was going to have to give up football, that his dad wanted him to graduate and go to law school.

Three years later, Buck graduated from law school and started a distinguished career. I've seen the letter Coach Bryant wrote him. He told him how proud he was of him coming to talk to him about giving up football, getting his degree, and starting a great professional life.

I hope that points out how tough Coach Bryant was on the practice field, yet how caring he was when it came to players.

It was a hard time for all of us, me included. I went to Alabama after setting records as a fullback at Woodlawn High School, records that stood until Tony Nathan came along and broke them. But after giving me a shot at fullback, Coach Bryant decided I should be an offensive lineman.

So I'm listed as an offensive guard.

We had a player, an offensive guard, who got in a fight during a practice with Jim Blevins, a military vet who was there as an offensive lineman. It was awful. Blevins knocked out his teeth and made a mess.

They didn't promote fighting, the coaches didn't, but if one broke out, well, nobody was quick to stop it. They wanted to find out who could play.

The next day, they put me on the board during a blocking drill with Blevins on the other end of the board. I fired out and tried to block him. He knocked me flat on my back.

They lined us up again, with assistant coach Pat James screaming and hollering. I fired out, got a good lick on Blevins and knocked him off the board.

Blevins reached for my headgear, attempting to pull it off. I remembered the day before, when he messed up another guy, and I got him down on the ground. I had an arm around his neck and my fist clenched. The next thing I heard was the whole team screaming, "Hit him . . . Hit him . . . Hit him . . ."

The coaches were letting us go at it. Coach Bryant, I guess, probably turned his head and looked the other way.

The prevailing story after that was Jim Blevins had a battleship on his chest and Jack Rutledge sunk it.

But that was the environment they wanted us in. They wanted some fighters, some tough guys, and the only way to find out who had what it took to win at Alabama, the Bryant way, was to let us go at it a little bit.

While we were going through all of that, we kept thinking what Coach Bryant had told us, that we'd win a national championship if we did what he told us to do. It was hard to believe. But the coaches he had on his staff were, for the most part, former players who had been through the same thing.

There wasn't any water, not a drop, and there wasn't any shade to save us from the sun. It was hard work.

I was lucky, I guess, because after getting on the first team as an offensive guard, I went to Coach Bryant and told him I had been dating the same girl for four or five years and planned to marry her. He said, "Jack, if you get married, you'll be on the scout team at the start of next season. I don't need any married players out there trying to win."

Well, I married Norma that summer. When preseason practice started, I was on the scout team. Then in the third or fourth game, we had an offensive guard get hurt. I was dressed with the varsity, and Coach Bryant tried to send me into the game.

I said, "Coach Bryant, I haven't played all year. I'd like for you to redshirt me. That'll give me three full seasons."

I don't know what made him agree to that, but he did. He put somebody else in the game. That gave me the chance to play on the 1961 team that won a national championship.

You just asked if the 1961 team had an arrogance about it, or an assurance that we were mentally tough and physically tough, superior to anybody we would play because of what we went through under Coach Bryant. The answer is no, because one of the things he preached about was that we should always be humble, no matter what success we achieved.

But I can assure you of one thing. If you made it through Paul Bryant practices, just the specialty periods at the start, you had it made in games. Those were easy, about like going to a picnic.

We had a good team in 1958. We had a better team in 1959. We had an exceptional team in 1960. But that team in 1961, well, we didn't show up for any game with any thoughts that we would lose. We beat everybody. We scored 297 points. We gave up twenty-five points. I'd say we were proof that Coach Bryant knew what it took to win a national championship.

18

THE ALABAMA YEARS

The things Coach Bryant taught me have followed me through life. They have impacted my marriage and the way I have raised my children.

—LEE ROY JORDAN, Alabama player

On January 1, 1963, University of Alabama linebacker Lee Roy Jordan made thirty-one tackles during a 17–0 victory by the Crimson Tide over Oklahoma in the Orange Bowl.

After watching that performance and being asked for a reaction, Coach Paul "Bear" Bryant said, "Lee Roy will get 'em if they stay between the sidelines."

Later, Bryant said, "Lee Roy is the best football player I've ever had."

Jordan was a Bryant prototype player. He was six-foot-one, stretching it, and weighed 205 pounds. He came from a small town, Excel, Alabama, and the only reason he became a collegiate star is because he wanted to be one. He played on Alabama teams that produced 8–1–2, 11–0, and 10–1 records—and the losses were by thirteen points to Tennessee, 20–7, and one point to Georgia Tech, 7–6. He went on to achieve Circle of Honor status with the Dallas Cowboys of the National Football League:

The way Coach Bryant taught was his greatest asset. He taught you about life. He taught you right from wrong. He taught you how to handle pressure situations. He taught you how not to jeopardize yourself as a result of your actions. He taught you to be constructive in the things you do. He taught you to establish goals and to work to achieve them. He taught you that there are ways to overcome limits you and others might put on you. He taught you that winners are few and far in between and that champions are even fewer in number. He taught you how to take a setback and turn it into something positive.

Look how those lessons worked for us at Alabama. We reestablished a proud program by winning under him. We won a national championship in 1961. We came within one point of winning a national championship in 1962. The people who played under him won national championships in 1964 and 1965 and should have been awarded another one in 1966.

I don't know what else can be said about his greatness as a coach, as a person, and as a leader. But I can tell you I took what Coach Bryant taught me and used it with the Dallas Cowboys, and I've used it since my retirement from football. Also, I've attempted to teach my children the same things about life that he taught me and attempted to teach everybody who played for him.

Without question, Bryant had his greatest era as a coach during his years at Alabama. His teams won six national championships and thirteen Southeastern Conference championships. Incredulously, there could have been more trophies in the case had a single fumble been recovered by a player in crimson or had a football bounced in one direction instead of another.

Indeed, it is a mark of greatness in football when accomplishments are measured as much in narrow defeat as in triumphant victory.

How is that explained?
Look at the figures below:

In 1958, his first year at Alabama, Bryant lost four games by a total of 25 points.
In 1959, Bryant lost two games by a total of 21 points.
In 1960, Bryant lost one game by 13 points.
In 1962, Bryant lost one game by 1 point.
In 1963, Bryant lost two games by a total of 6 points.
In 1964, Bryant lost one game by 4 points.
In 1965, Bryant lost one game by 1 point.
In 1967, Bryant lost two games by a total of 15 points.
In 1968, Bryant lost three games by a total of 28 points, two of them by a total of 3 points.
His teams got drubbed in 1969 and 1970, losing ten games by a total of 139 points.
In 1971, Bryant lost one game by 32 points.
In 1972, Bryant lost two games by a total of 5 points.
In 1973, Bryant lost one game by 1 point.
In 1974, Bryant lost one game by 2 points.
In 1975, Bryant lost one game by 13 points.
In 1976, Bryant lost three games by a total of 27 points, one of them by 21–0 at Georgia.
In 1977, Bryant lost one game by 7 points.
In 1978, Bryant lost one game by 10 points.
In 1980, Bryant lost two games by a total of 10 points.
In 1981, Bryant lost two games by a total of 7 points.
In 1982, his final season, Bryant lost four games by a total of 27 points.
All told, there were 232 victories, 46 defeats and 9 ties during his years at Alabama.

How can that be summarized? Of course: Hail to the Victors and Wake Up the Echoes—as well as Roll, Tide, Roll.

$\backsim$

Coach Bryant was disappointed, as much that night as I had ever seen him. He wanted to win that game badly.

—ARNS CALLERY,
Sugar Bowl committee member

Bryant considered Aruns Callery a dear friend. Often, he talked to him about victory and defeat. One such occasion was on the evening of December 31, 1973, just after Alabama had lost to Notre Dame in the Sugar Bowl. If ever there was a game the coach wanted to play over, it was that one, the first meeting between the two superpowers. Both were undefeated and untied. The Fighting Irish won 24–23 by completing a long pass out of their end zone when it appeared the Crimson Tide was poised to win with at least a field goal late in the fourth quarter:

> Paul sat in his hotel suite after that game and stared at the walls. He was disgusted. He was disappointed. He thought he had the better team and had let one get away he should have won.
>
> Paul told me that night that he had been convinced his 1973 team was his best in history, putting aside his 1966 team, but that he couldn't say that after it lost.

There rests an interesting thought about Bryant during the years he coached Alabama. Perhaps it is a mark of greatness when losses have such impact.

That is why what he accomplished during the remainder of the 1970s is so stunning. There were few losses to consider. He was at his best in 1977, 1978, and 1979, when the Crimson Tide posted 11–1, 11–1, and 12–0 records.

ᔑ

We felt like champions in 1977. We felt like champions in 1978. We knew we were champions in 1979.

—DAVID HANNAH,
Alabama player

David Hannah had an interesting career with the Crimson Tide. He lettered in 1975, missed the 1976 season with a knee injury, and starred in 1977, 1978, and 1979.

The 1977 team played a tough schedule. The loss was by seven points at Nebraska, 31–24, and the highlights were victories over Georgia, Southern Cal, Tennessee, and Ohio State in the Sugar Bowl.

✆

It was definitely something special when Coach Bryant and Coach Woody Hayes coached against each other in the 1978 Sugar Bowl. We won it, 35–6, and it looked a whole lot easier than it really was. Those were two great coaches. It was a privilege to play under Coach Bryant, and it was a privilege to help win that game for him. Of course, as always, we had a masterful game plan to use against Ohio State.

—MAJOR OGILVIE, Alabama player

The 1978 team played a more wicked schedule. The loss was to Southern Cal 24–14, and the highlights were victories over Nebraska, Missouri, Washington, Florida, Tennessee, and Penn State in the Sugar Bowl. **David Hannah** was on the bottom of the pile when Alabama held the Nittany Lions on consecutive rushes inside the 1-yard line to preserve a 14–7 victory:

> It's really unbelievable how that victory over Penn State shaped up. But it's exactly the type game Coach Bryant always talked about, winning with defense in the fourth quarter when the chips are down and a national championship is at stake.
>
> It's funny how during our pregame practice the day before that Murray Legg, a senior safety, said off the cuff,

"This is where the game is going to be won or lost." We were working on our goal line defense on the same end of the Louisiana Superdome that we stopped Penn State.

Then it was Murray who said, "This is a gut check" as Penn State got ready to make those runs on third down and

Photo by Barry Fikes

Paul "Bear" Bryant and Woody Hayes (right) shared the spotlight during the 1978 Sugar Bowl game. Alabama gave its coach a resounding victory and, of course, the championship trophy.

fourth down. That made Murray famous, I guess, because Alabama fans refer to that as The Gut Check.

But Murray wasn't the first person to say that. Coach Bryant used to talk about gut checks all the time at practice. I think that's why he got such a kick out of us winning like that, with two great teams fighting over about a foot of real estate.

Bryant had a lot of victories for which he was proud. But that was the one he liked best because of the same reasons Hannah talked about. Also, it was a wicked game from start to finish.

ॐ

Without a doubt, and there isn't even a close second, that was the toughest, roughest, most physical, and hardest football game in which I ever participated. It was hit or be hit from start to finish.

—MAJOR OGILVIE,
Alabama player on the 1979 Sugar Bowl

Jim Goostree, Alabama trainer, agrees in total:

The 1979 Sugar Bowl wasn't a place for anybody faint of heart, as Coach Bryant always said. It was his kind of football game. In fact, it was a football game that anybody who loves the sport would want to see.

If you had on an opposite colored jersey, you knew you were going to be hit. Everybody was fair game. The Penn State defense was brutal. The Penn State offense was like ours, methodical and grinding.

Ultimately, late in the game, our players had the opportunity to do exactly what Coach Bryant had always trained them to do. That defensive stand in the shadow of the end zone was phenomenal. It was his kind of football. He was pleased by that one in a major way. His players got to display what they had inside them.

Coach Bryant never was one to show any kind of favoritism. But he got a great deal of enjoyment watching those young men win the way they did that day. It was his way.

༄

I don't know if Coach Bryant liked coaching our 1979 team, but I think he liked watching us play. We had that great defense. Our offense just sort of pounded on people until we got in the end zone. Our kicking game was super. We had to come from behind to win over Tennessee and Auburn. Those are the type things he talked about a lot as he taught us about football and life.

—MAJOR OGILVIE, Alabama player

The 1979 team gave Bryant his last national championship. The highlights were victories over Georgia Tech, Florida, Tennessee, LSU, Auburn, and Arkansas in the Sugar Bowl. In 1981, **Bryant** reflected on the power of that team:

That team won every way imaginable. It won with offense. It won with defense. It won with kicking.

We had a defense in 1961 that acted like it was a sin to give up a point—not just a touchdown.

We had a team in 1964, with Joe Namath, that won every game, although the officials said Texas beat us in the Orange Bowl that year.

We had a productive offense in 1966, with Kenny Stabler at quarterback. I would have hated having to try to come up with a defense to slow those players down. The defense was great, too, because it pitched six shutouts.

We had an explosive offense in 1973. That 1977 team was classy, and it got better as the year wore on. We had a ton of talent in 1978, a team that had to fight through a schedule I arranged that was mighty demanding.

I don't have any idea how one of those teams would have stacked up against the others.

But they were bigger, stronger, and faster in 1979—and they didn't lose to anybody, not once.

༄

During the late 1970s the rock-and-roll group Steely Dan had a hit record entitled "Deacon Blues." The chorus says:

They got a name for the winners in the world
They got a name for those who lose
They call Alabama the Crimson Tide
Call me Deacon Blues.

Those lyrics came from studio musicians in Los Angeles, California, one of whom liked to watch Paul "Bear" Bryant–led Alabama play football.

19

THE TIRELESS MAN AT WORK

*No matter how successful he was, he was never satisfied.
Coach Bryant refused to rest on his laurels.*

> **—SAM BAILEY,** Alabama
> associate athletics director

Sam Bailey was as close to Paul "Bear" Bryant as anybody
who worked with him. They coached together at Texas A&M
and Alabama. Ultimately, the former became the associate
athletics director in charge of all Crimson Tide sports other
than football. Their offices were next to each other at
Memorial Coliseum in Tuscaloosa, Alabama. The morning
after the coach died in 1983, Bailey reflected on how tirelessly
Bryant had worked:

Coach Bryant never reached a plateau. We could be named
the national champion on Monday night, and he was back
at it early Tuesday morning, working to win another one. A
normal person would say, "We've had a great year and we've
done a good job, so I'm going to have a great summer." But
not him. He was never that way. He was driven to succeed
over and over. He worked just as hard after a 12–0 season as

he worked after a 6–5 season.

That's why there weren't many of those bad years. He was a strong leader who set a fast pace. We had to work hard with him just to keep up.

⟡

I was fortunate to have **Bryant** read a creed of excellence he developed for coaching clinics. He told high school and college coaches he often made the same points with players:

Players should be told they don't have to win, but that there's a great difference in the rewards associated with winning and losing.

Players should be told a football game cannot be prayed over, or played over, that once it's over the result has to be lived with for life.

Point out to players that only special people win consistently, that there is very little difference in being average and being a champion. Sometimes work ethic can make the difference as easily as the talent level.

Players should be told that a champion has a winning attitude on and off the football field. They should display that class before games, during games and after games. You can't be a champion for four quarters in a football game and be a loser in every other part of your life. A champion is a champion.

Make sure players know there's a totem pole out there that's crowded at the bottom and in the middle, but has plenty of room at the top. That's where a champion ends up, at the top of the totem pole, where the wind blows the hardest.

⟡

It did not matter if it sometimes got so warm he had to carry his sport coat during the pregame warmup, Paul "Bear" Bryant dressed sharp for games, a houndstooth hat included.

Photo by Barry Fikes

I would've carried all of my players off the field on my shoulders if they had let me.

—PAUL "BEAR" BRYANT,
after a historic victory

On November 28, 1981, Bryant became the most prolific winner in history at the collegiate level when his Alabama team defeated Auburn 28–17 at Legion Field in Birmingham. All the years of hard work paid off that afternoon.

When Bryant arrived for his postgame press conference, Auburn Coach Pat Dye was about to leave his meeting with the news media. The two rivals hugged.

"I want you to know Governor Jimmy Carter called me on the telephone in the dressing room," Bryant said to Dye, a Georgia native.

"Are you talking about President Ronald Reagan or . . ." Dye said.

"I'm talking about Governor Carter," Bryant said with an infectious grin. "I figured you'd appreciate that more."

"I'm not a politician, I'm a coach," Dye said with a grin. "But did President Reagan call you, too?"

"Why sure he called me," Bryant said. "I don't guess he has ever called you, has he?"

Bryant was having fun with the man he started in coaching, which was not surprising because he never lost sight of the contributions of the players and assistant coaches who labored under him. He credited them with doing the winning and said he directed traffic and tried to stay out of the way.

So it was appropriate that when he was asked about his players carrying him off the field on their shoulders after that historic victory he heaped praise on them. **Bryant** was particularly pleased that Alabama had to come from behind in the fourth quarter to defeat Auburn on national television:

Sure, coming from behind is a whole lot better. It's always great to win like that, better than going to the front and breezing through.

Players learn from experiences like that. Winning like they did today will help them somewhere in the future. There'll be a time when they'll get behind in life like they did today, at some point when they're trying to make a living and things aren't going good. They'll know what it takes to win the hard way.

That's why I should've been carrying them off the field today instead of them toting me to the center of the field. If I wasn't so old and tired, I would've done that, even if I had to stay here until midnight to get them all to the dressing room.

I'm that proud of them. I'm proud of our coaches, too.

🍥

After being associated with Coach Bryant, you want him to approve of everything you do in your life.

—TOM HARPER, Kentucky player

Tom Harper played for Bryant at Kentucky and went into the coaching profession. He was forty-nine years old on November 23, 1981, five days before his former coach became the winningest in history at the collegiate level. He was asked to comment about the man about to make history with victory number 315. He said:

> If you change jobs, you want Coach Bryant to approve. If you buy a house or a car, you want him to approve. If you get married, you want him to approve of your wife. I don't guess that's right, but that's how it is because he has always been willing to give so much of himself to his players.
>
> It's like a family, really. He had us feeling that way at Kentucky, as I'm sure has been the case with his players at Maryland, Texas A&M and Alabama. He equated football to life, from the first day, and that was his way of teaching players. When somebody cares that much about what might happen to you after your football playing days are over, well, it's only natural to want him to approve of what you do with your life.

ॐ

I'm a product of the Paul Bryant school of life, the Alabama football program, and I'm proud of that.

—JACKIE SHERRILL, Alabama player
and Mississippi State coach

To this day, Jackie Sherrill talks about Bryant as if he were a magician with a wand. After playing linebacker at Alabama from 1963 through 1965 and coaching at Iowa State, Pittsburgh, Texas A&M, and Mississippi State, he is more sure of the lessons he learned while starring for the Crimson Tide:

First of all, my first meeting with Coach Bryant was powerful. I was a high school senior in Biloxi, Mississippi and had pretty much made up my mind that I was going to Georgia Tech or Oklahoma. That changed when Coach Bryant came for a visit on the way to the Sugar Bowl in New Orleans.

We talked for about two hours and not once did he ask me to come to Alabama. That appealed to me. He just talked, and he listened to what I had to say. I don't recall saying all that much, but I was impressed by the way he cared about what I thought.

To this day, I think I was changing my mind and was going to Alabama the minute Coach Bryant shook my hand. There was something mystical about his grip.

Coach Bryant got more out of his players than any coach has in history. He made me think I was a better player than I was. He had the secret to that, a God-given talent, and I think it worked because he genuinely cared about us.

Coach Bryant had a way of making players feel important. You didn't just play for him. You learned from him.

It wasn't the big things he taught that made the strongest impact. It's the little things, subtle expressions about discipline and commitment, that tend to come back to people who played for him and help us in our professional lives.

I'm not sure I've ever seen a man so driven to succeed. He had a goal and he had a plan. He labored tirelessly. He put players first and developed the team concept, with every young man contributing to us winning.

It's impossible to explain because Coach Bryant had something no other coach has had—and it isn't something you'll find in books.

20
THE INNOVATOR

Coach Bryant drew play after play, sheet after sheet, on the plane trip home that night.

—**KIRK MCNAIR,** Alabama
sports information director

The University of Alabama football team had just completed a 24–24 tie with Oklahoma in the 1970 Bluebonnet Bowl, and the airplane carrying the Crimson Tide home from Houston, Texas, had been in the air only a few minutes.

Kirk McNair, the sports information director, was seated near Paul "Bear" Bryant:

Coach Bryant pulled out that big ol' brown briefcase, the one that looked like a suitcase, and went to work. He sat the briefcase on his lap and, as usual, got out a yellow legal pad and a felt pen. I was wondering what he was going to do, so I kept my eyes trained on him.

To my amazement, he started drawing the wishbone offensive formation against all kinds of defensive formations. Oklahoma had used that somewhat new form of attack against us that night and Coach Bryant had been impressed.

That was not a good year for Alabama football. Our record was 6–5–1, after a 6–5 record in 1969, and it was obvious what we were doing wasn't working. Coach Bryant knew that, too, and he was looking for the right answer.

Needless to say, Coach Bryant found it because Alabama had ninety-seven wins during the next nine seasons.

ॐ

It could be said the decision to go to the wishbone saved Coach Bryant's career, or extended it. I'm glad I was able to contribute to that because he was truly an exceptional coach. In fact, he took the formation to another level.

—DARRELL ROYAL, Texas coach

Darrell Royal, the great coach at the University of Texas, was the first to use the wishbone formation. He was more than pleased to assist Bryant in the implementation of it at Alabama:

Paul telephoned me not long after the 1970 season and said he wanted to learn more about the wishbone. His team was struggling, running the "I" formation and passing the football too much. That didn't fit his personality, not at all. The grind it out nature of our offense was more to his liking.

I told Paul I'd be glad to show him some game films and talk to him about the wishbone. We tried to decide where we could do that without drawing too much attention. Finally, I said, "Just come on out to Austin, and I'll take a film projector home with me. We'll lock ourselves away in the house and talk football. I'll tell my secretary not to forward any calls to the house. I'll tell Edith to tell anybody who calls that I'm not available."

After a couple of days, Coach Bryant was hooked on the

wishbone. He said, "Darrell, the only question I've got is how do you get your offensive linemen to pass block in that formation? I mean, how much time do you spend on that?" I said, "You don't teach 'em how to pass block." He was puzzled by that answer. I said, "Paul, nobody expects you to pass in the wishbone, so nobody is going to rush the quarterback. It's the element of surprise that does the blocking for your linemen."

Early in the summer, Paul telephoned me and said, "Darrell, we're going to the wishbone offense if you'll let your offensive line coach and your running backs coach come to Tuscaloosa and show my assistant coaches how to teach it. I'll let them address our clinic for high school coaches from the state, and that'll allow them to make some extra money. You need to come, too, and we'll play golf and have some fun while they work."

That's what happened. The other guys worked and Paul and I visited and played a lot of golf. We had fun, as always, and, to be honest with you, I really enjoyed watching the way Alabama ran that offense, mastered it, and expanded it.

֍

Coach Bryant showed John Forney and me the Texas training tape and said that was the offense Alabama would be using during the 1971 season. This was during the summer of that year. I was amazed. I asked him if he was going to put in a new offense in a month and he said, "Yeah, you're damn right."

—DOUG LAYTON, sports broadcaster

Bryant wanted to make the move for two reasons. He had a terrific running back named Johnny Musso, a gifted option quarterback named Terry Davis and a relatively strong offensive line led by powerful guard John Hannah. Also, the Alabama defense had been porous for two seasons, to put it kindly, and there was a need for an offensive attack that would enhance time of possession.

The first opponent in 1971 was Southern Cal, which was ranked in the top three nationally. The Trojans had defeated Alabama 42–21 in the first game of the 1970 season, a result that pretty much points out the previously mentioned shortcomings the Crimson Tide had at the time.

"There was a high degree of secrecy surrounding Alabama preparations for the 1971 regular season," said Doug Layton, who handled radio broadcasts with John Forney. "Coach Bryant had decided to tell John and me what was happening, the change to the wishbone, so we would be prepared on opening night in Los Angeles. He cautioned us to keep it under wraps. Given his stature, the way both of us felt about him, that was as much a command as a suggestion."

๑

When a rumor surfaced and somebody from the news media suggested Alabama was going to the wishbone, Coach Bryant said, in a sarcastic tone, "Yeah, that's what we're doing. We're going to nothing more than a running game." He skillfully sold the truth as a lie.

—**Charley Thornton,** Alabama
sports information director

Coach Bryant had told his staff Alabama was going to sink or swim with the wishbone offense. He meant it, too, because he had already guided recruiting efforts in that direction. He wanted centers and guards who could block at the point of attack, a quarterback who could run the option and a powerful fullback.

Thick tarps were put up around the practice field and managers stood guard to keep people from seeing what was going on during summer workouts. When the news media came to visit, like the SEC Skywriters Tour, when a lot of sportscasters and broadcasters arrived on campus together, the team went back to the I-formation and played pitch and catch. Coach Bryant didn't miss a trick when it came to deception.

Alabama, a longtime Southeastern Conference power whose rivals were more than glad to see being put to rest, went to Los Angeles as a prohibitive underdog. The Crimson Tide unleashed the wishbone offense and won 17–10, with ball control playing a vital role in the outcome. The regular season record that season was 11–0. Nebraska won handily 38–6 in the 1972 Orange Bowl, a national championship showdown, but Bryant and his program were back in step.

"It was unbelievable how shocked Southern Cal coaches, players and fans were that night," said Forney. "I remember Coach John McKay, who was one of Coach Bryant's best pals, pointing a finger across the field late in the first quarter, as if to admit his buddy has pulled a good one on him. Meanwhile, team managers had rushed into the Trojans' dressing room and had brought out chalkboards so the defensive coaches could try to figure out what Alabama was doing with that running attack.

"Even the Southern Cal broadcast team was infuriated. Doug and I enjoyed a good laugh when their guys started shaking their fists at us while seated in a press box booth next to ours. We had discussed the game with them the previous night, various points of strategy. Did we ever mention Alabama going to the wishbone offense? No way, which made it more enjoyable."

The move to the wishbone offensive formation sort of

took Bryant back to his roots as a coach. He had learned the Notre Dame Box under Coach Frank Thomas during his years as an Alabama player. He had always loved strong running, carefully calculated passing, powerful defense and a crafty kicking game. Near the twilight of his career, he was back where he started, more or less, and winning with more regularity.

🌀

I always thought Coach Bryant was a perfect example of contradiction when it came to strategy. He preached defense and kicking over and over, but he would spend about six hours out of every eight hours dabbling with offense. I think the wishbone offense fascinated him. With a lot of input from Mal Moore, the offensive coordinator, he searched for ways to improvise, to open it up and take it to a new level.

—**Kirk McNair,** Alabama Sports
information director

Alabama was still running the wishbone offense when Bryant coached his final game. The formation was broken much more at that time, and passing was more of a fancy, but the basics were still in place. The mix of power and speed captivated the imagination of fans.

But changing with the times, plus initiating changes in the sport of football as a whole, was always a Bryant forte. He was such an innovator he forced numerous changes in the rules—and used others to his benefit.

🌀

I want players who are agile, hostile, and mobile.

—PAUL "BEAR" BRYANT,
on his prototype player

In the early years Bryant won with small and quick players, which endeared him to fans. That enabled him to use a couple of plays that sort of became his trademarks.

Bryant particularly liked the quick kick, when on a down other than fourth he would let a halfback take a pitch from a quarterback and punt the football up the field. It was a field position ploy because nobody was back to handle the football after it was kicked and it would roll for several yards.

There were times when, with a strong defense at his disposal, Bryant would punt on third down. His reasoning was he could try again on fourth down in the event of a bad snap from center. If the field conditions were miserable, like wet and muddy, he would punt on almost any down.

The University of Utah was the first to use the "Utah pass," but Bryant utilized it often, especially during the 1960s, calling it the "whoopee pass." It is still popular today.

The quarterback takes the snap from center, either in the shotgun formation or at the line of scrimmage, and shovels the football to a running back or to a flanker who is in motion. The play normally is run between the tackles. If the football is dropped, it is termed an incomplete pass and not a fumble. That makes it a surprising and safe maneuver.

Vivid is the memory of Bryant calling the "whoopee pass" against Colorado in the 1969 Liberty Bowl. When the officials ruled an incompletion a fumble, he ran onto the playing field and argued long and hard. He went back to the sideline, after some serious coaxing, decided he had not spoken his piece and ran back onto the playing field to continue the debate.

The tackle eligible pass was a Bryant fixture. He ran it by moving a running back or flanker up to the line of scrimmage on one side, thus making him a tight end, and backing a tight end from the line of scrimmage on one side, thus making him a running back or flanker and making the offensive tackle an eligible pass receiver.

When rules were changed to mandate that eligible pass receivers wore certain jersey numbers, Bryant simply had extra jerseys on the sideline and let his offensive tackle change into one that was legal.

The tear-away jersey was another Bryant weapon that was eventually outlawed—after being invented by Russell Athletic by accident.

The jersey manufacturer was producing orange apparel for the University of Tennessee. On an afternoon when it rained, the dye got drenched and weakened the fabric. Suddenly, defenders were left holding pieces of cloth in their hands.

Bryant found that interesting and asked Russell Athletic to produce tear-away jerseys, but not by accident. When Auburn University Coach Ralph "Shug" Jordan, among others, complained loudly about his players not being able to yank down Alabama players by their jerseys, a rule was enacted that stated a player with a torn jersey had to leave the game. The Crimson Tide coach responded by letting his quarterbacks and running backs wear several tear-away jerseys at a time, so when one was ripped apart another one was in place.

Bryant was an early proponent of athletics dorms, where his football players lived together.

Bryant was a trailblazer in the almost total recruitment of in-state talent. He said, "A player from Alabama, with roots in the state, will play harder for the University of Alabama in the fourth quarter, when the game is on the line." Other coaches found that to be true and adopted similar plans.

Normally, we'd get a prospect if Coach Bryant got seated in front of a player and his parents, particularly the mother, during a home visit. He told the prospect he'd give him a fair chance to prove himself, that if he was good enough, he'd play at Alabama. Most of them responded to that, at least the ones with the type character he wanted. He'd tell the mother that he'd treat her son like his own, take care of him, and he meant that. That's what a mother wants to hear from a coach.

—CLEM GRYSKA,
Alabama recruiting coordinator

Bryant made use of messengers to send in offensive plays from the sideline. In the early years, he sent substitutes in with a play written on a sheet of paper. In the latter years, to the dismay of rivals, he made use of messengers in another manner. He had players who would run onto the field, deliver the play and run back to the sideline before the football was snapped.

❧

He was screaming at me a little, and I couldn't figure out what had happened. Finally, I got the message. He was happy with the touchdown, but the big thing with him was following instructions.

—LAURIEN STAPP, Alabama player

Former Alabama player Laurien Stapp was chuckling as he visited with sports writer Mike Fleming of the *Memphis Commercial Appeal* just before Bryant coached his final game in the 1982 Liberty Bowl. He was remembering a time when he carried a play into the Crimson Tide offensive huddle.

"Coach Bryant had about six plays listed on a sheet of paper and he circled the one he wanted," Stapp said. "He had one of them circled, but I didn't see that he had made a little scratch through it and had written on the back another play he wanted. I went with the original play and we scored a touchdown.

"Coach Bryant let me have it after that play, even after we had scored. He was really steaming. He put more emphasis on me following instructions than the touchdown."

Bryant is credited with organizing practices in a concise manner. He did not believe in the old approach, when the offense and defense scrimmaged and everybody else watched. He had everybody working at a station, in the interest of time, and, of course, he watched everything happening around him from an observation tower that became famous.

Most everybody has followed that lead.

ॐ

I begged Coach Bryant for several years to let me come to Tuscaloosa and observe his practice sessions.

—Johnny Majors, Tennessee coach

Normally, I'd make a trip to Birmingham every year to talk to the quarterback club down there, usually the week after our game with Alabama. Every year I'd ask Coach Bryant if I could come to practice and observe, maybe steal a little of his time and talk to him about staff management and practice management. I was intrigued by the way he did things, for obvious reasons.

Coach Bryant always had an excuse for me. He'd say this wasn't a good week for a variety of reasons. I wasn't naive enough to believe everything he said. I knew the importance he placed on the Tennessee-Alabama series.

But in 1981, to my surprise, Coach Bryant called me and invited me to come to practice. I went down there and had a delightful time. I watched how he conducted practice. I spent a few hours with him talking about coaching in general. I walked away from the experience much more knowledgeable when it came to staff management and practice management. I was impressed that he remembered me asking to come down so many times before that.

At that time, Alabama had defeated Tennessee eleven consecutive times, the longest streak of dominance in the treasured series. The following October, the 16th, the Volunteers defeated the Crimson Tide 35–28 in Knoxville, Tennessee, in the last game Bryant coached against the Big Orange. What is more, Majors won on the third Saturday in October in 1983, 1984, and 1985.

🌀

Coach Bryant always searched for the winning edge and usually found it. One of the more bizarre times came just before we played Auburn in 1961.

—BILLY RICHARDSON, Alabama player

The afternoon before we played Auburn, after we had our last practice session on the playing surface at Legion Field, there was a concern that our shoes weren't right, that we'd have trouble with our footing during the game. It was something about the way the grass was cut that made it a little precarious. I believe it was worn thin and sort of slippery.

Well, Coach Bryant pondered the problem, obviously, and we were told later he had called Fred Sington, an Alabama great in 1930 who had sporting goods stores all over the state, and asked him to round up a certain style of shoe and get every pair he could to Birmingham. In fact, Coach Bryant got in touch with the State Troopers' Office and arranged for the shoes to get an escort to the hotel where we were staying.

Early the next morning, on game day, Coach Bryant got several of us out of bed, quarterbacks, running backs, pass receivers and kick returners, and had us report to the hotel parking lot. When we got there we found all of these interesting black shoes. I believe the brand was Puma, and they had white stripes along each side and rubber cleats on the bottom.

We ran through some plays in the parking lot and everybody agreed those were great shoes. They were ideal for what we had in mind for the game. We got a big victory that afternoon, 34–0, and I remember those Auburn players looking at those shoes with expressions on their faces that said, "Oh no, it looks like you've gone one up on us again."

Without question, several coaches have studied the Bryant way of doing things and have found them superior. But one of his more memorable traits seems to have fallen by the wayside.

Bryant always dressed immaculately for football games. He wore a coat and tie and dress shoes on the sidelines, departing from that only on rare bad-weather days when he put on boots and rain gear over his clothes. He looked like a man who thought what he was doing was important, as surely he did.

21

THE BOWL GAME POWER BROKER

I told Paul that sounded good to me, that we'd get together in Memphis. As soon as we finished talking, I got on the telephone with a Sun Bowl selection committee member and said, "Nebraska will be glad to come to El Paso."

—BOB DEVANEY, Nebraska coach

Bob Devaney, the fabled University of Nebraska coach, said he will always be thankful for the 1972 Orange Bowl, a national championship showdown that featured unbeaten teams. His Cornhuskers won over Alabama 38–6 in Miami, Florida.

"It allowed me to save face in head-to-head battles with my buddy Paul Bryant," Devaney said.

Devaney felt that way because Alabama defeated Nebraska 39–28 in the 1966 Orange Bowl and 34–7 in the 1967 Sugar Bowl. Proof of his sincerity rests in what happened when Bryant attempted to match the Crimson Tide and Cornhuskers for a third consecutive year:

In the first game, the Orange Bowl, I honestly believe we had the best team. Alabama caught us with the tackle eligible pass, onside kickoffs and a lot more. Steve Sloan threw the football better for them that night that he ever had or ever did again. He had Ray Perkins and Dennis Homan catching passes. The game got off to a terrible start for us, with them taking a 24–7 lead, and we never got back in it.

Bryant had a great plan that night. They passed the football all over the field. They caught us off guard.

The second game, the Sugar Bowl, was a mismatch. We didn't have much business being on the field with Alabama. They were too fast for us and too good for us. They had Ken Stabler at quarterback. That was just the start because they had a hell of a football team, arguably the best in the nation.

We were okay, that's all, and they jumped on us on the first play and never backed up.

So after those two games, Bryant called me near the end of the following season. He said, "Bob, neither of us are good enough to get one of those big bowl game bids, so why don't we try to get together again?" I asked him what bowl game he thought would be good for both teams. He said the Liberty Bowl would be ideal because it was first-class and Memphis, Tennessee, is a place their fans and our fans could get to.

I told Paul that sounded good to me. Then that's when I called the Sun Bowl and told them Nebraska would accept an invitation to play down there.

At that point, Paul Bryant had hooked me enough.

֍

I don't know if "matchmaker" is the proper description. But Paul Bryant certainly knew what was going on when it came to all of the bowl games.

—SAM CORENSWET,
Sugar Bowl committee member

A story related to the 1967 Sugar Bowl game between Alabama and Nebraska comes from Sam Corenswet, whose father was president of the Sugar Bowl committee that year:

> The Sugar Bowl wanted Alabama in a major way that year, rightfully so, because the Crimson Tide had won the national championship in 1964 and 1965 and was unbeaten and untied. In fact, there was talk about the Rose Bowl lifting its relationship with the Pac-Eight and Big Ten to get Alabama back out there. I think they were having some kind of contract dispute with the conferences and thought that was an ideal time for a change.
>
> So the Sugar Bowl was a little in the dark when it came to Bryant's intentions. To protect ourselves, we talked to a few other programs, like Georgia, which had a 9–1 record, and Ole Miss, which had an 8–2 record. We wanted another Southeastern Conference team if we couldn't get Alabama. In fact, at one point we seriously considered Alabama and Georgia, which hadn't played during the regular season.
>
> One afternoon Bryant telephoned my father and said, "I want you to know you've got your match, Alabama against Nebraska." My father was ecstatic, yet concerned about the other programs we had talked to. He said, "That's great, but what about Georgia and Ole Miss?" Bryant said, "Don't worry about them. Ole Miss is going to the Bluebonnet Bowl to play Texas and Georgia is going to the Cotton Bowl to play SMU."
>
> I don't think Bryant arranged all of the bowl games, as some people have contended through the years. But, yes, by all means, he was a man who knew what was going on across the nation.
>
> We laughed about that many times because not only did the Sugar Bowl have the game we wanted, we could have announced a few other pairings, too.
>
> That brings to mind the first time we had Alabama when

it was coached by Bryant, in 1962, when the Crimson Tide defeated Arkansas 10–3.

We were courting Alabama hard. My father and three other committee members went to Tuscaloosa to visit with him. They were in his office when he stood up, announced that Alabama would accept our invitation and offered his right hand. My father said they would draw up the agreement and Bryant said, "All we need is a handshake. We'll be there."

That handshake started a wonderful relationship between Alabama under Bryant and the Sugar Bowl. He brought eight teams to New Orleans. He won seven times. The loss was by one point to Notre Dame, 24–23, and he could have won that one just as easily as he lost it.

ᔕ

It stopped raining as soon as Coach Bryant stepped onto the playing field.

—KENNY STABLER, Alabama player

Bryant had so much success in the Sugar Bowl that there was one afternoon when he even seemed to be in control of the weather, recalls Stabler:

When we got to the Sugar Bowl on the day we played Nebraska, it was cloudy and raining. That didn't work well for us because we were much smaller and much faster than they were, and we planned to pass a lot in the game, you know, take advantage of finesse. They had some big guys, mud runners, to use horse racing terminology, and we didn't want to play them on a wet field.

As soon as Coach Bryant appeared on the playing field just before the game started, the rain stopped and a ray of sunshine broke through the clouds. Our fans went crazy when they noticed that. I was a little shocked, too.

I was walking beside Coach Bryant and he said, "Kenny, on the first play, I want you to throw the football as far as you can to Ray Perkins on the left sideline." I chunked it out there, about thirty-five yards, maybe forty, and Ray caught it. A few plays later we were in the end zone and the rout was on.

People who weren't there don't believe that story about the rain stopping and the sun popping through the clouds. I was there. I saw it. I believe.

ॐ

We're proud of the bowl game heritage we have at Alabama. It's an important part of our tradition.

—Paul "Bear" Bryant,
on Alabama and bowl games

Bryant took Alabama to twenty-four consecutive bowl games, starting with the 1959 Liberty Bowl and ending with the 1982 Liberty Bowl. That was a national record that was extended in 1983, when the Crimson Tide played in the Sun Bowl under Coach Ray Perkins.

From January 1, 1926, through January 1, 2000, Alabama played in fifty bowl games and produced a 28–19–3 record. Bryant led the Crimson Tide to eight Sugar Bowl appearances, five Orange Bowl appearances, four Cotton Bowl appearances, four Liberty Bowl appearances, two Astro-Bluebonnet Bowl appearances, and one Gator Bowl appearance. He led Kentucky to four bowl game appearances: the Great Lakes, the Orange, the Sugar and the Cotton. He led Texas A&M to one bowl game appearance, the Gator.

His resume included twenty-nine bowl game appearances.

೪

Going to a bowl game was the primary goal at Alabama until winning a national championship replaced it. He didn't consider it a reward, either, at least not completely. He thought that once you got to a bowl game, you were obligated to win it.

—BILLY NEIGHBORS, Alabama player

Billy Neighbors played tackle on the first three Alabama teams that made bowl games under Bryant. They included a 7–0 loss to Penn State in the 1959 Liberty Bowl, a 3–3 tie with Texas in the 1960 Bluebonnet Bowl and a 10–3 victory over Arkansas in the 1962 Sugar Bowl:

Coach Bryant got pretty intense before bowl games. He was glad to be a part of a chosen few, because there weren't many bids to go around at that time, and he knew the television exposure would help the Alabama program grow in stature.

It was snowing in Philadelphia when we played Penn State in the Liberty Bowl. Most of us were colder than we had been in our lives. It was freezing and the wind was blowing. That's the day Coach Bryant got all of us southern boys all around a little heater in the dressing room at halftime and asked for volunteers to play the second half. He knew we were miserable trying to play those guys from Penn State who were accustomed to that type weather.

Coach Bryant was really on edge when we went to Houston to play Texas in the Bluebonnet Bowl. He might've felt that way because we were playing against Coach Darrell Royal, who had been a rival of his when he was at Texas A&M.

Regardless, nothing went right. Our airplane was late getting to Houston, which made him mad. Then we went to a team meeting to watch films of Texas, and the projector didn't work. He was furious. He picked up the projector and threw it against the wall, tearing it apart. That gave us a pretty good idea he thought the game was about as important as any we had played.

Then came the 1962 Sugar Bowl in New Orleans, a place all of us had heard about and wanted to see.

But Coach Bryant treated it like another game. We went to Biloxi to practice a few days before the game. Believe me, that wasn't like being in New Orleans. He took us to New Orleans the day before the game. We worked out in the stadium, went back to the hotel, under a curfew, and played the game the next day.

That was it. We won the game. We won a national championship. But what we experienced was a whole lot different than what players experience today when they go to the site of the bowl game, do a lot of sightseeing, and play the game.

I'm not saying what we did was bad. It was good. I'm proud to have been a part of a senior class that got Alabama winning again, that set the stage for the future.

Alabama was one of the top bowl game attractions from that point on, if not the most desired, because the Crimson Tide won with consistency and Bryant was a sideline delight for television networks and fans.

ॐ

Paul telephoned me at a restaurant in New Orleans. He said, "Aruns, I want you to read the newspaper tomorrow."

—ARUNS CALLERY,
Sugar Bowl committee member

We were at a hall of fame dinner for the news media at a restaurant on Canal Street when they told me Paul Bryant was on the telephone wanting to talk to me. I answered the telephone and he said, "Aruns, I want you to read the newspaper tomorrow." I asked him what was up. He said, "Just read the newspaper. You can read, can't you?"

I laughed, hung up, and went back to dinner.

The next morning, there it was, an article in the newspaper in which Coach Bryant challenged Notre Dame to a game in the Sugar Bowl.

That's what we wanted. That's what he got us, a great matchup on December 31, 1973.

Never mind that Alabama lost that game and went eight consecutive bowl games without winning, from the 1968 Cotton Bowl through the 1975 Orange Bowl, because the Crimson Tide turned that around and won seven of the last eight it played under Bryant. He was still calling the shots as far as pairings were concerned until his last bowl game, the 1982 Liberty Bowl.

As an example, consider these comments he made to staff members on November 11, 1980, four days before Alabama played Notre Dame in Birmingham. The Crimson Tide had lost one game that season, 6–3 to Mississippi State, and that defeat ended a 28-game winning streak.

Bryant was already thinking about what bowl game the Crimson Tide might choose to play:

I'm getting forty calls a day from people wanting to know what I know about the bowl game pairings. I don't know what's going on right now, nor do I want to know until we get finished with our game against Notre Dame. We can't make a decision until then. If we get beat by Notre Dame, there might not be anybody out there who wants us.

On the other hand, I know what our players are thinking.

If we've got a chance to play for another national championship, they'll want that matchup, no matter where it's staged.

If we don't beat Notre Dame, I want us to go wherever the players want to go. I want them to have some fun—sooner, later, depending on the climate or whatever.

I don't want to deal with this bowl game business right now, but I've got to start making some plans. In fact, I've got to go over to the president's mansion after we get finished here and let him know what to expect.

Alabama lost to Notre Dame 7–0 that week, then won over Auburn 34–18 to complete a 9–2 regular season. The next game was the Cotton Bowl, a 30–2 win over Baylor, as orchestrated by the famous coach with clout.

22
THE MEDIA DARLING

I was stunned and impressed by how candid Coach Bryant was with me, how he never sidestepped an issue. He talked openly about the good and the bad. He didn't back up one time while addressing his life and his life as a football coach.

—JOHN UNDERWOOD, author

Paul "Bear" Bryant was, for the most part, a favorite subject of the news media. He had a way of delivering quotes in a homespun, compelling manner. He could take the sport he loved, football, and equate it to life and war. He had a lifestyle that was interesting, to say the least, disciplined at times and undisciplined at times, and he never attempted to hide either aspect.

Some sports writers and sports broadcasters considered him a manipulative person. Many of those never recognized him for who he really was because they were too busy attempting to figure out why he said things and why he did things.

Bryant made a cover story for many magazines, *Sports*

Illustrated and *Time* among them. He was followed closely by all the major newspapers and television networks. Editorial cartoonists found his face appealing.

Photo by Barry Fikes

But while he adored such attention, he was more comfortable dealing with state and regional sports writers and sports broadcasters. He loved hosting an annual golf event for sports writers and sports broadcasters from Alabama. He looked forward to an annual outing with news media reps from Alabama, Florida, Georgia, Tennessee, Kentucky, Mississippi, and Louisiana who traveled in a group to Tuscaloosa, Alabama. Some years he hosted the news media reps at a family house on Lake Martin near Alexander City, Alabama, and there were a few times when he kept a party alive by moving it from a local motel to his house.

The news media loved Paul "Bear" Bryant. Here, he is being interviewed by CBS Sports just before the start of the 1981 Cotton Bowl.

Bryant had his favorites in the news media. Billy Reed of the *Lexington Herald-Examiner* was probably the first person to make that list. Mickey Herskowitz of the *Houston Post* was probably the second person to make that list. He covered the boot camp at Junction for the *Houston Post*. Benny Marshall of the *Birmingham News* was on that list. He got closer to the coach than all of the other newspaper reporters and columnists. Also on the list were Tom Siler of Knoxville, Fred Russell of Nashville, and Charles Land of Tuscaloosa. Without doubt, Keith Jackson of ABC Sports was close to him.

But John Underwood of *Sports Illustrated* is clearly the journalist Bryant favored the most. He is the person he chose to ghost write his autobiography, *Bear: The Hard Life and Good Times of Alabama's Coach Bryant*, which was published by Little, Brown and Company in 1975. It chronicled his life through the end of the 1973 football season in the first person.

The book was the result of a five-part series the extremely talented and highly personable Underwood wrote for *Sports Illustrated*. That work appeared in print many years after the sports writer was introduced to Bryant and found him refreshing, an out-of-the-ordinary individual.

Considering the love Bryant had for baseball, perhaps he was impressed because **John Underwood** had written *My Turn at Bat*, an autobiography with Ted Williams. Regardless, a warm friendship was established and the author has a multitude of memories related to the coach:

Because the folks at *Sports Illustrated* pretty much gave me a free hand to pursue story subjects, I've been able to meet a lot of sports stars through the years. But I've never met one quite as interesting and entertaining as Paul Bryant.

I got to know Paul because of Alabama football. I don't think there's a better team sport than football, the way it teaches ups and teaches downs, and I've always favored the college level.

I guess it was in the early 1960s, after Alabama won the national championship in 1961, that I went to Tuscaloosa the first time to interview Paul. It was a grand introduction. I think he was impressed that I was prepared and was willing to ask questions beyond the mundane. I know I was impressed with his answers, how he was so totally honest and forthright. Regardless, he spent a lot of time with me.

After a few trips, Paul opened up even more. He'd let me

stay in the athletics dorm, and he invited me to stay at his house. I did that one night, which was extremely enjoyable. He'd let me sit in on staff meetings from time to time.

I was just a kid and he was a legend. I was taken by the fact I could ask any question, and he would answer it.

Without question, Paul was a joy to be around—and I certainly saw a lot of him through the years.

ॐ

His real motivating power didn't come in the dressing room just before a game. It came earlier in the day, during the team meal at the motel.

—JOHN UNDERWOOD, author

I can remember being there when his players ate the pregame meal. That's when he said the things that really got to them.

Also, I recall he usually invited a member from the University of Alabama faculty to be a guest at those meals. He told me he did that because he truly believed the football program should be an integral part of the entire university. I specifically recall the dean of the English Department being there on one occasion.

Coach Bryant got up to make his speech and, as usual, he delivered it in that low, growling voice. The players were leaning forward in an effort to hear him. I don't recall exactly what he said that morning, but it was darn sure inspiring.

It was quiet in the room as he spoke. In fact, I recall one of the players knocking over a glass of water. It sounded like Niagara Falls as that water dripped to the floor while Paul was talking. That's how captivating he was that morning.

As everybody left the dining room, the dean of the

English Department told me, "If I could get my students in the palms of my hands like Coach Bryant can, I would teach for the rest of my life for nothing."

I understood what the dean meant. Coach Bryant could definitely get the attention of his players.

꩜

Coach Bryant wrote three words on the note pad and drew heavy lines under them. I was curious, obviously.

—JOHN UNDERWOOD, author

I was in Atlanta one year for an Alabama game against Georgia Tech. It was Friday night, and I decided to go down and knock on his door at the motel, just to say hello. He answered the door, wearing his pajamas, and invited me in.

He was listening to a football game on the radio, Miami and Florida State, I believe, and he was making notes from the play-by-play. George Mira was the Miami quarterback then, a player Coach Bryant really respected.

I was amazed how Paul could carry on a conversation with me and scribble notes as we talked and he listened to the game. Then he wrote three words on the note pad and drew two heavy lines under them. I was curious, obviously. I leaned over to see what he had written. He had written "Miami can't win" in a margin beside the other notes he was recording.

Well, Miami lost the game something like 21–0. He had written those words when the game was still in the first quarter. So tell me how he knew that just from the play-by-play he had heard on the radio.

꩜

Coach Bryant had the man's face jammed down on the table and he had a grip on his right hand.

—JOHN UNDERWOOD, author

I don't think it's a secret that Coach Bryant liked to have a good time. That was particularly the case when it came to shooting craps in Las Vegas. He was a good player, too, about as good as he was coaching football.

We were out there during the early 1970s, which is one of the places we met to do interviews for the book. On other occasions we'd go down to the Florida Keys or over to his cabin on Lake Martin near Alexander City, Alabama.

Paul was having a big time at the craps table, doing well, and he was roaring a little at the time. I was standing on his right when I heard a commotion, a loud thud. When I looked up, I was amazed by what had happened to the man standing on his left side.

Coach Bryant had the man's face jammed down on the table, right in a pile of chips, and he had a grip on his right hand. With his left hand, Coach Bryant had literally hoisted the man onto the craps table.

Guess what we found in the man's right hand? It was Paul's wallet. The guy was a pickpocket artist who had chosen the wrong victim.

Anyway, after that mess was sorted out the crap games continued. I think we were there three days, doing a lot of work and having a lot of fun.

From Las Vegas we went to Pepperdine University near Los Angeles, where Paul was going to lecture a group of coaches. He was worn out, looking drained, and I was a little worried that he wasn't up to the challenge. I knew he wasn't feeling good.

But he got to the podium and was making a marvelous talk, again in that low, growling voice. The coaches were straining hard to hear what he was saying.

Then Paul stopped for a few seconds, in silence, before saying, "I don't know how to say this, but is there a doctor in the house?" That's when he collapsed, the time the national headlines speculated he had a heart attack.

I rode to the hospital in the back of an ambulance with him. He was conscious, although weak, when he handed me his wallet and said, "John, take care of this for me."

I decided I better see what I was taking care of, not to be nosey, just so I could make a proper accounting when he got back on his feet. There was a wad of 100-dollar bills in there, at least 30, maybe 40, his take from the craps table the night previous.

As everybody knows, Paul didn't have a heart attack. He was just exhausted from having a little too much fun after working as hard as he did all of the time.

Paul worked about as diligently on the golf course as he did other places. That was particularly true when he got a group together at Indian Hills Country Club in Tuscaloosa.

The first day I was invited to play, the first thing I noticed was three golf carts waiting for us. He didn't play a foursome, not always, rather on that day a sixsome. I guess you could say he made up the rules as he went.

Then we got on the first hole, a narrow par four, and he said, "John, you're up. Hit 'em until you get one you like." I was lucky. The first tee shot was in the fairway. I said, "I'll take that one."

Paul must have hit a dozen tee shots before he was satisfied with one. Most of the other guys did the same thing. By the time we went to hit our second shots, that fairway looked like a mushroom bed, there were so many golf balls on it.

But that was one great round of golf. Those guys went back and forth at each other all afternoon. They were placing bets, side bets and emergency bets. I was scared to death.

The way I had it figured, I could win or lose three bucks, or I could win or lose four hundred bucks.

You know, some people hear stories like that about Paul Bryant and become critical. They don't understand he was a man who worked hard and played hard, enjoyed life to its fullest, and, more surprising to a lot of folks, he was a religious man and a compassionate man.

That brings to mind another story.

We were at Lake Martin doing some work on the book. There was a nice lady there who cooked meals for us. One morning we were talking while she was preparing breakfast.

When she called us to the table, Paul took a seat, bowed his head and said grace. He did it that way all the time, which might surprise some people. He thought his religion was important and sometimes talked about it in private quarters. He just didn't wear it on his sleeve for everybody to see.

In fact, there's a trailer to that breakfast scene. After Paul said grace, he looked at his eggs and said, "Damn, those things look like puppy dog ears."

٩

I said, "Paul, I don't think I want any part of this series if you're not going to talk about that."

—JOHN UNDERWOOD, author

The only time I can recall Paul and me having a serious difference of opinion came while I was preparing the series for *Sports Illustrated* that led to the writing of the book. He had read the first three parts, and I flew from New York to Lake Martin to let him review the last two parts.

The fourth part dealt with his problems with the *Saturday Evening Post*, the game fixing charge from the early 1960s, the deal with Wally Butts of Georgia. I don't think anything hurt him more than that article, his wife, Mary Harmon, too, and the memory of it was sort of painful.

I gave Coach Bryant and Mary Harmon a copy of the fourth and fifth parts and they went to bed. The next morning he came out of the bedroom for breakfast and said, "John, Mary Harmon doesn't want to recollect any of that *Saturday Evening Post* stuff. I don't want to, either."

I said, "Paul, I don't think I want any part of this series if you're not going to talk about that." I was serious, too, and maybe a little hurt by it. He had been totally honest with me. He hadn't backed up on anything. I wasn't jumping up and down, yelling, but I was prepared to suggest to the managing editor that we forget the series if he wasn't going to talk about that.

Finally, Paul said, "Let me talk to Mary Harmon some more about the matter. I'll take it back to her for reconsideration."

I returned to New York that day. A couple of days later, Paul telephoned me. He said, "John, you can put it all in there, everything."

I never asked what made Mary Harmon change her mind. I would guess he simply told her it was best to put it all out there because there wasn't anything to hide.

My conversation with Underwood continued for quite a while, two old friends talking about the genuine Bryant. We agreed controversy was prominent during his coaching career. We concluded his ability to overcome it and to win for almost four full decades added to his greatness.

"I've seen a lot of great sports figures through the years," Underwood said. "I've followed college football more closely than anything else. I haven't seen another person anything like Paul 'Bear' Bryant. He was unique in his accomplishment."

Bryant was not considered such a darling by every person from the news media. A few considered him arrogant. A few considered him unapproachable. A few considered him unpredictable. A few have carried their early negative impressions forward and did their jobs with such civility that nobody had reason to believe there were ever any problems.

Two good examples come to mind, both highly respected sports columnists, Clyde Bolton of the *Birmingham News* and Furman Bisher of the *Atlanta Journal*.

Bolton was fairly early in his newspaper career when quarterback Joe Namath arrived on the University of Alabama campus in 1961. As a sophomore, he starred on a powerful Crimson Tide team. After an early season performance, the newspaper columnist was interviewing him after a game, with every good reason. Bryant walked through the dressing room and screamed, "Get away from that sophomore before you ruin him!"

Bolton was more embarrassed by the unexpected outburst than he was angered by it. He wrote many glowing columns and articles about Bryant and Alabama. A true professional, he told only a few people about the humiliation he felt that afternoon when the football coach was, without doubt, crass in his behavior.

In fairness, I believe Bryant would have apologized to Bolton if he had learned the sports columnist had been damaged by the outburst.

Bisher was on the point when the aforementioned "bad blood" developed between Alabama and Georgia Tech during the 1960s. A fine journalist, he wrote what he perceived to be the truth. His sources were not always accurate, which put him at odds with Bryant.

Later, Bisher traveled to Tuscaloosa to interview Bryant.

He sat in a reception area and waited for several hours. When he inquired about when he might be admitted to the office, he was told it would be only a little longer. He waited until the advent of evening, when he was informed the football coach had left for the day.

Like Bolton, Bisher wrote glowing columns about Bryant and Alabama after he had been treated in such a rude manner. He, too, is a consummate professional.

I never got to ask Bryant about the behavior he displayed as it relates to two sports columnists I consider friends. I certainly would have had I known about the incidents before he died.

But, at the same time, I know Bryant treasured his association with the news media, and he gave us all a hell of a lot more great information that led to columns and articles than reasons to consider him an impolite man—a point on which both my offended pals graciously concur.

23

THE FAMILY MAN

As a husband, Paul "Bear" Bryant was attentive. When the "hotline" telephone in his office at Memorial Coliseum rang, he knew the chances were good Mary Harmon Bryant, his wife, had something important on her mind.

The married couple had endured a lot. In the early years, when he pretty much worked around the clock, she once said, "Paul, I wish you had become a ditch digger." She had grown weary of practically singlehandedly taking care of two children, a son and a daughter.

"But I don't want to be a ditch digger," Bryant said that morning. "I want to be a football coach."

Mary Harmon Bryant laughed when talking about how Paul Bryant looked on those rare occasions when he was at home long enough to play with the children. "He looked like a clumsy ol' elephant flopping around on the floor," she said. "He didn't know what to do or how to act."

As a father, Bryant was much more accessible than most people believe. He was busy, yes, but if Paul Bryant Jr. or Mae Martin Tyson needed him, he was quick to respond—even if it had to be by long distance telephone on occasion.

As a grandfather, Bryant excelled in all areas, as pledged

by his only grandson, Marc Tyson.

Tyson recalls getting football bowl game tickets as a Christmas gift every year. "The best part about it was getting to go to the games and stay with Papa," he said.

Tyson recalls sharing a love for baseball with his grandfather. "We took a trip one summer and watched the Cincinnati Reds, the Boston Red Sox, and the New York Yankees play home games. That was a wonderful week.

Tyson recalls fishing with his grandfather, and the wonderful conversations they had about life.

Then there was a football game.

"One of the funnier things I remember about Papa was how he came to the first high school football game I played," Marc Tyson said during a campus newspaper interview while a student at the University of Alabama. "It was in Brookstown, Georgia, when I was in the eleventh grade. Papa wanted to come to the game, but was afraid he'd make me nervous. So he tried to sneak in.

"Papa was going to bring a newspaper to the game, sit in a corner of the grandstands and look through the newspaper. I can't believe he thought nobody would notice him reading a newspaper during a football game.

"Papa did come to the game. It didn't make me nervous. It gave me confidence."

∽

"A tie is like kissing your sister."

—PAUL "BEAR" BRYANT,
on the importance of winning

As a brother, vows **Louise Goolsby**, Bryant was tough at times and tenderhearted at times—and never out of touch:

My husband Odis and I went down to an Alabama-Tennessee game at Legion Field in Birmingham. Paul was standing down on the field during pregame warmups, leaning on the goal post, as he always did, and I wanted to see him bad. The folks with us suggested I go down to the fence and holler at him.

Finally, I mustered up enough courage. When Paul saw me, he walked over to me, hugged me, picked me up off my feet and kissed me right there in front of all of those people.

I was so proud when he did that, one of the proudest moments in my life. So, see, the man who said a tie is like kissing your sister really didn't mean it literally.

I hated to bother Paul at that moment because he was so busy with the game. I really hated it after people saw him talking to me and started running that way. It created a mob scene because they didn't know I was his sister. I mean, there was a throng of folks running his way.

But Paul took time to visit with those fans, particularly to satisfy the children in the crowd. The kiss was one thing. That made me more proud of him.

Paul always made me proud. There were times during games when I would want to stand up and scream, "There's my brother out there coaching Alabama." In fact, I almost got tackled because of my pride at another Alabama-Tennessee game, this one in Knoxville.

We went to the concession stand for a soft drink and ran into a drunk. He was ranting and raving about Paul. He was a Tennessee fan, intoxicated, and he was saying, "That Bryant is the greatest coach who ever lived." I looked at the man and said, "I know. I agree." I thought he was being serious. Then Odis said, "She should know because the coach is her brother."

That was the wrong thing to say. Suddenly, that Tennessee fan wasn't so complimentary of Paul. He changed in a snap. I thought he was going to maul me.

I'm rarely surprised by the reactions I get when people learn I'm Paul's sister.

I was at our country club in Nashville one afternoon when a lady came over to me and said, "I just heard something I want to ask you about. Are you really his sister?" I said, "If you're talking about Paul Bryant, yes I am." She patted me on the back and said, "I just want to touch you. I admire that man."

That lady was Mrs. John J. Hooker, the wife of the millionaire businessman and politician.

ॐ

I always watched Paul during games, not the games themselves.

—Louise Goolsby, sister

Paul used to put on a show during games, particularly early in his career. That made a lot of folks pay attention to him. I remember one game during which he literally ran onto the field to argue with an official. They had to delay the action for a long time. If I remember correctly, that got him forty-five yards in penalties before he settled down. He used to throw his hat to the ground a lot, too.

Paul mellowed during his latter years. That was good to see, I thought, but I hated seeing him after games during that time. He was so bushed, literally worn out. His shirt was all ruffled, his tie was loose and his face looked so tired.

Obviously, my brother never quit putting everything he had into winning until he coached his last game. I don't think there are many people who put so much into their profession—even when it took away time from his life.

ॐ

Our family had a magic-like affection to it.

—LOUISE GOOLSBY, sister

I didn't see Paul much while he was coaching because he stayed so busy all the time. But he telephoned all of us a lot. He and I stayed in touch more than the others because we exchanged letters and talked on the telephone every now and then. He would've been there had any of his sisters or brothers needed him.

I normally wrote Paul extremely long letters, several pages, and my husband told me one evening he didn't think Paul read them because he was too busy. Well, I saw Paul at a football game, visited in his hotel suite, and I said, "Odis doesn't believe you read my letters." Paul looked at me, as if he was surprised, and said, "Honey, not only do I read them, I read them three or four times. You keep them coming my way."

Paul was a great brother. He wasn't perfect, not by any stretch. I always thought his frankness was a little bold at times, particularly when things were going bad for his team. But let me tell you something. Behind that tough shell there was a warm and compassionate man with a tender heart.

I'll tell you when I saw Paul at his most tender moment. It makes me cry when I think a lot about it.

Paul, Mary Harmon, and the children were on a vacation when our mom had a stroke. He quickly flew to the hospital and went to her room. Standing beside her bed, he started crying. He took her hand in his and said, "Sweetheart, this is the first time I've squeezed your hand that you failed to squeeze mine."

I'll never forget seeing Paul so crushed that day.

We had good Christian parents who taught us to love God. From them we got an appreciation of faith that has helped all of us through life.

—LOUISE GOOLSBY, sister

Goolsby said she and Bryant had a special relationship as children because they were close in age. During a videotaped interview on file at the Paul Bryant Museum on the University of Alabama campus, she recalls them arriving home from school after a lengthy walk, grabbing a couple of sweet potatoes from an oven in the kitchen, going outside and sitting under an oak tree and talking:

If Paul had a fault when he was young, the only one I can remember is he was a little hardheaded at times. But he was a deep thinker, even back then. He always seemed to be thinking about something important, even while we talked. I asked him once what he wanted to be when he grew up. He said he might want to become a doctor.

Obviously that changed after he was introduced to football.

It's true all you've heard about Paul and our mother riding a wagon to Fordyce to sell vegetables, eggs, and butter. That was particularly hard on them during winter. He was only eight years old, or thereabouts, but he had to go because he was the only one who could drive the team of mules. Our father used to bake bricks and put them in a croaker sack to keep them warm on those trips. But there were a lot of days when he would literally have to pick up Paul when they got home and take him into the house because he was so frozen.

I think that's why Paul drew so much inspiration from our mother. They spent so many hard hours together. He truly admired her, as we all did. She was a strong lady and a caring lady who prayed more than anybody I've known.

Our father, Monroe, was not well. Nobody ever figured out what was wrong with him because our parents didn't believe in doctors. There were times when our father just had to sit around because of high blood pressure. There were times when he would simply disappear in the middle of the night. We would find him the next morning wandering through the woods.

Our father was a good man, a spiritual man, and a loving man. He taught us discipline. He just wasn't much of a provider because he couldn't keep up a work pace.

I'll tell you how kind our father was. We had some share-croppers on our land who helped us chop and bale cotton and farm some other crops. Our father loved those folks. We all did. So he would tell them to go into Fordyce to our uncle's general store, get whatever their families needed and charge it to his account. They literally broke him, all of the time, but he never said a word about it.

I think Paul learned a lot from that because he never took advantage of anybody during his entire life.

We didn't have much, but we didn't feel poor because we worked as a family for all we did have. We all had chores to do. Paul took care of the horses, cows, and pigs every day. He had to get up early to do that. In the afternoon, he brought the horses into the barn, fed them and turned them out. He chopped cotton and plowed the fields. He picked potatoes. Later, he added odd jobs in Fordyce to his weekly routine. He had several stores he worked for because people liked him because he was friendly. They got a kick out of him, too, because he was so big and a little clumsy and would knock over things all the time.

There were a bunch of us children, but all nine of us weren't at home at one time. Some of the older ones were out on their own. I remember six of us being there with our mother and our father.

We didn't live in a log cabin, like some people have said. We had a house with three bedrooms, a big kitchen and a room running through the middle. The girls slept in one bedroom, and the boys slept in one bedroom. It was comfortable enough, yet hot as blazes during the summer and cold as ice during the winter.

Mostly we raised what we ate. We had pigs and cows, plus chickens for eggs and another kind of meat. Our mother had a huge garden. So we had meat, vegetables, and milk. We didn't have a lot of variety when it came to meals, but none of us came close to starving to death.

Clothes were another matter. Our mother made us dresses out of old sacks. She would bleach them, cut them by pattern and pass them on to us. We had some pass-along clothes, too, and they didn't always fit just right or match just right.

We went to church at Smith Chapel, not far from the house, like a few blocks by city standards. We would walk because it was so close. I'll never forget how mad Paul used to get when somebody would come home for Sunday lunch because the adults always ate first and the children ate what was left. He always complained about only having a few chicken wings by the time his turn at the table arrived.

Paul and I spent a lot of time talking about those times during his latter years. We laughed about it and joked about it.

There was one evening before an Alabama football game when my husband Odis and I stopped by his suite at the hotel where his team was staying. There was a table in a corner with fancy finger foods on trays. I went over to fix a plate, and when I walked back past Paul, who was sitting in a big chair, he grabbed me and sat me on his lap.

Paul said, "Honey, this sure does beat plowing and chopping cotton. Don't you think so?"

I agreed with him. Then he said, "Sugar, your ol' brother has everything he needs now."

I looked at him and said, "Paul, do you really?"

Paul knew I was talking about his spiritual life. He never did answer me. He just smiled.

I learned later how spiritual he had become late in his life. He might have gone away from it at one point, but he came back to it.

In fact, that tiny little church in the country we went to as children got a renovation because of his contributions to it. I didn't know that until after Paul was gone.

24

THE BUSINESSMAN

Paul "Bear" Bryant achieved wealth during his lifetime, by fairly modest standards, but he was never considered an astute businessman. His chief attribute, a good one, was he was willing to listen to friends who had achieved success and a son, Paul Bryant Jr., who had done the same.

At some point during the late 1970s, the *Tuscaloosa News* published the salaries of state employees. One of the numbers provided was the annual base income of Bryant. It was $99,999.96, a paltry sum for a man who had done so much—definitely a low amount given the money paid coaches today.

I walked into Bryant's office one morning and plopped four pennies on his desk.

"What in hell is that about?" Bryant said.

"I wanted to make you a six-figure man," I said. "I read in the newspaper where you were four cents short."

Maybe people in Birmingham, sixty miles away, heard his laughter. In West Blocton, roughly half the distance, they definitely did.

That brings to mind another story.

One of the first things Bryant enjoyed after a practice was a cup of orange drink and a cigarette. He was provided the former. As for the latter, he said, "Alfred, have you got a spare smoke?"

This went on for several months until I finally said, "Damn, Coach Bryant, you're a millionaire and you're breaking me a nickel at a time."

Bryant promised repayment. He kept bumming cigarettes. Ultimately, he provided me with a job that, after about two weeks, got me even on the Marlboro 100s he smoked.

But on a higher level of finance, he listened to people more in tune. The folks at Coca-Cola and Golden Flake improved his standing considerably. He had other contributors, in that regard, but those were the base.

Then there is Ziegler, the meat packing company, with Jimmy Hinton in leadership. His friend took him under his wing, so to speak, and the results were phenomenal. He rarely served as a spokesperson, which was his desire, as well as that of his good pal, and the partnerships netted dividends.

Of course, Bryant was blessed to have a son, Paul Bryant Jr., who had a magical touch. He knew a lot and he worked a lot. He put his father on some deals that worked.

The coach had a seat on many corporate boards of directors.

Whether Bryant knew much about the business world is open to debate. But he read the stock market reports like a football game plan, in newspapers and on television.

Bryant left the University of Alabama a lot of money when he died, a thank you note with dollar marks included. In keeping with his personality, he wanted the actual sum to remain a mystery.

In 1981 Bryant became a pioneer of sorts when he allowed Golden Eagle Enterprises of Selma, Alabama, to handle "endorsements" for him. The company, directed by Bill Battle, a former Alabama player and Tennessee coach, reviewed and approved or rejected products that used the coach's name or likeness. This was during the peak of his popularity, as he moved toward a historic victory number 315.

That partnership between Bryant and Golden Eagle sort of opened the floodgates, leading to all of the trademark licensing we see today in collegiate sports. Eventually, Battle founded Collegiate Sports Licensing and turned it into a business empire. Other groups followed—hence we have just about everything other than the term "50-yard line" registered as a trademark, and almost every college program has a group representing it in marketing endeavors—for a nice percentage of gross revenue.

I doubt Bryant would have liked business being conducted as it is today, at least to the current extent, because he was a fan's man, and he was smart enough to realize such marketing partnerships significantly drive up the cost of goods for consumers. In fairness, they have curtailed the production of numerous shoddy products.

The marketing of Bryant in 1981 and 1982 brought a flurry of products into the marketplace—interesting items. There was a "Bear" Bryant Commemorative Van that sold for between $20,000 and $25,000, depending on the desired accessories. There was a "Bear" candy bar that sold for fifty cents. There were collectible stuffed bears that ranged in price from $20 to $2,500, depending on the size and quality. There was a bronze bust that sold for $4,500. There was a lot more.

But there never was a "B.J. and the Bear" advertising campaign, as desired by a man who owned a champion dog. The man wanted to offer the animal for stud service and wanted Bryant to appear in pictures with it.

Bryant made few appearances as a commercial pitchman, at least on television. He did participate in a campaign for South Central Bell, the telephone company, to rave reviews. With approval from the Public Service Commission, that group produced and sold a limited number of telephone faceplates commemorating victory number 315.

Bryant derived much of his outside income from appearances, such as an almost annual Super Bowl analysis in Las Vegas with former Michigan State coach and good friend Duffy Daugherty. It was at one of those that his companion on stage produced a memorable line.

After talk centered on the controversy Bryant had throughout his career, Daugherty said, "Bear might or might not be the best football coach who ever lived, but he sure has caused the most commotion."

25
THE SUDDEN DEPARTURE

The memory I have of Coach Bryant from the last couple of months of 1982, as I was about to become the next coach at Alabama, is of a man who was totally spent. He was tired. He was sick. He had spent himself totally for a lot of years, and he had done that with a singular purpose—to help others learn how to win.

—RAY PERKINS,
Alabama player and coach

☙

I talked with Coach Bryant a lot during the 1982 regular season as he contemplated his retirement from football. He was tired and he was sick. But he made himself get through that final season. By God, he was that tough. He had decided he wasn't ready to quit, not without getting through that year. I'm sure he knew he was limited in time, but he wasn't going to give it up until he could get that final victory.

—LEE ROY JORDAN,
Alabama and professional player

Paul "Bear" Bryant definitely had several physical and emotional struggles during his final season coaching football, 1982, and he seemed to be as concerned about the future of the University of Alabama as he was about himself.

The year started well enough, with five consecutive victories, but the strain began taking a toll. The Crimson Tide had a 7–4 record when it went to the Liberty Bowl to claim a 21–15 victory over Illinois in his final game. The coach was as fatigued as those around him had noticed.

๖

Paul "Bear" Bryant was considering his final game as University of Alabama football coach. These were his thoughts on December 28, 1982, one day before the Liberty Bowl:

> I've tried to stay away from thoughts about my last game, actually, to keep from getting tied up in it.
>
> But I'm sure that by tonight I won't be able to sleep, and tomorrow morning I'll be smiling while my gut is growling and hurting.
>
> Tomorrow night, after the game is over, it'll take me to about Monday morning to realize it's over for me as a coach.
>
> Yeah, the big thing I'll realize is I won't be going back to it, not ever again. I don't know how that'll feel. I haven't felt that for the last forty-something years.

๖

It was probably the most historic football game that has been played in modern time.

—**BUD DUDLEY,**
Liberty Bowl founder and friend

We were inundated for press credentials and tickets to the 1982 Liberty Bowl. We had people who wanted to be a part of it, an international audience, and our press box and stadium were too small to accommodate everybody. That was a major disappointment for me because a truly great man was honored in victory that night.

After the game, we had to have our press briefing in a large tent because the dressing room area was so small. Charley Thornton, the former Alabama sports information director, helped us with that and did a magnificent job.

It was the most meaningful press conference I've seen. It took us a while to get Coach Bryant there, and he was worn out, obviously, but people were cheering and he was masterful.

⑤

Coach Bryant told me he thought he had exhausted his usefulness in coaching and didn't desire to do much else.

—MIKE WHITE, Illinois coach

Because he was a bit embarrassed by the attention he was receiving at the Liberty Bowl, Bryant went out of his way to share the spotlight with Coach Mike White and his Illinois team. That meant they had some memorable conversations:

Coach Bryant made me feel special by telling me he truly enjoyed being around me that week. But the Liberty Bowl was his day, as it should have been, and that's more meaningful since he died so quickly after it.

I remember telling Coach Bryant how I had thoroughly enjoyed watching him at work that week, how much I had learned from the experience. I was impressed by the strength of the man, at that point a sick man, the class of the man, and the humility of the man. Seeing him and being around him had a profound effect on my life.

When it was all over and time to go home, Coach Bryant gave me a hug. I'll never forget that moment.

ᔕ

I'm proud of our players for winning because, as I told them before the game, people are going to remember them for this game, whether they like it or not.

—Paul "Bear" Bryant,
on the Liberty Bowl victory

Bryant said the victory "in the last roundup" would make his retirement more pleasant. Then he said, "That's true whatever time I have left—years, a year, or whatever."

ᔕ

It was like a movie scene, really, with Coach Bryant seated in a straight chair in the middle of a large hotel room. He was reflecting on the game a couple of hours after it had ended. It was a small crowd. For some strange reason, not very many people came by for the reception.

—John Forney,
broadcaster and friend

Coach Bryant was gray, ashen, and he turned to me and said, "John, was it a good game for television?" I said, "Gosh, Coach Bryant, it was great. We came from behind to win, it was a tribute to you, and nobody will ever forget seeing you get carried off the playing field like that." He said, "Well, I'm glad to hear that."

I told Coach Bryant we had arrived at the hotel at the same time his players had, and they were jumping up and down, excited and full of themselves for winning. Coach Bryant looked at me and said, "John, the worst thing in the world for them would have been us losing tonight. I'm just so pleased it worked out like it did."

That one tore me up. There was the man of the hour thinking about those kids.

What I saw the last year of his life was a man in very bad health, yet a determined man who willed himself through the last several months of his life.

—LINDA KNOWLES, secretary

Three people outside of his family were closest to Bryant down the stretch in his life: his secretary, Linda Knowles, his longtime friend and confidant, Billy Varner, and Alabama trainer Jim Goostree:

Only the will to live carried Coach Bryant through that last season. He was so ill. There were days when I got extremely concerned about him making it. He would lie down in the morning and at noon for naps, then go to football practice in the afternoon. There were times during the latter part of October that I thought he wouldn't wake up.

Then one day Dr. Bill Hill, his cardiologist, came by the office for a visit. Coach Bryant buzzed me and asked if I could get Jim Goostree to bring up some Band-Aids. I told him I had some in my desk, that I could bring them in if he wanted.

When I walked in his office, I noticed Dr. Hill had given him an injection. Miraculously, from that day it seemed like he got better, albeit gradually.

About three weeks before we played Auburn in the last regular season game, Coach Bryant seemed to be coming around. He got better every day. After the Auburn game, I thought, "Wow, he's going to be okay. We're over the crisis." In fact, the day he announced his retirement in December, he looked as good as I'd seen him look in several months. He was full of spirit. He was in complete control.

Then about six weeks after that, about a month after the Liberty Bowl victory, I went home from the office on a Monday afternoon at about four-thirty not knowing I'd never see Coach Bryant again.

Bryant went to the hospital that night. Less than two days later, he died.

၆

It was so unexpected at that time. He was here, then gone.

—Billy Varner, confidant and friend

I was shocked when I heard Coach Bryant had passed away because I had seen him an hour or so before. I had been at the hospital all of Tuesday night, and he was doing better, it seemed. I had taken his daughter, Mae Martin, to see him Wednesday morning, and he was joking and laughing.

When I took Mae Martin back to Coach and Mrs. Bryant's house, I said, "Well, this looks good. I can go home for a while." When I got home, I called Linda to let her know where I was, and she told me he had taken a sudden turn for the worse. I hurried back to the hospital. When I got there, he was gone.

၆

The most touching thing I have ever been through was Coach Bryant's funeral, particularly the processional as it moved down what is now known as Paul Bryant Drive, the street that runs beside Bryant-Denny Stadium.

—JIM GOOSTREE, Alabama
trainer and associate athletics director

There was such an outpouring of sympathy the day we laid Paul Bryant to rest. It was a heart-rending experience, seeing little children and their moms and dads lining the thoroughfares in Tuscaloosa after the funeral service at First United Methodist Church. I remember seeing little children first, but there were nurses and surgeons lined up, too, plus people from all walks of life.

I thought how among those several thousands of people, that there were many, most of them, in fact, who didn't know Paul "Bear" Bryant but loved the man just the same. I looked into many faces that had never seen an Alabama football game. But they loved Alabama football and, goodness, how they respected Coach Bryant and what he had meant to them.

It's difficult, if not impossible, to put into words what that entire scene meant to me. It was a monument to his greatness.

⑤

I remember passing by a little house, and there was a man on his front porch. He was wearing overalls and sweeping. But when that processional rolled past, he stopped what he was doing. There were tears rolling down his face. I doubt that man ever saw Coach Bryant, or met him, but he was crying for that man so many people loved. That was a sad time for a lot of people, an uncountable number, thousands upon thousands who loved Paul Bryant.

—LINDA KNOWLES, secretary

295

❦

He meant a lot to so many people.

—JOHN FORNEY,
sports broadcaster and friend

I was stopped in my tracks when I heard Coach Bryant had died. That's not unlike a lot of people.

One thing about Paul Bryant, he had a unifying effect on a multitude of people in one state and, to a lesser degree, to people across the nation. He was a one-of-a-kind person, which certainly separates him from the masses.

I'm honest about it in that I know if you were against him, the enemy, there were things you could criticize—and there were people who did do that. But when you weigh the positive influence he had during his lifetime, his critics are shallow, at best. But there's one thing I know for sure: If Paul Bryant liked you, you had the staunchest of allies known to mankind.

❦

I sat in the Methodist church in Tuscaloosa and cried and cried during my brother's funeral.

—LOUISE GOOLSBY, sister

I've got a picture of Paul in my house, and many times I've passed by it and said, "Honey, I think I know where you are. I think you're with Jesus."

Then one Wednesday night, Odis and I were at a prayer meeting dinner. When everybody finished eating, some of the men went outside to smoke. I went to get a cup of coffee. A church member I didn't know by name came up to me and said, "Aren't you Coach Bryant's sister?" I told him I was.

The man was a good friend of Steve Sloan, the former Alabama player under Paul and the former Vanderbilt University coach. He told me a story that Steve, a good Christian man, had told him after my brother died.

Steve was coaching at Duke at the time. He was new on the job there. This was during Paul's final years. Paul was in Chicago for some kind of meeting. He telephoned Steve and said, "Steve, I need to see you." Steve told him how busy he was with a new job, but Paul insisted and said, "Steve, I need to see you." Finally, Steve got on an airplane and went to see Paul.

The man said the conversation Paul and Steve had was spiritual. He assured me my brother had come back to God, if indeed he had ever strayed.

I knew then Paul was in heaven.

26
THE MAN REMEMBERED

About a decade ago, I was challenged with the responsibility of writing lyrics for a theme song for *The Legacy Lives* video-tape about the years Paul "Bear" Bryant served the University of Alabama as its football coach.

It was an arduous chore. The deadline was tight—two days—and the words did not come easily, at least at first.

But they did come.

These are those words:

He arrived from backwoods Arkansas
To play for the mighty Crimson Tide
Not knowing his fame as a coach
Would grow as deep as it is wide.

He was a genuine hero whose legacy
Will never die or slip away
Coach Bryant, we all will remember
How your Alabama teams played.

And his hands were made of granite
His eyes were like hot steel
On his head he wore a houndstooth
In his heart there pounded a will.

From his mouth came precious lessons
Pearls of wisdom for boys who played
The secrets to winning championships
For those who miss him so much today.

I Remember Paul "Bear" Bryant

Now The Bear taught them how to win
By preaching prices to pay
Insisting they always show class
Every day and in every way.

From his tower he watched them grow
Champions known as the Crimson Tide
As his fame as a football coach
Grew as deep as it is wide.

His hands were made of granite
His eyes were like hot steel
On his head he wore a houndstooth
In his heart there pounded a will.

From his mouth came precious lessons
Words of wisdom for boys who played
The secrets to winning championships
For those of us who miss him so much today.

They all remember their leader
Snake, Bob, Ozzie and the rest
They call Paul Bryant a superstar
As a coach the very best.

The sport has changing faces
As different heroes come and go
But the big man from Alabama
Is the best we'll ever know.

—Al Browning

THE FINAL WORD

You think of somebody like Paul "Bear" Bryant, who had such a huge aura surrounding him, the person he was, and you think he would live forever.

When he died, the first things that came to my mind were, perhaps, his thoughts:

"Well, I've broken all the records. I've done all I can do as a coach. Maybe it's time to go."

But a civilian, not a football coach, I don't think Paul Bryant could have been or would have wanted to be.

I'm sure Coach Bryant said it's time to go on to something else, up there—somewhere.

It was unfortunate, his death, a shock to a lot of us. But while everybody has to die at some point, to me it's like he's still around and might always be.

—KENNY STABLER, 1991

INDEX